"Tell the Next Generation":
ESSAYS ON CHRISTIAN EDUCATION AT HOME AND IN SCHOOL

CORNELIS VAN DAM

Copyright © 2024 by Cornelis Van Dam

"Tell the Next Generation": Essays on Christian Education at Home and in School
by Cornelis Van Dam

All rights reserved solely by the author. The author guarantees all contents are original and do not infringe upon the legal rights of any other person or work. No part of this book may be reproduced in any form without the permission of the author. The views expressed in this book are not necessarily those of the publisher.

Published by Providence Books & Press
Box 3, Site 15, RR2 Barrhead, Alberta, T7N 1N3
www.providencebookspress.com

Book design by Studio of Sarah

All quotations are from the English Standard Version (ESV) unless otherwise indicated.

NIV84 = the New International Version (1984)

NASB = New American Standard Bible (2020)

Any transliterations from the original languages of the Bible are done according to the guidelines described in *The SBL Handbook of Style*, 2nd edition (2014), 56–60.

ISBN 978-1-7382729-6-9 (Softcover)

ISBN 978-1-7382729-7-9 (Ebook)

Library and Archives Canada Cataloguing in Publication

Title: "Tell the next generation" : essays on Christian education at home and in school / Cornelis Van Dam.

Names: Van Dam, Cornelis, 1946 - author

Description: Co-published by Lucerna Publications. | Includes bibliographical references and indexes.

Identifiers: Canadiana (print) 20240438108 | Canadiana (ebook) 20240438116 | ISBN 9781738272969 (softcover) | ISBN 9781738272976 (EPUB)

Subjects: LCSH: Christian education—Canada. | LCSH: Home schooling—Canada.

Classification: LCC LC40 .V36 2024 | DDC 371.04/2—dc23

Dedication

*In memory of Dr. Jelle Faber,
Professor of Dogmatology and the first
principal of the Canadian Reformed
Theological Seminary (1969-1989) who also
tirelessly promoted Reformed education.*

Recommendations

Cornelis VanDam has gifted the Christian community with a compilation of revised and updated works that provide practical, relevant, and confessional clarity to the home, school, and church, as it collectively instructs the next generations.

The reader will gain an appreciation for the clarity of scripture, as its enormous power shapes minds, influences culture and equips the reader to navigate the ever-changing narratives of our times. The necessity of verbal communication clarity is explored in depth, and the detailed appendices provide a gold mine for further encouragement, pedagogical research, and teaching perspective.

Highly recommended.

> **Harry Moes** – Credo Christian High School Principal (retired) and current British Columbia Ministry of Education School Inspector

I read Telling the Next Generation with much appreciation and enjoyment. I loved how it worked with enduring messages and brought them to life in the contexts of today. I loved how it affirmed the cause of engaging with the children and young people of the church to tell them of God's wonderful works and to connect that to the challenges they face in growing up and finding their place in the world. I loved how it brought churches, families, and schools together to build synergy together for our young people, mindful of where they and we all are headed. I loved the shepherding tone and the calm reasoning that pervaded the work. I can only highly recommend it.

> **Alwyn Terpstra** – Reformed Education Coordinator for Free Reformed School Association (Western Australia)

Embark on a profound exploration of Christian education with this enlightening collection of essays that skillfully dissect the "why" and "how" of nurturing faith-based learning. Written from a Reformed perspective, each essay serves as a guiding light, offering clarity on the roles played by the home, school and church in shaping the spiritual and intellectual development of the next generation.

From the detailed description and analysis of the roles of the home, school, and church to the nuanced exploration of challenging topics like homeschooling, each essay provides invaluable insights for navigating the fundamental questions surrounding Christian education. Two essays specifically delve into the power of language within a Biblical context, while another three explore the intricate relationship between science and the Bible, offering profound insights into understanding God's special and general revelation and the relationship between faith and reason.

"Tell the Next Generation" is an indispensable resource for anyone seeking guidance on the topic of why and how to educate the next generation for service to the Lord. Whether you are a teacher, parent, home schooler or a board member, these essays provide excellent and accessible resources for navigating the fundamental questions surrounding Christian education in both the home and school settings.

Dr Derek Juan Swarts – CEO Free Reformed School Association (Western Australia)

Dr. C. Van Dam shares carefully considered biblical, ever timely, reflections. Topics concerning Home-School-Church relationships are addressed in a pastoral, yet scholarly manner. Each very readable essay facilitates insightful and ongoing discussion on "things that we have heard and known, that our fathers have told us." This collection highlights a biblical worldview with practical reformed approaches for nurturing covenant youngsters and teenagers. It is enthusiastically recommended!

Dr Art Witten – Retired Christian High School Teacher and Covenant Canadian Reformed Teachers College Instructor.

Foreword

Dear reader,

You are about to embark on a special journey. A journey shaped by a love for *"tell[ing] the next generation the praiseworthy deeds of the LORD"* (Ps. 78:4) and by a desire to keep the generational chain, from ancestors, via parents, to children, and children's children, intact.

The author has dedicated this book to the memory of Dr. Jelle Faber, one of his former teachers at the Canadian Reformed Theological Seminary.

Jelle Faber was himself a recipient of Reformed Christian education. Born to God-fearing parents, his education was shaped by attending Reformed elementary and secondary schools, the Funenschool and the Gereformeerd Gymnasium, in Amsterdam. He then completed his undergraduate and graduate theological studies at the Theologische Hogeschool in Kampen. Rev. Jelle Faber was also a teacher. In responding to his calling as a pastor, teaching catechism students formed a joyous aspect of his ministry. In addition, he taught for many years as a part-time teacher at the Gereformeerd Lyceum in Rotterdam. In 1969, together with his wife and children, he left the Netherlands in order to take up his task as the first Principal of the Canadian Reformed Theological Seminary in Hamilton. There his teaching was not limited to the classroom, but spilled over into the informal but lively daily teatime conversations during which students and professors interacted with each other. He also offered evening lectures to college and university students and other interested listeners. In many ways, Dr. Jelle Faber was a catalyst of Reformed Christian education. He provided strong leadership for the advancement of Reformed Christian elementary and secondary schools in Hamilton. He felt strongly that in order to teach covenant youth, teachers had to be well prepared for the task. He was instrumental in designing summer courses for teachers and participated enthusiastically in the efforts that led to the establishment of Covenant Canadian Reformed Teachers College.

In turn, we express our deep gratitude to Dr. Cornelis Van Dam who himself dedicated much time and effort to speaking and writing on matters of faithful teaching and learning. It is often said that in educating the youth of Christ's Church, Reformed education functions in unity of purpose between home, school, and church. Within God's covenant community, teaching the next generation is a distinct privilege and responsibility. Therefore it is our prayer that this book may serve as a tool for parents, teachers, and pastors as they seek to "tell next generation."

Christine van Halen-Faber

CONTENTS

Analytical Outline	3
Preface and Acknowledgments	7

Part A: The Task Of Christian Education

1.	Fathers and Mothers: at Home and at School	11
2.	Education in the Home, School, and Homeschooling	35
3.	The Home as Nurturer for Identity, Worship, and Renewal	63
4.	The Privilege and Challenge of Educating Children with Disabilities	87

Part B: The Importance Of Language

5.	The Gift of Language: Corrupted and Redeemed	103
6.	Education in the Word in an Age of the Picture	125

Part C: Science And Education

7.	The Bible and Science: God's Revelation in His Word and Creation	147
8.	A Lesson from Galileo's Trial	169
9.	Faith and Reason	177

Part D: A Challenge For Teachers And Graduates

10.	The Nurturing Rains	199
11.	Getting Dressed for the Job	207

Appendices

A.	Decisions of Dort Regarding Education	217
B.	A Christian School's Mandate	221
C.	Original Publication Information	224

Select List of Works Cited	227
Scripture Index	233
Author Index	241

ANALYTICAL OUTLINE

Part A: THE TASK OF CHRISTIAN EDUCATION

1 Fathers and Mothers: at Home and at School
    The Teachers
        The Parental Task
        Other Teachers
        School Parents
    The Purpose of Education
        Preparation for Life in Fullness
        Imparting True Wisdom
    Ways for Attaining this Purpose
        Life-Producing Discipline
        Memory Work
        Meaningful Interaction
    The Ongoing Challenge

2 Education in the Home, School, and Homeschooling
    The Historic Reformed Emphasis on Godly Education
    The Baptismal Vows and Consequences
    The Threefold Cord and Homeschooling
        Homeschooling: The Pros and Cons
        Christian School: The Pros and Cons
        Decisions and Consequences
        In Mutual Educational Service
        The Indispensable Place of the Church
    In Conclusion

3 The Home as Nurturer for Identity, Worship, and Renewal
    Realizing a Clear Identity
        Children of God
        Gender Identity
            The Gender Ideology Offensive
            Christian Parental Response

    Practicing Family Worship
        Time and Place
        Scripture Reading
        Prayer
        Singing
    Family Nurturing the New Creation
        Heart and Mind
        Joy in the Lord

4   **The Privilege and Challenge of Educating Children with Disabilities**
    What is the Sense of Living with Disabilities?
        Uncertainty and Certainty
        An Office to Perform
        In It Together for Blessing
    Home and School Responsibilities
        The Teaching Task
        Experiencing Joy
    Concluding Comments

Part B: THE IMPORTANCE OF LANGUAGE

5   **The Gift of Language: Corrupted and Redeemed**
    The Origin and Power of Language
    The Corruption of Language
        "As Were the Days of Noah ..."
        The Need for Discernment in Educating in a Corrupt Culture
    The Redemption of Language
        The Need to Prepare the Heart
        The Use of Songs
    In Conclusion

6   **Education in the Word in an Age of the Picture**
    The Priority of Verbal Communication both Oral and Written

The Teaching Task
    The First Place of the Spoken and Written Word
    The Clarity of Verbal Communication
    The Word and Faith
The Place of the Visual
The Second Commandment
Memorizing Scripture
The Enduring Task

Part C: SCIENCE AND EDUCATION

7   The Bible and Science: God's Revelation in His Word and Creation
    The Issue
    What Does General Revelation Reveal?
    The Need for Special Revelation
    The Wise Men from the East and the Star
    Psalm 19 and the Laws of Nature
    Some Principles in Using Scripture
    The Place of Science in Understanding Scripture
    In Conclusion

8   A Lesson from Galileo's Trial
    What Was the Issue?
    The Situation Today
    The Question of Proof
    In Conclusion

9   Faith and Reason
    Luther's Ninety-Seven Theses
    Three Approaches
        Fideism
        The Historical-Critical Approach
        Evidentialism

A Reformed Understanding: Van Til's Contribution
The Starting Point
Implications of this Starting Point
Faith and Reason

Part D: A CHALLENGE FOR TEACHERS AND GRADUATES

10 **The Nurturing Rains**
The Truth from God
Like Rain, Like Dew
Important Principles
Like a Rock, Like an Eagle

11 **Getting Dressed for the Job**
The Decision
Getting Dressed as a Christian
The Critical Question

APPENDICES

A The Decisions of Dort (1618–19) Regarding Education

B A Christian School's Mandate
Purpose and Foundation
Specific Aims and Overviews

C Original Publication Information

Preface and Acknowledgements

No Reformed parent will question the enormous importance of the education we give to our children whom God has entrusted to our care. Over the years I have had the opportunity to write and speak on aspects of Christian education. An earlier version of most of this material has been published elsewhere and is now brought together in a revised form in the hope that it may serve a wider audience. The title of this book is a quotation from Psalm 78:4 (NIV84).

I have benefited from the input, critique, and feedback of those with expertise in their fields of work. I am indebted to Keith Sikkema of the Covenant Canadian Reformed Teachers College in Hamilton, Ontario, for his willingness to critique and give feedback on all the material in this publication. His input has been of great benefit. I am also thankful to many others.

For chapter 1, I am grateful for the feedback provided by Dr. Sean Schat, Assistant Professor of Education at Redeemer University.

For chapter 2 on homeschooling I have benefitted from a 2019 Facebook discussion on this topic initiated and led by Monica Oosterhoff of Vineland, Ontario, who also invited my interaction with the views presented. I have also profited from the input of Leonard Bergsma of Heritage Resources in Carman, Manitoba, on an earlier draft of this chapter, and more recently from Rev. Jan de Gelder, minister emeritus of the Redemption Canadian Reformed Church of Flamborough, Ontario.

For chapter 4 on educating children with disabilities, I received help from Bert VanGoolen, recently retired as Executive Director of the Anchor Association in Ontario which provides long-term support to those with developmental disabilities in a supportive Christian environment and also from Wendy Smeding of Guido de Brès Christian High School in Hamilton as well as Henry and Annelies Homan who know the life reality of dealing with a special needs sibling.

For chapters 7 to 9, I have benefited from feedback provided by Dr. John Byl, Professor Emeritus of Mathematics at Trinity Western University.

Needless to say, I alone am responsible for the views expressed in this book.

I greatly appreciate the willingness of Dr. Christine Van Halen-Faber, daughter of Dr. Jelle Faber, to write a foreword to this publication.

I thankfully acknowledge permission from William Gortemaker to use material that first appeared in Clarion and here appears in revised form, from Rev. W. Huizinga to use material from *Fathers and Mothers at Home and at School* to which he held the copyright, and from Guido de Brès Christian High School to include their mandate in this book.

I acknowledge my debt of thanks to Margaret Alkema, librarian at the Canadian Reformed Theological Seminary, who is always ready to help whenever that is necessary and to Dr. Gijsbertus Nederveen who carefully read through the entire manuscript and suggested improvements. The willingness of Andrew Schouten of Providence Books and Press to publish this material is greatly appreciated as are the skilful labors of Mary DeBoer in her editorial work and Sarah Tiemstra of Studio of Sarah in preparing the material for publishing.

PART A

THE TASK OF CHRISTIAN EDUCATION

CHAPTER 1

Fathers and Mothers: at Home and at School

The task of educating our children and preparing the next generation for service to the Lord in all of life is an incredibly important undertaking. No responsibility from God is more important for the well-being of those who will exercise their office and calling in the home and in society after us. Each generation is faced with this challenge. It is more than that. Educating the next generation is a holy duty that God himself has entrusted to us as Christians.

A survey of some of the basics of how we go about living up to God's expectations in preparing the next generation is the focus of this chapter. We will consider the responsibilities of those charged to educate and how they are to live up to their duty, as well as the goals and methods of education involved.

The Teachers

There are two main groups of teachers that concern us: the parents and those who give instruction outside the home in schools. As we shall see, these two groups are closely identified in Scripture.

The Parental Task

It is an irrefutable fact that the Lord God gives parents the holy charge to educate their children in the fear of his name. They are the first ones who have this responsibility. There is no way they can evade it. Already way back in the patriarchal era, God said of Abraham: "I have chosen him, that he may command his children and his household after him to keep the way of the LORD by doing righteousness and justice, so that the LORD may bring to Abraham what he has promised him" (Gen 18:19). Furthermore, after the LORD God had given Israel his laws and decrees at Mount Sinai, he solemnly charged his covenant people:

> And these words which I command you today shall be on your heart. You shall teach them diligently to your children, and shall talk of them when you sit in your house, and when you walk by the way, and when you lie down, and when you rise. You shall bind them as a sign on your hand, and they shall be as frontlets between your eyes. You shall write them on the doorposts of your house and on your gates. (Deut 6:6–9)

Similarly, we read in Psalm 78 that the LORD

> established a testimony in Jacob and appointed a law in Israel,
> which he commanded our fathers to teach their children
> that the next generation might know them, the children yet unborn,
> and arise and tell them to their children so that they may set their hope in God
> and not forget the works of God, but keep his commandments.
> (Ps 78:5–7)

Thus the parents had the holy obligation to teach their offspring the way and will of the LORD.

This duty concerns both the father and the mother. One can think of the proverbial admonition: "Hear my son, your father's instruction, and forsake not your mother's teaching" (Prov 1:8; similarly 9:20). It was also the mother of King Lemuel who taught him (Prov 31:1).

Already in Old Testament times, parents were helped with teachers outside their homes. Let us briefly consider schools in ancient Israel and then look at how the instructors and their teaching are described.

Other Teachers

Not much is explicitly stated in the Old Testament about formal education outside the home. This relative silence is, of course, not surprising since it is not the purpose of Scripture to inform us of such details. There are, however, a number of factors that we should take into consideration when trying to understand the situation in ancient Israel.

We do know that the tribe of Levi, particularly the priests, were charged with teaching Israel the ordinances and laws of God.[1] We may, therefore, assume that the Levitical cities (cf. Num 35:1-8; Josh 21) functioned as important centers of learning.

Furthermore, prophets were involved in education by teaching and preaching. Scripture informs us of prophets who lived together in various places as "sons of the prophets" under the leadership of Elijah and later Elisha.[2] We can assume that these so-called "schools of the prophets" had an educational function in keeping alive the knowledge and worship of the true God in the northern tribes in a time of apostasy. A similar situation seems to have existed earlier in the days of Samuel with the destruction of Shiloh. Bands of prophets were then active (1 Sam 10:9–13; cf. 3:1; also see 19:20). Later Isaiah can speak about his teaching and disciples (Isa 8:16; cf. Ezek 33:30-33).

Finally, wise men or sages can be mentioned as being involved in teaching, perhaps by attracting followers who learned from them. "The lips of the wise spread knowledge" (Prov 15:7). Their sayings were collected as in the Book of Proverbs. "Besides being wise, the Preacher also taught the people knowledge, weighing and studying and arranging many proverbs with great care. The Preacher sought to find words of delight, and uprightly he wrote words of truth … They were given by one Shepherd" (Eccl 12:9–11). Not much is known about these sages or their activities.

But did schools, that is, some sort of education outside the homes, exist? Are the above not geared more to the "religious"? What about

---

1 Deut 31:10–13; 33:10; Lev. 10:11; 2 Chron 17:7–9.
2 1 Kings 20:35; 2 Kings 2:3,5,7,15; 6:1–2; cf. 1 Kings 20:35; Isa 8:16; Edward J. Young, *My Servants the Prophets* (Grand Rapids, MI: Eerdmans, 1952), 83–94.

instruction with a broader interest? To begin with, it would appear that one must not underestimate the importance of the Levitical cities as centers of learning. Although the Levites were charged by God to teach his revelation to his people (Deut 33:10), there are factors that could suggest that instruction did not stop there. After all, the Levitical cities apparently served as administrative centers and Levites had responsibilities in "the affairs of the king" (1 Chron 26:29-32). It would be most reasonable if at least some of the Levitical cities included scribal educational centers, which besides teaching writing also taught administration and other skills necessary to keep the royal bureaucracy going. Such schools existed in Egypt and Mesopotamia as early as the third millennium BC. There is reason to assume that Israel had similar means of educating when the following factors are taken into consideration along with those already mentioned.

Literacy was widespread. God's demands had to be written on the doorposts of Israel's homes (Deut 6:9; cf. 27:2–8), implying that the average Israelite could do this. The young man from Succoth, who happened to be captured by Gideon, was able to write down the seventy-seven names of the officials and elders of that city for his captor (Judg 8:14; also cf. e.g. Josh 18:4, 8–9).[3] Furthermore, school exercises dating from before the first millennium BC to the exile have been found in Israel.[4] Also, judging from architectural and related evidence throughout Israel, technical education must have been available in Israel as well.[5] It is, therefore, not surprising that most scholars appear to agree that education outside the home took place in schools of some sort in ancient Israel.[6] The first actual

---

3 Alan R. Millard, "An Assessment of the Evidence for Writing in Ancient Israel," in *Biblical Archaeology Today: Proceedings of the International Congress on Biblical Archaeology Jerusalem, April 1984*, preface by A. Biran (Jerusalem: Israel Exploration Society, 1985), 301–12, esp. 308; J. Kaster, "Education, OT," in *The Interpreter's Dictionary of the Bible*, ed. George Arthur Buttrick (Nashville, TN: Abingdon, 1962), 2:30; Felix Höflmayer, et al., "Early Alphabetic Writing in the Ancient Near East," *Antiquity* 95, no. 381 (2021): 705–19.

4 André Lemaire, *Les écoles et la formation de la Bible dans l'ancien Israël*, OBO (Fribourg, CH: Éditions Universitaires, 1981), 7–33; cf. Isa 28:9–13 which seems to allude to a classroom setting.

5 B.S.J. Isserlin, "Israelite Architectural Planning and the Question of the Level of Secular Learning in Ancient Israel," *Vetus Testamentum* 34 (1984): 169–78. It is also important to note that the sophisticated culture of Egypt and that of Canaan and ancient Israel had ties from earliest times until the destruction of Jerusalem. See Philip Zhakevich, *Scribal Tools in Ancient Israel: A Study of Biblical Hebrew Terms for Writing Materials and Implements*, History, Archaeology, and Culture of the Levant (University Park, PA: Eisenbrauns, 2020), 160–68.

6 André Lemaire, "The Sage in School and Temple," in *The Sage in Israel and the Ancient Near East*, eds. John G. Gammie and Leo G. Perdue (Winona Lake, IN: Eisenbrauns, 1990), 167.

mention of schools occurs in the apocryphal book Sirach (51:23) which can be dated about 190–175 BC.[7] The synagogue became the center of public Jewish education since that is where the law was taught. There is evidence to suggest that compulsory attendance at elementary schools was established by the first century BC.[8] In New Testament times every effort was made for all Jewish children wherever they lived to attend elementary school (to age 15).[9]

It is of interest for us to know how the teachers who taught children outside the home were characterized.

School Parents

The Bible uses a term to describe teachers which we seldom employ. A teacher is called "father" and the students are known as "sons" (and therefore also "daughters"). According to this terminology, students in school not only have parents at home, they also have a "father" at school. Considering the enormous influence teachers have on students—they are like pliable clay in their hands—such terminology is quite fitting. Teachers literally mold the lives and ideas of their pupils as a parent would.

The term "father" is quite an honorable way to address someone in Scripture. That is why, for example, David respectfully spoke to King Saul as to a father (e.g. 1 Sam 24:11). It is, therefore, not surprising that teachers as honored members of the community be given this title. When Elijah was taken up into heaven by a whirlwind, then Elisha cried: "My father, my father! The chariots of Israel and its horsemen!" (2 Kings 2:12; cf. 6:21). The meaning of the term "father" as used here includes the meaning of teacher, especially when one considers that Elisha was a student of Elijah and that the students of the prophetic schools were, as noted earlier, called the "sons of the prophets" (cf. 2 Kings 2:3,5). The teacher was the "father."

---

7   Lemaire, "The Sage," 166.
8   S. Safrai, *The Jewish People in the First Century: Historical Geography, Political History, Social, Cultural and Religious Life and Institutions*, eds. S. Safrai and M. Stern, Compendia Rerum Iudaicarum Ad Novum Testamentum (Assen, NL: Van Gorcum, 1976), 947–48.
9   A.W. Morton, "Education in Biblical Times," in *The Zondervan Pictorial Encyclopedia of the Bible*, gen. ed. Merrill C. Tenny (Grand Rapids, MI: Zondervan, 1976), 2:211.

Similarly when David wanted to give instruction, he set himself up as a father. "Come, O children [lit. sons], listen to me; I will teach you the fear of the LORD" (Ps 34:11). These "sons" are not his natural offspring, but are the saints (cf. v. 9). We find a similar usage of the term "father" in the book of Proverbs. In Proverbs we often hear the voice of a teacher to his pupils, as that of a father to his sons (Prov 2:1; 3:1 etc.).

Similar terminology is found in the ancient Near East. In ancient Sumer, the land which came to be known as Babylonia, texts dating from about 2,000 BC indicate that the head of a school was among other things called a "school-father" and a student was called a "school-son."[10]

In the New Testament, the Lord Jesus called students of the Pharisees who perform exorcisms "sons" of the Pharisees (Matt 12:27). Paul, a student of Gamaliel, a Pharisee, identified himself as "a son of Pharisees" (Acts 23:6).

It is noteworthy that in the book of Proverbs it is not always obvious whether the natural father or the teacher father is referred to. In Proverbs 1:8, the biological father is obviously in view: "Hear, my son, your father's instruction, and forsake not your mother's teaching." But elsewhere it is not always so clear whether the biological or teaching father is meant. The reference can be to either the one or the other.[11] The fact that some of the passages (e.g. 3:1,11,21; 4:1 etc.) are open to debate whether it is indeed the natural father or the teacher father who is speaking indicates that in a sense the distinction between the two types of fathers is in Proverbs somewhat blurred. The use of this parental terminology underlines the fact that the parental character of the education to be received is essentially the same, whether that be given at home or at school. This important point is underlined by the common purpose of education at home and at a school.

---

10 Samuel Noah Kramer, *The Sumerians: Their History, Culture and Character* (Chicago, IL: University of Chicago Press, 1963), 232; see also Kaster, "Education, OT," 2:27.

11 So, e.g., Paul E. Koptak, *Proverbs*, The NIV Application Commentary (Grand Rapids, MI: Zondervan, 2003), 72; W. H. Gispen, *De Spreuken van Salomo*, Korte Verklaring der Heilige Schrift (Kampen, NL: Kok, 1952), 1:25; also see H. Haag, "*bēn*," in *Theological Dictionary of the Old Testament*, ed. G. Johannes Botterweck, Helmer Ringgren, and Heinz-Josef Fabry, trans. David E. Green, et al (Grand Rapids, MI: Eerdmans, 1975), 2:152.

The Purpose of Education

Children were to be taught the great deeds of God (e.g. Deut 6:6-9) as well as the practical skills of life. Common thinking in Judaism was that a man who did not teach his son the Law and a trade, that is, the ability to work, reared him to be a fool and a thief.[12] Israel's education was structured so that boys could earn the bread and butter and girls could be prepared for their future task in the home.

But apart from these more or less obvious objects of education, what was the underlying goal, the ultimate reason for teaching children spiritual truths and practical skills? Two interrelated purposes can be mentioned: to prepare them for life in fullness and to impart true wisdom. Both are related to their relationship with God and life with him, now and forever.

Preparation for Life in Fullness

The practical education was religious since the fear of the LORD is the basis of all knowledge and wisdom (Prov 1:7). The Bible does not separate the practical and the spiritual. This life and the life to come is one continuum. The Heidelberg Catechism puts it well. We "begin in this life the eternal Sabbath" (QA 103).[13] The great duty of the father and the mother was to see to it that their sons and daughters could live, that is, make a living before God in obedience to him and so receive the covenant blessing of a long life, yes eternal life! The practical and the spiritual belong together and are to be integrated. Just as fathers and mothers were God's instruments to bring about physical life, so also they are to be instruments to give eternal life.

---

12 William Barclay, *Educational Ideals in the Ancient World* (Grand Rapids, MI: Baker, 1959), 16. Josephus, a Jewish historian (c. AD 37–100) in contrasting the very practical education of the Lacedaemonians and Cretans on the one hand and the much more theoretical education of the Athenians on the other hand, wrote in *Against Apion*, 2.172–173 that the Jewish education combined both. *Josephus, The Life; Against Apion*. With an English translation by H. St. J. Thackeray, Loeb Classical Library (Cambridge, MA: Harvard University Press, 1926), 360–63.

13 *Book of Praise: Anglo-Genevan Psalter* (Winnipeg, MB: Premier, 2014), 555.

If we see this as the root meaning of what it means to be a parent, also when speaking of education, then the implications of a teacher being called a father are quite staggering. Israel, and later the Jews, saw that clearly, especially when professional teachers more and more took over the education of children. In view of the awesome life-giving function of a father, one can understand how an ancient Jewish exposition even dared to place the relationship of the student to his teacher father higher than the student's relationship to his physical father, "for his father did but bring him into this world, but his teacher that taught him wisdom brings him into the world to come."[14] This is, of course, a wrong dilemma, for the biological father has the same duty, but the point is that teachers were rightly held in great respect.

Now if education had as its goal to make life possible now and forever, both practical and spiritual, then what children really need to learn is biblical wisdom.

Imparting True Wisdom

Such biblical wisdom is found, for example, in the book of Proverbs. The imparting of wisdom is both a daily and long-range goal. It would take us too far afield to discuss Proverbs at any length, but it will be profitable to deal briefly with a highlight or two from Proverbs 1:2–7 and draw some conclusions for the teaching task today. The book of Proverbs certainly has something to tell us.

The purpose and main point of Proverbs is:

To know wisdom and instruction,
    to understand words of insight,
to receive instruction in wise dealing,
    in righteousness, justice, and equity;
to give prudence to the simple,
    knowledge and discretion to the youth—

---

[14] *The Mishnah*, trans. and ed. Herbert Danby (Oxford, UK: Oxford University Press, 1933), 350 (Baba Metzia 2:11).

> Let the wise hear and increase in learning,
> > and the one who understands obtain guidance,
> to understand a proverb and a saying,
> > the words of the wise and their riddles.
> The fear of the LORD is the beginning of knowledge;
> > fools despise wisdom and instruction. (Prov 1:2–7)

The overall meaning of this passage is clear. A key word that demands our attention is "wisdom." This word is rich in meaning in Proverbs as well as in the Old Testament generally. It signifies in the first place wisdom as we generally understand it: good sense, insight, and prudence (e.g. 2 Sam 20:22, 1 Kings 2:6; 3:28). It is also an attribute of those who appreciate the value of time and use it wisely (Ps 90:12). This wisdom comes from God, especially in fearing him (Prov 1:7; 9:10; Ps 90:12; 1 Kgs 3:28).

In the second place, the Hebrew term for wisdom also means technical ability, for example, in working with different fabrics and metals. Those who were to make the holy garments for Aaron were endowed by God with "the spirit of wisdom," that is artistic skill (so lit. Exod 28:3). This wisdom, therefore, has also its source in God (e.g. lit. Exod 31:3; 35:31).[15]

As is evident from the wide scope of Proverbs, which seeks to impart wisdom (Prov 1:2), wisdom concerns all the areas of life. Although rules are not given for every conceivable situation, the guidance and principles given are clear enough (e.g. on the harlot and drunkenness) to grant wisdom and practical help for the twentieth century in evaluating literature, music, and the offerings of the mass media. The wisdom of Proverbs is not speculative philosophy. It is practical life wisdom, with life understood in its fullest sense as we have seen earlier—life before God in all its practical and religious ramifications. There was in Israel no dilemma of theoretical speculation and practical knowledge. All wisdom is life wisdom.

---

15 The Hebrew term for "wisdom," *ḥokmâ* is sometimes translated literally in the ESV, but is often translated with "skill" or similar terms in other translations in the passages that concern us now. But it is important for understanding the biblical notion of wisdom to realize that the word for "wisdom" is literally used in passages which are relevant for our topic, such as Exod 31:6 which lit. reads "in the hearts of all who are wise of heart I have put wisdom;" Exod 35:26 "whose heart lifted them up with wisdom;" 1 Kings 7:14 "filled with wisdom."

This wisdom is to be taught. There would be little rationale for much of Proverbs if this was not so. Listen to Proverbs 4 on parents teaching this wisdom.

> Hear, O sons, a father's instruction,
>   and be attentive, that you may gain insight,
> for I give you good precepts;
>   do not forsake my teaching.
> When I was a son with my father,
>   tender, the only one in the sight of my mother,
> he taught me and said to me,
>   Let your heart hold fast my words;
>   keep my commandments, and live.
> Get wisdom; get insight;
>   do not forget, and do not turn away from the words of my mouth.
> Do not forsake her, and she will keep you;
>   love her, and she will guard you.
> The beginning of wisdom is this: Get wisdom,
>   and whatever you get, get insight. (Prov 4:1–7)

There are conditions for teaching and learning wisdom. As is clear from Proverbs 4, the law is to be the norm and the subject matter. Furthermore, effort and discipline are needed. Acquiring wisdom is not automatic.

The place of the law is central as norm and the object of study. The Hebrew word for "law" is *tôrâ*; but the term also means "direction," "instruction," and "teaching."[16] The subject matter is instruction that gives direction. In this way life before God and for God is taught. The teaching must be authoritative for it is the way God has shown in his Word. Today we would say that the Bible and its implications for our entire life must be taught.

---

[16] David J. A. Clines, ed., *The Dictionary of Classical Hebrew* (Sheffield, UK: Sheffield Academic Press, 1993–2016), 8:612–16; Ludwig Koehler, Walter Baumgartner, and Johann Jakob Stamm, *The Hebrew and Aramaic Lexicon of the Old Testament*, trans. and ed. M. E. J. Richardson (Leiden, NL: Brill, 2001), 1710–12.

The fact that the normative Word of God is taught means that teachers cannot engage the students in such a way so that they will seek the truth together according to their own insights, as is often done in secular education. God's truth and norms are the basis of all instruction. Now this goes contrary to our sinful human nature and, therefore, the authority of the Word needs to be brought to bear. Life experience and the book of Proverbs show that there is resistance to this authoritative teaching of divine wisdom. But this is what fools do. They "despise wisdom and instruction" (Prov 1:7). As the rest of Proverbs 1 shows, the fool is rebellious, not just against his father, but also against God, for the wisdom at issue is the wisdom whose source is God. Since "the fool" is inside all of us by nature, the instruction in God's wisdom needs a lot of effort. This fact is also evident from the Hebrew term used for instruction (*musar*, e.g. in Prov 1:2–3). It also means "training" and has the idea of discipline. The instruction is, therefore, a teaching accompanied by correction and reproof, an instruction presented with authority. But all the work involved is worth it!

The knowledge given with this teaching of true wisdom ultimately concerns God and one's relationship to him. Indeed, the instruction in the law and will of God can be described as teaching "the fear of the LORD" (cf. Ps 19:7–11). It is something that can be taught. As David put it when speaking of instructing about God's norms: "I will teach you the fear of the LORD" (Ps 34:11–14). And so educating in God's wisdom entails the knowledge of God himself and the correct attitude of humble and reverent submission to his will. Without the LORD, there is no true knowledge and wisdom. "The fear of the LORD is the beginning of knowledge" (Prov 1:7); that is, true understanding is only possible when one submits to the LORD and his revelation. This true knowledge is not something which one can sit back and wait for. No, effort is needed! It needs to be taught and learned. Teaching, discipline, and the application of authority is needed, as well as effort by the student. As we read in Proverbs 2:1–7:

> My son, if you receive my words
>   and treasure up my commandments with you,
> making your ear attentive to wisdom
>   and inclining your heart to understanding;

> yes, if you call out for insight
>   and raise your voice for understanding,
> if you seek it like silver
>   and search for it as for hidden treasures,
> then you will understand the fear of the LORD
>   and find the knowledge of God.
> For the LORD gives wisdom;
>   from his mouth come knowledge and understanding;
> he stores up sound wisdom for the upright;
>   he is a shield to those who walk in integrity. (Prov 2:1–7)

So wisdom comes from God and it is only made one's own by listening to him in reverent submission.

In Proverbs, wisdom is also personified, especially in chapter 8. Wisdom speaks and says: "The LORD possessed me at the beginning of his work, the first of his acts of old. Ages ago I was set up, at the first, before the beginning of the earth" (Prov 8:22–23). When God created the world, "then I [wisdom] was beside him, like a master workman, and I was daily his delight" (Prov 8:27). This personification can be seen as a preparation for the New Testament revelation of Christ as the true wisdom. Christ is the wisdom of God (1 Cor 1:24) and God has made him our wisdom (1 Cor 1:30). In Christ are hid all the treasures of wisdom and knowledge (Col 2:3).[17]

To summarize, wisdom is life wisdom in the fullest sense of the term. He who finds wisdom finds life (Prov 8:35). This wisdom is only acquired in the fear of the LORD, for the fear of the LORD is the beginning, that is the first and controlling principle, of knowledge (Prov 1:7). True knowledge is only attainable in God, in knowing and fearing him. Wisdom, knowledge, and teaching are therefore very much bound up with one's relationship to God. In knowing God and understanding his ways, will, world, and handiwork are true insight, discretion, prudence, and understanding found. There is really no such thing as objective true

---

[17] For a more detailed discussion on the personification of wisdom in Prov 8 and Christ, see Cornelis Van Dam, *In the Beginning: Listening to Genesis 1 and 2* (Grand Rapids, MI: Reformation Heritage Books, 2021), 71–76.

knowledge by autonomous man. Only with reference to the God of this world and all its contents and facts, can there be true knowledge and understanding.[18] With such an orientation, one can truly be educated for life, here and now before God and in his service in this world as his responsible children. Only then can one savor true life and enjoy the beginning of life eternal.

Ways for Attaining this Purpose

There are several means to help achieve this purpose of being equipped for the full life that can be mentioned: life-producing discipline, memory work, and meaningful interaction.

Life-Producing Discipline

Because the teacher as father or mother has to impart to children the fear and wisdom of the LORD, that is, true life, therefore the authority of a teacher must be life-producing. It must be exercised as a parent would do it, with love, encouraging the pupils in the Lord. Students, the "sons" and "daughters" must sense a teacher's great affection for them, as well as a deep commitment to their high calling to prepare them for life before God. The exercise of discipline and authority must not be stifling, but life-producing, not discouraging but encouraging for the students. One sometimes reads of overzealous teachers who make all kinds of rules which cannot be enforced. Then such a teacher is not a school "father" or "mother" but a police officer. As the saying goes: "If you act like a warden, your students will behave like prisoners." Something of the beauty of a family atmosphere must be present in the school, for the teacher is as a parent and the teaching is for life instruction. After all, properly seen, the school is ideally nothing but an extension of the home.

---

18 Cf. John Calvin, *Institutes of the Christian Religion*, ed. John T. McNeill, trans. Ford Lewis Battles, Library of Christian Classics (Philadelphia, PA: Westminster, 1960), 1.1.2 (pp. 37–38) where Calvin says that we cannot even know ourselves without knowing God.

The nature of such life-inducing authority does not, of course, mean a lack of discipline, as teachers know only too well, for the student sons and daughters are inclined to sin. For them accepting the direction and teaching for life here on earth and starting a life eternal neither comes naturally nor easily. But the discipline can never simply be a conditioning, a making of something from a blank slate. Baptized sons and daughters are recipients of God's covenant promises and a school father or mother has the holy obligation to recognize that reality and encourage the true life in Christ. Solomon could, therefore, extol the virtue of godly discipline. "Whoever spares the rod hates his son, but he who loves him is diligent to discipline him" (Prov 13:24). Solomon often spoke in a somewhat humorous way, as illustrated by the translation of Proverbs 23:13-14 given by Old Testament scholar H. J. Schilder: "Do not withhold discipline from a child; give it to him with a stick. Don't worry. It won't kill him! Just give him a spanking. You will save his life from death."[19]

While the Lord gives parents the freedom to discipline their children with a physical spanking, today's teachers should not use any corporal punishment lest they leave themselves open to possible charges of abuse in today's climate of children's rights. It goes without saying that in the case of parents, physical discipline should be a last resort and appropriate if administered. However, godly parental disciplinary action is in a totally different category from child abuse which unfortunately does occur under the guise of discipline. Such abuse is to be severely condemned. But to ban any appropriate parental spanking would be to deny biblical wisdom.[20] When the author of the book of Hebrews writes of discipline by a father, he noted that "for the moment all discipline seems painful rather than pleasant, but later it yields the peaceful fruit of righteousness to those who have been trained by it" (Heb 12:11). Today's teachers, enabled with the professional training they have typically received, should be able to discipline their students and achieve their goals in the classroom without having to resort to physically spanking them.

---

19 My translation from his Dutch version in H.J. Schilder, "Education and Upbringing in the Old Testament (II)," *Almond Branch* 1, no. 2 (November 1970): 16.

20 See, e.g., the views and guidelines of a Christian psychologist from Focus on the Family, Jared Pingleton, "Spanking Can Be an Appropriate Form of Child Discipline," *Time*, 16 September 2014, found at https://time.com/3387226/spanking-can-be-an-appropriate-form-of-child-discipline/.

Memory Work

To be equipped for a full life of service to God, the importance of memorization should not be underestimated.

Scripture makes clear that parents have the obligation to entrust the great deeds of God to their children. To state it differently, God's works have to be written on their hearts (cf. Deut 6:6–9). In Old Testament times much was therefore undoubtedly committed to memory. Nowadays memory work is often viewed with disdain. But it was and still should be a very important means by which the father and mother can fulfill their task. Also the school parents should require their students to memorize, for with memory work great principles are at stake.

Psalm 78 illustrates how two principles are involved in the need to memorize God's saving work. The first is that the LORD's deeds need to be transmitted and remembered. The psalm enjoins God's people: "tell to the coming generation the glorious deeds of the LORD, and his might and the wonders that he has done" (Ps 78:4). Furthermore, God

> commanded our fathers
>   to teach to their children,
> that the next generation might know them,
>   the children yet unborn,
> and arise and tell them to their children,
>   so that they should set their hope in God
> and not forget the works of God,
>   but keep his commandments;
> and that they should not be like their fathers,
>   a stubborn and rebellious generation. (Ps 78:5–8).

The above words also illustrate a second principle, namely, that the children learn from the sins of the past and be encouraged in true obedience to God.

It was therefore important that the fathers tell their children the great deeds of the LORD, lest they forget the LORD and stray from his ways. Fathers were repeatedly told to keep on telling the LORD's doings to their children, whether they were sitting, standing, lying down, or rising (Deut 6:7–9). In this way, God's works would be committed to memory. It is interesting to note that this continual instruction and the memorization that went with it resulted in later generations being able to speak about the Exodus with details that were not even mentioned in the written Mosaic records of the events being remembered. The LORD could, therefore, use these details of the memorized accounts to be included in his Word at a later stage. So, for example, one can find in Psalm 77:18–19 a reference to thunder during the crossing of the Red Sea which we do not read about in Exodus.[21] Clearly the fathers had an important task.

Now one could say that memory work is less important today. After all, there was some urgency in passing on God's great deeds to the next generation by way of memorizing in Old Testament times because written copies of God's Word (as far as it was then put in writing) were probably relatively scarce. In all likelihood only the priests and the wealthy had access to written copies of what was their Bible at the time, if the example of the Middle Ages before the advent of printing can give an indication of the situation that then transpired. It is possible, therefore, that for many the Scriptures constituted the memorized words of the LORD as they had been handed down by their parents and the priests.

Such reasons for downgrading the importance of memorization today do not hold water. The great importance of memorizing God's great deeds and Scripture passages is that, by being immersed in Scripture, students are enabled to grow in the knowledge and fear of the LORD. Knowing God's Word by memory enables them to "think God's thoughts after him."[22] Scripture needs to be internalized and made, as it were, part of their DNA, their very identity. Then a student is enabled to see reality from God's point of view. For that to be possible it is, of course, obvious that whatever Scripture students are asked to memorize must be relevant and applicable

---

[21] W. H. Gispen, *Mondelinge overlevering in het Oude Testament* (Meppel, NL: B. Ten Brink en M. Stenvert & Zoon, 1932), esp. p. 38.

[22] The phrase is from Cornelius Van Til, *A Christian Theory of Knowledge* (Phillipsburg, NJ: Presbyterian and Reformed, 1969), 16; also see William N. Blake, "Van Til's Vision for Education," in *Foundations of Christian Scholarship: Essays in the Van Til Perspective*, ed. Gary North (Vallecito, CA: Ross House, 1976), 103–16, esp. 108.

to their lives, as well as being age-appropriate.²³ Furthermore, parents and teachers must also know those assigned passages from memory as well and so underlining that what the students are learning is meaningful for one's walk of life with the LORD. Not to do so sends the message to them that such memory work is not all that important. Once you get out of school you can forget it, just as the parents and teacher did!

The great and constant challenge of teaching is to shape the thinking of those being taught to be oriented around the LORD and what he has said and done. All the subjects need to be anchored in and permeated with the language and presuppositions of the Scriptures. In a real sense, both home and school parents mediate the wisdom and knowledge of God's Word to their children as it concerns the different subjects. To grow in biblical wisdom is to be constantly challenged to see all things pertaining to one's life through the lens of God's revelation to us. That is the only real antidote to the pervasive secularization of so much thinking and writing today.²⁴

In sum, the importance of memorization cannot be overestimated. The downplaying of memorization is a recent development as is the notion that truth can exist meaningfully in a book, to be used for reference purposes as needed instead of in a person's mind.²⁵ These trends must be resisted. The Word needs to be internalized so that it shapes our life habits. The psalmist said: "I have stored up your word in my heart, that I might not sin against you" (Ps 119:11). David noted that the law of God is in the heart of the righteous and so "his steps do not slip" (Ps 37:31). The truth and relevance of God's Word must never be divorced from life. They need to be integral to it.

---

23 Cf. J. Marion Snapper, "Memorization in Church Education," *Calvin Theological Journal* 16 (1981): 43–44.
24 Cf. the stimulating work of Harry Blamires, *The Christian Mind* (London, UK: SPCK, 1966); Harry Blamires, *Recovering the Christian Mind: Meeting the Challenge of Secularism* (Downers Grove, IL: InterVarsity Press, 1988); Harry Blamires, *The Post Christian Mind: Exposing Its Destructive Agenda*, foreword by J.I. Packer (Ann Arbor, MI: Servant, 1999).
25 See Marion Snapper, "The Dethronement of Memory in Church Education," *Calvin Theological Journal* 13 (1981): 44–47; also see Barclay, *Educational Ideals in the Ancient World*, 23–24, 40–43.

Meaningful Interaction

In order to internalize the Word and make remembering it an integral part of one's mindset means that there must be meaningful interaction between both home and school parents and those entrusted to them. Teaching is not a one way street. God encouraged those who were learning to ask questions. It is striking that God would sometimes use memorials to arouse the curiosity of the children to help them know and remember his saving works. For example, twelve stones were placed in the Jordan River where Israel miraculously crossed on dry ground into the Promised Land as well as twelve on the shore. The point was that when children would later ask their parents concerning these memorials, they would learn and be reminded of God's great deeds (Josh. 4:1–10, 20–24).

God also used the annual festivals to ingrain into the minds of his people his saving work and its impact on their lives. The Passover was also a memorial about which children could ask questions and so learn of God's saving work for his people in delivering them out of Egypt (Exod 12:26–27). The Feast of Weeks or Pentecost was a time to rejoice in the LORD as families and community and remember their bondage in Egypt from which they had been delivered (Deut 16:9–12). The Feast of Booths was a time to remember their desert wanderings when they lived in temporary shelters en route to the Promised Land (Lev 23:33–43). Through such feasts, the LORD regularly brought his saving works into the very fabric of their lives so that it became part of who they were.

Today the regular celebration of the Lord's Supper also serves in part as a memorial to God's salvation in Christ, and children are free to ask questions about it as well. Indeed, they should be encouraged to do so. It brings the redemption in Christ closer to their world and life experience. The same goes for the sacrament of holy baptism whereby God signifies his claim on us as his precious possession. It is a wonderful teaching moment for the children which can profoundly shape their view of themselves and their outlook on life.

In passing on the riches of salvation in meaningful interaction with those in our charge, we can also learn from the use of memory aids in the book of Proverbs. The strategic use of striking stories or unforgettable sayings can be very effective in helping students to remember. Who will readily forget, for example, this characterization of the lazy sluggard. "As a door turns on its hinges, so does a sluggard on his bed" (Prov 26:14). Or who cannot fail to remember the description of the loose woman luring a young man without sense (Prov 7:6–21). The result is: "All at once he follows her, as an ox goes to the slaughter" (Prov 7:22). Our teaching should ideally be vivid and refreshingly vigorous. Such instruction will be more readily remembered. It will also make the students think. Indeed, if students are to be taught true wisdom and knowledge and grow and mature for a full life before God, then they must be taught to think through issues and struggle with questions under the guidance of their parents and their school parents.

When students start asking more sophisticated questions, the issue of the relationship between faith and reason comes up. What is the relative place of each? God has given us the ability to perceive problems and think critically. Inquiring children are a great gift.

The use of our reason must, of course, always be subject to God's revelation in Scripture. We proceed from the basis of biblical truth. We believe the Scriptures. Faith seeks understanding. Our reason can never be an autonomous entity. Cornelius Van Til has correctly said that "the gift of logical reason was given by God to man in order that he might order the revelation of God for himself. It was not given him that he might by means of it legislate as to what is possible and what is actual."[26] In other words, all our thinking is to be subject to Scripture.

Parents and teachers can reason with their children or students about the revelation of God, but only in faith. That is the condition and the beginning point. Then one can proceed and ask about the why and how. Faith and reason do not compete. The latter serves the former to the extent that we are allowed to explore as far as Scripture permits us to go. But by ordering God's revelation and thinking it through, a gold mine of insight and knowledge and wisdom can be discovered and related

---

26 Cornelius Van Til, *An Introduction to Systematic Theology* (Phillipsburg, NJ: Presbyterian and Reformed, 1979), 256.

to the subjects being taught. All parents and teachers of God's sons and daughters must constantly be busy with God's revelation. Are we not to love the LORD with all our heart, soul, and mind, that is, with all the strength and faculties that God has given us? (cf. Prov 23:26). The basic attitude and methodology of starting with and being subservient to Scripture in meeting the questions of the day must be firmly implanted in the student's mind. They need this manner of approaching issues to function in a biblically wise manner as adult Christians.[27]

And finally, to mention this point one more time, for all interaction to be meaningful it must, of course, be both practical and relevant. What is taught should be related in some way to real life needs. There should be no false dichotomy between theoretical and practical education. The notion of abstract knowledge, unrelated to the realities of life, was unknown in Israel. As the book of Proverbs illustrates, wisdom was intensely practical. The relevance of the education given at school must be clear to the students. They must know, for example, why the study of history is important, even though it seems so remote from the present. Unless the students know the practical need of their studies, how can they be expected to apply the knowledge they have gained?

The Ongoing Challenge

The LORD has entrusted our children to us. He has also claimed them for himself and he has given his Word as the ultimate resource for raising them in the fear of his name. Scripture sets the goals and norms of their education. The ongoing challenge is to integrate the Word into all of life so that the great deeds of God resonate within our daily life as well as that of our children. To achieve that end, the Bible must be far more than a reference tool, to be consulted as the need arises. Its truths and standards must become second nature to us and our children. To achieve that, God has given both home parents and school parents.

---

27 See further on faith and reason, chapter 9.

The LORD directed parents to incorporate the fullness of his revelation into all of life. Parents were to speak all day of the LORD and his greatness and love. It was to come naturally to speak in this manner because their hearts were to be full of love for the LORD. God exhorted them to teach their children diligently at home, on the road, during the day, and at bedtime his works and love. These were to be imprinted on their very hearts and minds (Deut 6:4–9).

Many parents are also blessed with the availability of a Christian school. It can be of great help to the instruction received at home. In the controlled atmosphere of an educational institution, the "fathers" and "mothers" teach students subjects all day long in the light of God's Word. Here the great deeds of God can be transmitted in such a way that they are not left forgotten in a book, but are relevant and meet the needs of the day. At school all facts, whatever the subject may be, can in one way or another be related to the LORD and his plan for us and the world. Then teaching is *torah*, giving direction for life, yes, for the full life in Jesus Christ on this earth, but which is at the same time the beginning of life eternal.

Ideally such a Christian school is a Reformed school. It provides the closest association with the ideals and beliefs of the children's parents attending a Reformed church. After all, Reformed schools are confessional in character since the teaching is based on the Reformed confessions. Such schools are also very consciously covenantal. They stress their close association to the local Reformed church community and the parental promises made at the baptism of their children. There can, of course, be situations where sending children to a Reformed or a Christian school is not possible. In that case the option of home schooling should be considered. More about that in the next chapter of this book. Parents can, however, also be compelled by circumstances to use a local public school. This can happen for a number of reasons, such as the inability to homeschool, a long geographical distance from the nearest Christian school, or a child with special needs who can only be accommodated in programs available in a public school. In that case, Christian parents need to monitor ever so closely the education their children receive at such a secular school since teachers exercise considerable molding power over their students.

Also teachers in a Christian school obviously have an enormous influence over their students. These "fathers" and "mothers" at a Christian school take on a tremendous responsibility and exert considerable control in shaping their "sons" and "daughters." They are the "parents" away from home. This fact has important repercussions. They fill the lives of their "sons" and "daughters" in a very real way. Daily and systematically, with the authority and discipline which come with a school situation, the students are worked on, at a time when they are most productive and attentive. When the biological parents see them after school, their children have already given their best. The potential impact of the "fathers" and "mothers" in school is therefore immense and should never be underestimated. Life direction is given in the school. Yes, life—which must include eternal life.

Such is the impact that the successful teacher literally molds his "children" in his image, just as a biological parent has children in his or her image. This can and does happen in the classroom. Teachers are like parents. They give life instruction and influence the life outlook and the very image of their students.

One can sense that this state of affairs can raise problems. A teacher's influence is immense. Is it not too great? Do parents not have the first right to influence? Do their sons and daughters not belong to them? An Aramean story recounts how a mother took her child to school and entrusted him to the teacher with these words: "His flesh is yours, his bones are mine." That is, the teacher is given the authority to teach and discipline the child, but the child belongs to its parents. The flesh is given to the teacher, even to be beaten, if necessary, but the bones, the basic structure, remains with the parents.[28]

There is something sound about this approach, for the teacher is not to remake the child he receives; the child belongs not to the school but

---

28 For this account, see Rousas J. Rushdoony, *Intellectual Schizophrenia: Culture, Crisis and Education*, preface by Edmund A. Opitz (Grand Rapids, MI: Baker, 1961), 126–27.

to the parents. We are reminded that the first five or six formative years are in the parental home.[29] This is also of comfort if one happens to be living where Christian school education is not possible. However, the fact that children belong to their parents is also a reminder that we cannot just leave our children in the care of the "parents" at school without any further involvement, no matter how good the school is. The school is to be an extension of the home; that's where the real father and mother are. Therefore parents must be very much involved with the teachers at school.

This involvement does not mean interference. It means praying for the teachers. It means using the channels available to show interest in their work and to find out how our children are doing. Positive involvement also implies good communication from school to home so that parents can reinforce what their children are taught in school and so that students receive a unified education. Parental involvement also means ensuring that teachers are well equipped so that they can do their calling as effectively as possible. It means above all that our children clearly see that there is no competition between their home parents and the school "parents" but that in the unity of the faith both are equipping the child in full obedience to the Lord in all areas of life.

This unity of home and school is the beauty of true Christian education. The "problem" of the teacher molding students in his or her image is then in a sense always limited. For when our children are molded in the image of the teacher, it should not be a direct source of concern, for both the "father" in the school and the father at home have another Teacher to whom they both submit and whose image they seek to be. He gives true wisdom, yes, he is true wisdom. He gives and is life, even life eternal (1 Cor 1:30). He was not called "father" as a title of honor, as teacher, for his teaching ministry revealed the great Father in heaven. Those who saw him, the Lord Jesus, were to see the heavenly Father (John 14:9), and those who obeyed him would be the image of Father on earth (Rom 8:29; Col 3:10)! And is it not the image of *that* Father that we seek to impress on our sons and daughters, also in school?

---

29 For more on the importance of the home, see chapter 3.

CHAPTER 2

Education in the Home, School, and Homeschooling

Education rightly occupies a very important place in the life of Reformed parents. It is a matter of critical significance. Within this context, an issue that continues to raise all sorts of fundamental questions and challenges is the matter of homeschooling.[1] What is the proper role of the family with respect to the education of our children? How does homeschooling relate to Christian schools? In considering such questions, we need to put the issues in perspective. We will, therefore, first step back and review some of the history of Reformed education in the home, school, and church. We will subsequently consider the blessings and challenges that are involved with homeschooling—for the family, the Christian day school, and the church family.

The Historic Reformed Emphasis on Godly Education

As we saw in the previous chapter, God entrusts parents with the holy duty to educate their children in the fear of his name. As parents were God's instruments to give physical life to their offspring, they are also to be one of his most important means to give their children life with

---

[1] A book that raises important legal questions about parental and state responsibilities and how they relate is James G. Dwyer and Shawn F. Peters, *Homeschooling: The History and Philosophy of a Controversial Practice*, The History and Philosophy of Education Series (Chicago and London, IL: University of Chicago Press, 2019). For a critical review, see Michael Wagner, "Parents on Perpetual Probation," *Christian Renewal* 37, no. 14 (28 June 2019): 30–32. Homeschooling has the attention of think tanks such as Cardus and the Fraser Institute to mention but these two examples. See their websites (www.cardus.ca and www.fraserinstitute.org) and search "homeschooling."

God, eternal life. For this enormous task, fathers and mothers had help in biblical times. Other teachers were involved, including the Levitical priests, but the key responsibility lay with the parents. This fact is underlined by the way teachers outside the home were called "fathers."

In the context of this discussion, the great Reformation of the sixteenth century was incredibly important for the church's reaffirming the critical central place that parents had for the education of their children in godliness. Within the Reformed heritage, a key influential voice in realizing the enormous importance of education and the place of the home and the church community was John Calvin. He stressed that parents were responsible for the education of their children, but so was the community of believers. Schools were also important and were to support the parental education in the home. This meant that the school teachers were to be Reformed and that the parents, that is the congregation, had control over what was taught in the schools.[2] There was, therefore, a very close supportive relationship between the parents, church, and school in providing the education for the children. These Calvinist notions had great influence on the synodical decisions of the Reformed Churches in the Netherlands during the sixteenth century with respect to the nurture and upbringing of the covenant youth, also by means of schools.[3]

Of far-reaching impact for the education of subsequent generations were the decisions of the great Synod of Dort (1618–19) as formulated in their seventeenth session on November 30, 1618.[4] The Synod stated

---

2   Stefan Ehrenpreis, "Education and Pedagogy," in *The Calvin Handbook*, ed. Herman J. Selderhuis (Grand Rapids, MI; Cambridge, UK: Eerdmans, 2009), 428–29; also see Peter Y. De Jong, "Calvin's Contribution to Christian Education," *Calvin Theological Journal* 2 (1967): 162–201.

3   For the sixteenth century synodical decisions, F. L. Bos, *De orde der kerk toegelicht met kerkelijke besluiten uit vier eeuwen* ('s-Gravenhage, NL: Uitgeverij Guido de Bres, 1950), 86–87; for a brief overview in English of the synods involved, William den Hollander, "The Great Reformation and Education," *Clarion* 67 (2018): 440.

4   *Acta, of handelingen der Nationale Synode: in de naam van onze Heere Jezus Christus: gehouden door autoriteit der hoogmogende heren Staten-Generaal der Verenigde Nederlanden te Dordrecht in de jaren 1618 en 1619: hier zijn ook bij opgenomen de volledige beoordelingen van de vijf artikelen en de Post-Acta of Nahandelingen*, reprint of the original Dutch edition of J.H. Donner and S.A. van den Hoorn (Houten, NL: Den Hertog, 1987), 41–43. An abridged English translation is found in Appendix A of this book, based on Henry Barnard, ed., "Scheme of Christian Education, Adopted at the Synod of Dort, on 30th of November, 1618," *The American Journal of Education* 5 (1858): 77–78.

that three modes of educating or catechizing were to be used: in the home by the parents, in the schools by the teachers, and in the churches by the ministers, elders, and catechists, especially appointed for this purpose. About the parental task, the synod stated:

> The office of parents is to diligently instruct their children and their whole household in the principles of the Christian religion, in a manner adapted to their respective capacities; earnestly and carefully to admonish them to the cultivation of true piety; to engage their punctual attendance on family worship, and to take them with them to the hearing of the Word of God. They should require their children to give an account of the sermons they hear, especially those on the Catechism; assign them some chapters of Scripture to read, and certain passages to commit to memory; and then impress and illustrate the truths contained in them in an easily comprehensible manner, adapted to the tenderness of youth. In this way they are to prepare them for being catechized in the schools, to encourage them, and to promote their edification.[5]

The Synod of Dort also underlined the great importance of schools. It was decided that "schools, in which the young shall be properly instructed in the principles of Christian doctrine, shall be instituted, not only in cities but also in towns and country places where up to this time none have existed. The Christian magistracy shall be requested to see to it that well-qualified persons may be employed with adequate remuneration." Teachers had to be active members in good standing in a Reformed church and were required to sign a subscription form "professing their belief in the Confession of Faith and the Heidelberg Catechism, and promising that they will accordingly give catechetical instruction to the youth in the principles of Christian truth." These teachers also had to ensure that those in their charge were not just acquiring head knowledge but that what they learned had to be instilled in their hearts and minds.

---

5   This and subsequent translations of Dort's decisions on education are found in Appendix A as noted in the previous footnote. The Dutch original text for this and subsequent quotes are found in *Acta Dordrecht 1618–19*, 41–43.

The third mode of educating involved the church. Ministers and elders had to ensure that parents discharged their educational duties and were required to supervise the teachers in the schools, ensuring that the instruction was up to their expectations. Furthermore, "the ministers, in the discharge of their public duty in the church, shall preach on the Catechism. These sermons shall be comparatively short, and as accessible as practicably possible, for the comprehension of children as well as adults." Ministers also had the responsibility to gather together those capable of being instructed and "explain to them the articles of the Christian faith, and catechize them according to the circumstances of their different capacities, progress, and knowledge."

The Synod of Dort was convinced that if the minister, and by implication others as well, who were involved in teaching the Christian faith, exercised their duties properly then "abundant fruit of their labors shall be found in the growth of religious knowledge and holiness of life to the glory of God and the prosperity of the church of Christ."

Today we may be the beneficiaries of this rich Reformed tradition in passing on the treasures of the faith to the next generation with these three important means of educating the youth: the family, the school, and the church. Much of this heritage comes together in the vows parents take at the baptism of their children.

The Baptismal Vows and Consequences

The classic Reformed baptismal form, which dates back to the sixteenth century, includes three questions that parents need to answer prior to their child receiving the sacrament of baptism.[6] The third question asks "do you promise as father and mother to instruct your child in this doctrine, as soon as he (she) is able to understand, and to have him (her) instructed therein to the utmost of your power?"[7]

---

[6] For the history of the text of these questions, see P. Biesterveld, *Het gereformeerde kerkboek*, rev. by T. Hoekstra (n.p.: Het Gereformeeerd Traktaatgenootschap "Filippus", 1931), 173–80; B. Wielenga, *Ons Doopsformulier* (Kampen, NL: Kok, 1906), 235–38.

[7] *Book of Praise*, 598.

The first promise that parents make is that they will instruct their child as soon as he or she is able to comprehend. That starts very early. Indeed, humanly speaking, a child's first five or six years are extremely important in terms of shaping a child's outlook on life. Such early training in the fear of the Lord is one significant way that God works faith in the hearts of little ones. In holy baptism, God claims the child as his own. In the parent's response to God's promises, they vow to do all in their power to give the child, whom God had entrusted into their care, back to God so that his divine claim can be realized in the life of the child. This parental vow is an awesome and demanding obligation. Its seriousness comes into focus in the prayer that follows the baptism. After thanking God, the Father, for the forgiveness of sins and his adopting us as his children, the prayer continues: "We pray through your beloved Son that you will always govern this child by your Holy Spirit, that he (she) may be nurtured in the Christian faith and in godliness, and may grow and increase in the Lord Jesus Christ."[8] In a 1941 speech on the office of parents, professor B. Holwerda noted that this baptismal prayer means that parents are in the service of the Holy Spirit as his instruments to raise the children in a Christian way. Their office is to lead the children to being Christians in the full sense of the word; that is, that their children may also be enabled to do their task and calling before God. Parents cannot sit back and say: "It is all grace whether you believe or not. The Holy Spirit will work the faith. We cannot do it." This may sound somewhat pious but it entirely misses the point that the Holy Spirit wants to use the parents to work the faith in their offspring and equip them for a life of service to God.[9]

The second promise that parents make in their vow is to have their child instructed in the Christian faith to the utmost of their power. This promise concerns in the first place the instruction given by the church. The Synod of Dort (1618-19) rightly underlined the teaching task of the church. The catechetical office of the church reminds us of Calvin's characterization of the church as the mother of believers. With reference to the church he wrote:

---

8 *Book of Praise*, 599.
9 B. Holwerda, *De betekenis van verbond en kerk voor huwelijk, gezin en jeugd* (Goes, NL: Oosterbaan & Le Cointre, 1958), 81, 84.

let us learn even from the simple title "mother" how useful, indeed how necessary, it is that we should know her. For there is no other way to enter into life unless this mother conceive us in her womb, give us birth, nourish us at her breast, and lastly, unless she keep us under her care and guidance until, putting off mortal flesh, we become like the angels [Matt 22:30]. Our weakness does not allow us to be dismissed from her school until we have been pupils all our lives.[10]

Calvin therefore went on to say that "it is always disastrous to leave the church."[11] This powerful metaphor underlines how crucial the educational ministry of the church is. It is central to its task. Catechetical instruction can, therefore, never be simply a matter of passing on information about God and the salvation in Christ. Rather, it involves interacting with the children and youth and involving them in God's promises and encouraging their believing response. It also includes preaching the doctrines of the church with the help of the Catechism.[12]

It is important to note that the parental baptismal vows are made in a public worship service. The entire congregation bears witness to the baptism and hence they are all involved. Their participation in the baptism is also assumed in the prayer after the sacrament has been administered when petition is made to the "Almighty, merciful God and Father" that the one baptized "may be nurtured in the Christian faith and in godliness, and may grow and increase in the Lord Jesus Christ."[13] Since being a member of the church includes the obligation of "building up the body of Christ, until we all attain to the unity of the faith and of the knowledge of the Son of God" (Eph 4:12–13), everyone in the congregation has the obligation, as opportunities arise, to help the newly baptized member of

---

10 Calvin, *Institutes*, 4.1.4 (p. 1016).

11 Calvin, *Institutes*, 4.1.4 (p. 1016); for a detailed study of the concept, Jaeseung Cha, "Calvin's Concept of the Church as *mater fidelium* (Mother of Believers), Viewed through his Concept of Accommodation," *Journal of Reformed Theology* 9 (2015): 182–201.

12 See on Calvin's catechetical teaching and preaching Elsie Anne McKee, *The Pastoral Ministry and Worship in Calvin's Geneva*, Travaux d'Humanisme et Renaissance (Geneva, CH: Librairie Droz, 2016), 222–32; also Peter Y. De Jong, "Calvin's Contribution," 162–201.

13 *Book of Praise*, 599.

the church to grow in Christ. Indeed, by way of example, the United Reformed Churches in North America (URCNA), have included in the liturgy of baptism the question to the congregation: "Do you, the people of the Lord, promise to receive this child in love, pray for him/her, help care for his/her instruction in the faith, and encourage and sustain him/her in the fellowship of believers?" To which the congregation responds: "We do, God helping us."[14] The form for baptism of the Orthodox Presbyterian Church has a similar exhortation to the entire congregation that it commits to assisting the child who has been baptized and its parents in its Christian nurture.[15]

It is obvious that besides being of help to each other as those baptized and claimed by the Lord God in Christ in the simple ordinary things of life, the matter of education is also very much implicitly included since it belongs to enabling the nurture in the Christian faith for which the congregation prayed. This obligation is made explicit in the liturgical forms for baptism just mentioned with their asking the congregation for its commitment to the nurture of the child who was baptized. Now one might object that being required to make such a vow may entail promising more than one is capable of fulfilling. To get around that difficulty, an alternate way to involve the congregation is to introduce a charge to all those present at the baptism. For example, the Reformed Churches in the Netherlands (Liberated) have added to their form for baptism, prior to the final prayer, this appeal to the congregation:

> And you, beloved brothers and sisters, receive this child (this brother/sister) with love into the congregation. Know yourselves called to support these parents (him/her) through your intercessory prayer and example. Also be ready, wherever necessary and possible, to help this child (this brother/sister) to grow in the faith, grace, and knowledge of our Lord Jesus Christ, because "we have all been baptized in one Spirit and

---

14 URCNA, "Liturgical Forms: Baptism of Infants - Form 1 and 2." found in https://formsandprayers.com/liturgical-form/.
15 *The Book of Church Order of the Orthodox Presbyterian Church* (Willow Grove, PA: The Committee on Christian Education of the Orthodox Presbyterian Church, 2011), 146.

thereby have become one body" (1 Cor 12:13). May the Lord help us in this by his Spirit.[16]

Such corporate responsibility for the nurture and instruction in the Christian faith can include the establishing and maintaining of Christian schools where that is possible. Indeed, the very fact that the parents vowed to have their child or children instructed in the Christian faith to the utmost of their power implies using Christian education when that is possible. The communal obligation understood at baptism for the spiritual and educational well-being of all the members of the congregation has led to the establishment of Christian schools.[17] Indeed, the matter of Christian education has had the attention of Reformed churches for centuries.

As noted earlier, the Synod of Dort (1618–19) mentioned schools as one of the modes of education in the faith. This Synod also included in its Church Order Article 21 on the issue. "Everywhere consistories shall see to it, that there are good schoolmasters who shall not only instruct the children in reading, writing, languages and the liberal arts, but likewise in godliness and in the Catechism."[18] The wording reflects the seventeenth century Dutch context when there were no parental schools, and institutions of education were controlled and supported by the government which was then committed to the Reformed faith. There was no clear separation between church and state. Consistories could have influence with the governing authorities in ensuring the appointment of solidly Reformed teachers. That situation did not last and the subsequent centuries saw the devastating influence of rationalism in the so-called Enlightenment. This development negatively impacted both churches and schools.

---

16 *Acta van de Generale Synode Zwolle-Zuid 2008–2009 van de Gereformeerde Kerken in Nederland*, Artikel 55 (my translation); found at http://www.kerkrecht.nl/node/20. A very similar charge was adopted by the Canadian Reformed Church at Abbotsford, British Columbia on May 8, 2017 (email from Karlo Janssen, November 26, 2021).

17 See J. G. Woelderink, *Het doopsformulier* ('S-Gravenhage, NL: Guide de Bres, 1946), 367; also W. W. J. Van Oene, *With Common Consent: A Practical Guide to the Use of the Church Order of the Canadian Reformed Churches* (Winnipeg, MB: Premier, 1990), 272.

18 Both the original text and this English translation of this article are found in Idzerd Van Dellen and Martin Monsma, *The Church Order Commentary* (Grand Rapids, MI: Zondervan, 1941), 92–93; for the complete Church Order of Dort, http://www.kerkrecht.nl/node/439.

Current church orders, therefore, reflect the different context that is ours today in which we have independent Christian schools established and supported by the parents and the Reformed community. Government schools are secular and churches have no input as to who is hired to teach in the public schools. Indeed, such input is not a responsibility of the churches and any such advice to the government would be outside their jurisdiction. The responsibility for education should be with the parents in the first place and not the government (cf. Deut 6:6–9; Ps 78:5–7). Thus Christian parents control the schools they have established. Article 58 of the Canadian Reformed Church Order is, therefore, typical of current Reformed church orders when it removes the primary responsibility for the education of covenant children from the consistories to the parents. Article 58 reads: "The consistory shall ensure that the parents, to the best of their ability, have their children attend a school where the instruction given is in harmony with the Word of God as the church has summarized it in her confessions."[19] This wording does justice to the fact that the parents are the first in line with the duty of instructing their children in the faith. It is also good to remember that God's Word never charges government with the responsibility to rear children. The children do not belong to the state but to the parents.[20]

The Threefold Cord and Homeschooling

We have seen that there are traditionally three strands that come together to form a strong bond for educating covenant children in the Lord: the home, the church, and the school. The reality of strength in numbers, here seen in the different institutions that work for the same goal, reminds us of the proverb that is applicable here: "a threefold cord is not quickly broken" (Eccl 4:12). The strands are not all of equal value, but working together

---

19 *Book of Praise*, 657. This formulation is similar to the one that was used in Article 21 of the Christian Reformed Church, Van Dellen and Monsma, *The Church Order Commentary*, 92. Also see, e.g., for the Church Order of the Free Reformed Churches of Australia, Clarence Bouwman, *Spiritual Order for the Church* (Winnipeg, MB: Premier, 2000), 144.
20 See further Van Dellen and Monsma, *The Church Order Commentary*, 92–95.

provide a strong unity. There is no doubt that the education received at home is of the greatest importance. The children belong to the parents and they have the first and most important obligation to educate their offspring and prepare them for life in fullness. This crucial fact that the parents and not the state have the ultimate authority for the education of their children needs to be kept in mind.[21] This reality also supports a homeschooling model for education. But there are of course other factors to consider.

What is the place of the Christian school? What about the communal responsibility, as witnessed at baptism, for those children who are unable to be homeschooled for whatever reason? What is the educational role of the church for education? Before attempting to answer these questions, let us first step back for a moment and do a brief inventory on the pros and cons of homeschooling, the place of school education with its own pros and cons, and the varied responsibilities of the traditional three strands forming the educational cord, and so try to come to some coherent and responsible understanding of a biblical approach to the responsibilities for educating God's children.

In the discussion that follows, homeschooling refers to what has traditionally been identified as such where parents make the conscious choice to educate their children themselves in their homes. Such homeschooling is different from the situation that developed during the COVID-19 pandemic when many parents were forced to do the schooling at home themselves. It was not their free choice. Both parents and teachers were suddenly faced with a situation that was imposed on them with the result that the quality and continuity of education were in many cases undermined. This state of affairs did, however, result in more families making the choice for traditional homeschooling.

---

21 Although the state can have an interest in the education of children, Christians should be very critical of its role with respect to education. The state cannot prepare children for a life of service to God and one's neighbor; indeed the state often opposes Christian values. John M. Frame, *The Doctrine of the Christian Life, A Theology of Lordship* (Phillipsburg, NJ: P&R Publishing, 2008), 436–49. For arguments based on Enlightenment notions of self-determination that the state has the ultimate authority over a child's education, see, e.g. Dwyer and Peters, *Homeschooling*, 135–47, 156.

Homeschooling: The Pros and Cons

Homeschooling has burgeoned, especially during the COVID-19 pandemic. Even before the outbreak of the corona virus, nearly two million American children were homeschooled, representing 4 per cent of all school children. According to Statistics Canada only about .7 percent of Canadian children were homeschooled in 2018–19,[22] but also in Canada homeschooling is catching on.[23] There are some obvious reasons and attractions for Christians to opt for homeschooling. Wayne Grudem has helpfully listed the key ones as follows.[24]

1. According to Scripture, parents have the first responsibility and they should do the teaching themselves rather than delegate it to others.

2. The most significant learning occurs in companionship, and parents are the best companions.

3. A child's companions in a public or Christian school may not be the best influence on the child. "Bad company ruins good morals" (1 Cor 15:33).

4. Training in moral standards and personal character is just as important as academic training. Parents are the best at teaching moral standards and character.

5. Studies show that homeschooled children on average show excellent educational achievement. Increasingly helpful and sophisticated aids for parents doing the homeschooling help to achieve this outcome.

---

[22] For the American figure, see Dwyer and Peters, *Homeschooling*, 1; for the Canadian number, Statistics Canada, "Vast Majority of Students Attended Public Schools Prior to the Pandemic." found at https://www150.statcan.gc.ca/n1/daily-quotidien/201015/dq201015a-eng.htm (October 15, 2020).

[23] Paige MacPherson, "Homeschooling on the Rise in Every Province." found at https://www.fraserinstitute.org/blogs/school-enrolment-in-canada-part-3-homeschooling-on-the-rise-in-every-province (February 4, 2021).

[24] Wayne Grudem, *Christian Ethics: An Introduction to Biblical Moral Reasoning* (Wheaton, IL: Crossway, 2018), 384–85; Grudem and his wife decided against the homeschooling option and helped establish a Christian elementary school (p. 385).

6. Homeschooled children do have opportunities for social interaction with other children. Sometimes local schools will allow their participation in certain activities such as sports teams.

7. Families who homeschool find great joy and family interaction in the process. This appears to be one of the strongest reasons why many parents homeschool. It strengthens family bonds that last a lifetime.

Other advantages of homeschooling that one hears from time to time include:

8. Without peer pressure, children can learn to think for themselves and develop confidence.

9. Flexible scheduling means making the most efficient use of time and allows for other edifying activities.

10. The tutorial method of teaching is very effective and can encourage the child's full potential.

In view of this impressive list of positive reasons to homeschool, it is small wonder that more and more parents are embracing this method of education for their children as the best one. There are, however, some important considerations which can cause one to pause and reflect whether to take this route or not.

In the first place, the time commitment is enormous which the primary educator in the home is usually unable to honor. Although Scripture gives both parents the responsibility to educate their children (Prov 1:8), the father has the first responsibility. God "commanded our fathers to teach their children" (Ps 78:5) and the apostle Paul exhorted fathers to bring up their children in the discipline and instruction of the Lord (Eph 6:4). But if the father has full-time work to support his family, he cannot normally homeschool and fulfill this part of his educational responsibility. This raises the question whether there is more than one responsible and biblical option for educating the children, such as a Christian school as a supplement to the education given in the home[25] and whether homeschooling is always the best alternative. When homeschoolers list the positives, they usually speak of parents (in the plural) being the educators and all the advantages this entails. But in fact, when the decision is made to homeschool, it is usually only one parent, the mother, that actually does the teaching of the curriculum. Given the nature of her position in the home, the entire schedule of a family will to a large degree be determined by her priorities and needs as a mother and educator of the children and this can have consequences that need to be factored in. This observation leads to a second consideration that can give pause.

The task of homeschooling can be stressful and lead to burnout, especially for mothers who have many domestic responsibilities and also do the lion's share of the homeschooling. This is one of the conclusions which Jennifer Lois, a sociologist, made on the basis of an extensive eight year study of the effects of homeschooling on mothers. Although a majority of homeschoolers experienced a honeymoon period when everything was working well, in most cases they eventually suffered from stress. Such stress was caused by being overwhelmed in terms of what all had to be done within a limited time, as well as coping with the ambiguity about their different roles as a mother, a teacher, and as a homemaker and how to manage these different identities. It could be emotionally draining to juggle the different roles, especially when expectations did not materialize.[26]

These research findings are not all that surprising given the fact that many mothers who do homeschooling were not specifically trained to handle all the courses that are now their responsibility. To take on the task of homeschooling on top of everything else that conscientious mothers do is inevitably to add stress. If such stress is unsustainable and results in mothers not doing what Scripture makes clear is expected of them as a wife and mother, the homeschooling should be reconsidered since there is no biblical command to homeschool. Author Rebecca VanDoodewaard has rightly noted that "when a legitimate option [like homeschooling]

---

25 An observation also made in Noel Weeks, *The Christian School: An Introduction* (Edinburgh: The Banner of Truth Trust, 1988), 6.
26 Jennifer Lois, *Home is Where the School Is: The Logic of Homeschooling and the Emotional Labor of Mothering* (New York, NY: New York University Press, 2013), 95–113.

crowds out essentials [like obeying clear biblical commands], it means that the option is no longer legitimate."[27]

A third consideration that can make parents pause and think some more before homeschooling, especially in the higher grades, is the specialized knowledge that is needed to do justice to the courses and make them understandable to the students. Average parents with no special training in certain subject areas may find themselves out of their depth when their children start asking questions for clarification because they cannot follow the material given to them. Although homeschooling teacher aids keep improving, the fact remains that teachers who have studied a particular subject area are going to be better able to answer some of the tougher questions that students ask and engender a greater confidence and enthusiasm in the minds of the students in what the teacher is telling them.

There have in the past been concerns about the social isolation that homeschooled children may experience. Studies however have shown that such concerns do an injustice to the homeschooled children. Richard G. Medlin, Professor of Psychology at Stetson University and a specialist in homeschooling, has extensively reviewed recent research on the socialization of homeschooled children. Based on the available empirical evidence he concluded that

> the socialization experiences homeschooled children receive are more than adequate. In fact, some indicators—quality of friendships during childhood, infrequency of behavior problems during adolescence, openness to new experiences in college, civic involvement in adulthood—suggest that the kind of socialization experiences homeschooled children receive may be more advantageous than those of children who attend conventional schools.[28]

---

27 Rebecca VanDoodewaard, "Before Homeschooling, Let's Think Like Christians." https://gentlereformation.com/2021/01/25/before-homeschooling-lets-think-like-christians/ (posted January 25, 2021).
28 R.G. Medlin, "Homeschooling and the Question of Socialization Revisited," *Peabody Journal of Education* 88, no. 3 (2013): 292; also see R.G. Medlin, "Homeschooling and the Question of Socialization," *Peabody Journal of Education* 75, no. 1–2 (2000): 107–23.

Although the concern of socialization is not really an issue for homeschoolers generally speaking, the context of Christian homeschooling necessitates an additional observation. Keith Sikkema has rightly noted that "It is problematic to shield children from the covenant community to which they belong. Learning to live as part of this community as well as in this imperfect world does not happen in isolation, but requires experience and community."[29] This observation also needs to be taken into account in any discussion on the social aspect of homeschooling.

Christian School: The Pros and Cons

Homeschoolers have some compelling arguments, in spite of the negatives that have also been mentioned. What can be said in favor of sending children to a Christian school instead of homeschooling? To be sure, some of the attractions of homeschooling are also applicable to sending children to a Christian school. These include: children experiencing Christian companionship and finding lifelong Christian friends and so strengthening the church family bonds in the communion of saints; good teachers being role models for students; academic excellence generally characterizing Christian schools compared to public schools. Such similar advantages of educating children at home or at a Christian school should not be a great surprise since a Christian school is a parental school working in the service of the parents who fund and support the school in every possible way. Teachers are chosen with a view to providing the type of God-centered education that parents would want to give their children at home. Such a school is an extension of the home.

Besides these attractions, Christian schools also have the following in their favor.

1. The fact that parents have the first responsibility does not prevent them from receiving help from others. There is no shame for parents who do not feel up to this task or are simply too busy

---

[29] Keith Sikkema, "Home Schooling in View of John Calvin: A Study in Education and Communion of Saints," unpublished Master of Education thesis (St. Catharines, ON: Brock University, 2004), 168; this resource can be accessed by going to https://dr.library.brocku.ca and using the search function.

to delegate qualified teachers to help in the education of their children. The history of Reformed education, as noted earlier, underlines this reality.

2. A school is able to draw on more specialized skills in the various subject areas so that more questions raised by children can be answered adequately. There is, therefore, a greater possibility that justice will be done to the full range of biblical impact on all the different subjects than would be possible within a homeschooling context.

3. Children may have additional Christian role models in their teachers which will help in their growth as Christians. They will not only learn to imitate the example of their parents, but also those of their teachers who embody the Christian life in contexts that are both different and instructive.

What are the perceived disadvantages of sending children to a Christian school? Two important ones come to mind.

1. Since the children are being educated at school, there is a potential for less than optimal parental involvement in the nurture and education of their children. Parents with busy schedules and many demands on their time may conclude that since the school takes care of the education of their children, they do not need to be too concerned about that aspect of their lives. Nothing could be further from the truth. Schools are a help and supplement to the education that parents provide and can never be a substitute. Parents remain the first educators in their homes as they guide their children to the goal of maturity in Christ. A school can never replace the Christian education that children should receive from their parents. The home and not the school is also best equipped to deal with personal issues and the children's growing in Christian character simply because the children are with their first educators, their parents, under far more and varied circumstances than with a teacher at school. Parents should, however, be and remain involved as much as possible in what the school is teaching. Schools value the continued participation of parents.

In short, parents need to be aware of and resist the temptation of thinking that sending their children to a Christian school relieves them of their educational task. A school can never replace the home. It is simply a help for the Christian parental calling.

2. Although schools can be places where lifelong relationships are made, they can also hinder or even harm relationships. Ross Mountney, a former school teacher who became disillusioned with the school environment and eventually started homeschooling, noted that children in school are in an enforced age-restrictive grouping which continues for years. The downside is that cliques form and bullying seems to be fairly common. You can be made fun of if you seek to interact outside the group with those not of your age. Her observations may or may not be true depending on the student. Some thrive in a school setting, others do not. But it is a fact that there is a certain artificialness of being confined to a certain social group which can have a negative impact on a student's experience. The teacher plays a very important role in facilitating positive social interchange among the students, also in recess periods.[30]

If both homeschooling and Christian schools are biblically justifiable ways for parents to educate their children, and they are, how should one decide which route to follow? Furthermore, what do we do when there is conflict among Christians about the choices parents make; for example, when those supporting a local Christian day school seek to pressure homeschoolers to send their children to this school?

Decisions and Consequences

When Scripture is silent on a particular aspect of Christian life and allows for different avenues to attain a certain goal, the route one takes often comes down to personal circumstances and preferences. At the same

---

30 See Ross Mountney, *Learning Without School: Home Education* (London, UK; Philadelphia, PA, 2009), 91; similar concerns were expressed in Sikkema, "Home Schooling," 110–11. An extensive 2018 American report documented a rise in bullying: Jen Wilka, "Opinion: Bullying is on the Rise, Survey Shows. How Did We Get There?" see https://hechingerreport.org/opinion-bullying-is-on-the-rise-survey-shows-how-did-we-get-here/.

time, the consequences of the decisions made also need to be kept in mind. This freedom to make choices and the need to reckon with the aftereffects of choices made are also part of the mix in any decision whether to homeschool or to send one's children to a Christian school.

One of the most important considerations is the welfare of the children. Parents who decide to send their children to a Christian school will probably be convinced that they have neither the time nor the talent for personally educating their children at home. In some cases, homeschooling might be possible for the first few years, but definitely not for the higher grades. Parents choosing for school education will have decided to deal with any negatives their children may experience in a Christian school should such issues come up.

Other parents will take a personal inventory of their circumstances and decide that they have the time to homeschool and pursue that route. They will also be convinced that they have the necessary mental, intellectual, and organizational capacity to handle this and that the homeschooling resources available to them will be adequate. Indeed, Christian homeschooling resources have come a long way and give indispensable help from the earliest grades through high school. Some parents may not be completely comfortable with homeschooling for any number of reasons but because of a child's bad experiences at school, such as bullying or unqualified teachers, may reluctantly decide to educate their children themselves and try to navigate any downsides of this approach as they arise.[31]

Another significant factor that can influence the decision to homeschool is finances. Christian schools are expensive. A family after some soul searching may decide to homeschool mainly because the financial requirements for sending their children to the local Christian school are prohibitive. They simply lack the funds and so they will do their best to try to homeschool under less than ideal circumstances and with trepidation. However, if finances are the decisive factor, parents should pause and reflect before going ahead on an uncertain homeschooling

---

31 For these and other reasons for starting to homeschool see Sikkema, "Home Schooling," 110–13, 116.

journey. In the circle of believers a deficiency in finances is not a good reason to embark on homeschooling because such a decision is not taken with the conviction that this is the best option for the child or children. The fellowship of believers can and should supply the parents with the necessary financial resources so that such a family can send their offspring to the local Christian school. Such sharing can be done through the ministry of the deacons which Christ uses to circulate the gifts, including the financial, within the congregation. The willingness to make resources available for the common good is one of Christ's gifts to the church. It is a privilege and no shame to receive such assistance with a view to the education of the future generation. As a covenant community Christians are in the educational task together and also money is ultimately God's to be used to his glory.[32]

Once homeschooling functions in a congregation with one or more families opting for this method of educating their children, the question arises how supporters of homeschooling and the local Christian school should relate to each other. Tensions and even latent hostility can easily arise, especially if the local Christian school desperately needs all the help it can get.

A basic truth that all need to keep in mind is that everyone on both sides of the issue is committed to giving their children a Christian education. This fundamental fact needs to be kept in mind to prevent false dilemmas. In a sense one could say that Christian day schools are an extension of the home and in essence homeschools. In Christian schools, parents seek help in their educational responsibilities and delegate some of them to teachers, school fathers and mothers (as noted in chapter 1). Both homeschoolers and those sending their children to a Christian school have the same goal in mind—to raise their children in the fear of the Lord for a life of service to his glory. They are not rivals but allies with a common purpose.

Since everyone agrees on these fundamentals, all need to work together with a unity of purpose. Before criticizing homeschoolers, those supporting Christian schools need to reflect and honestly ask some basic questions.

---

32 See further Cornelis Van Dam, *The Deacon: Biblical Foundations for Today's Ministry of Mercy* (Grand Rapids, MI: Reformation Heritage Books, 2016), 183–85.

What are my motives in criticizing homeschooling parents? Is it simply that we need their tuition to help support Christian education for all so that it is a bit easier financially for us? Is it jealousy—wishing that we had the talents needed so that we could do the same and even save money in the process? Are we being fair in exerting pressure against homeschoolers and unnecessarily causing tensions in the fellowship of believers? After all, is it not a biblical principle that parents take control of the education of their children? More positively, have we ever asked ourselves how we can support and be a source of encouragement to parents who take on the awesome responsibility to teach their children at home? The work and commitment involved is truly phenomenal. Are there ways that the larger community of believers and the Christian school in particular can be of help to such parents? Are there resources and facilities that we can share with homeschoolers? Could we invite homeschoolers to participate in special school programs or concerts such as at Christmas and Easter? These type of gestures go a long way to building bridges and enhancing the unity and well-being of the communion of saints.

Homeschoolers should also do their part in reaching out and seeking the welfare of Christian fellowship. They should not speak negatively about the local Christian school and its teachers or disparage and slight the place of this institution, but recognize it as an incredible and valuable gift that God has made possible. Indeed, homeschoolers should think of ways that they can support such a school, financially or otherwise; for instance, by participating in drives to promote and enhance its facilities, of which they may very well also become beneficiaries. They should also not isolate themselves or become cliquish and adopt an attitude of condescension and superiority over those unable, for any number of reasons, to homeschool. They should also not become activist recruiters for the homeschooling movement. Furthermore, homeschoolers need to keep in mind that the homeschooling method of education, like the day school method, is no guarantee that the children will become model believers, as some homeschoolers may imply or assume.[33] Homeschoolers also need to

---

33 See, e.g., the sad and poignant testimony of homeschooler Scarlett Clay, "Homeschool Will Not Save Them." https://www.desiringgod.org/articles/homeschool-will-not-save-them (posted March 7, 2018).

be honest and carefully monitor their homeschooling experience to assure that they are doing justice to their own expectations in using this avenue to prepare their children for a life of holy service.

In Mutual Educational Service

Since both the Christian day school and homeschooling have the same goal, we must see these two modes of education as being in partnership with each other and supporting each other. With parental responsibility for the education of their children being an undisputed bedrock principle of Christian education, parents are free to choose the type of education they give their children according to their convictions, gifts, and circumstances.

At the same time, since Christians form a fellowship in the Spirit, these two modes of education should not exist in isolation from each other, but should be of mutual support and encouragement. After all, it is God himself who has brought members of the same church together. Being in a fellowship of believers brings obligations. The apostolic command still holds true: "Let each of you look not only to his own interests, but also to the interest of others" (Phil 2:4). Perhaps it is helpful to illustrate this altruistic principle with some real life examples, in addition to those already given.

A family decides to homeschool simply because they feel, after much family counsel on the matter, that homeschooling is a more appropriate way for them to raise their children, at least for say the first four or five years. They have decided that they have the gifts, time, and discipline to proceed with this and keep it up. They are convinced that the advantages of homeschooling are such that for them it would be irresponsible not to choose this manner of educating their children. Those who support the Christian school should accept that decision as one taken in good faith. We should not unnecessarily harass each other on matters of conscience. Furthermore, the Christian school could show its support of such a family's decision by offering them access to some of the school's resources such as the library, teaching resources, and the privilege of a periodic professional evaluation from the Christian school of the family's homeschooling program. In this way, school supporters would show their goodwill and in the process enhance the good relationships in the church community.[34]

How can a homeschooling family show their commitment to the educational goals and values of the Christian school? If finances were not a factor in deciding to homeschool, such a family could show their support for the covenantal education offered in the schools with regular financial contributions to the school. Such gifts would signal to the school community that their decision to homeschool was not taken from a sense of individualism—caring only for themselves without any regard for the rest of the fellowship—but taken in the full awareness of their obligation to support the ongoing needs of other parents who depend on the Christian school for the education of their children. Such giving would engender much goodwill and harmony within the church and enhance the fellowship. It would also help ensure the continued viability of the local Christian school which has possibly served many generations of children and could hopefully continue to do so, especially since such a school is the only realistic option for most parents.[35]

Apart from choosing either Christian school or homeschooling, one could also envisage a situation in which parents bring their concerns about teachers or the course material to the attention of the school. The problems may be of such a nature that one possible resolution is that the school actually advises the parents to homeschool either some or all of their children to overcome the obstacles they are struggling with. At the same time the school can offer to assist them in any possible way so that the children get the best possible education.[36]

---

34 In one case, a Christian school offered registration to homeschoolers that would give them privileges such as access to the school library, and for an appropriate fee, participation in select programs, field trips, special events, and other benefits. Paul S. MacDonald, "Christian Schools and Home Schools," *New Horizons* 11, no. 8 (1990): 2–3. For a discussion on Christian school and homeschool collaboration, see Sikkema, "Home Schooling," 83–85

35 It speaks well of homeschoolers who continue to financially support the local school, as, e.g., recorded in Sikkema, "Home Schooling," 132–33.

36 Such a situation is envisaged in Sikkema, "Home Schooling," 168–69, also 174; an example; a special needs child may be far better of being educated at home. See Jane Lowe and Alan Thomas, *Educating Your Child at Home* (London, UK; New York, NY: Continuum, 2002), 131–40.

In light of potential tensions between those who make different choices for educating their children, there is another factor that we need to take note of as Reformed believers. Our situation today is quite different from the days of the great Synod of Dort (1618–19) and its decisions on education in the schools. In those days parents were by and large not able to provide their children with the education that schools offered. With the rise of educational standards for the entire population in western society, what was not possible then can be possible now. Parents with the necessary education are often able to teach their children at home. Furthermore, the great amount of Christian homeschooling resources available makes it possible even for less talented parents to do a respectable job of educating their children, especially for the equivalent of the first years of elementary school.

In view of the enormous change of circumstance, the question does arise whether the traditional Dort Church Order in its different current forms needs to be emended. A typical reading is Article 58 of the Canadian Reformed Church Order. "The consistory shall ensure that the parents, to the best of their ability, have their children attend a school where the instruction given is in harmony with the Word of God as the church has summarized it in her confessions."[37] The question arises whether it might be better not to specify that the teaching has to be done in a school. Such a change would prevent unnecessary friction and misunderstanding in the church and give more clarity for the elders when exercising their office within the congregation. Article 58 could then read: "The consistory shall see to it that the parents, to the utmost of their power, make sure that their children receive instruction that is in harmony with the Word of God as the church has summarized it in her confessions." Such a change in wording would also be consistent with Dort's biblical emphasis that the parents have the first responsibility for the education of their children, an emphasis echoed in other synodical decisions as well.[38] A change in the

---

37 *Book of Praise*, 657. Also see, e.g., the Church Order of the Free Reformed Churches of Australia, Bouwman, *Spiritual Order for the Church*, 144.
38 The suggestion to revise Article 58 was raised in Sikkema, "Home Schooling," 175, also see 65–66; for synodical decisions emphasizing the parental role see Bos, *De orde der kerk*, 86–87. I thank Rev. Jan de Gelder for the precise wording of a possible revision of Article 58, part of which reflects the third question of the Form for Infant Baptism used in the Canadian Reformed Churches which asks the parents to promise to instruct their child in the church's doctrine "to the utmost of your power." *Book of Praise*, 587.

Church Order along these lines would also be in accord with the notion of Christian liberty within the congregation on matters not specifically mandated in Scripture.

The Indispensable Place of the Church

An edifying discussion on the importance of education, whether in the form of homeschooling or day school, would be impossible if it did not take place within the communion of saints, united in one faith by the Holy Spirit. It is by virtue of the fact that we are all Christians, members of Christ's church, that a constructive dialogue can occur keeping in mind the apostolic injunction. "Walk in a manner worthy of the calling to which you have been called, with all humility and gentleness, with patience, bearing with one another in love, eager to maintain the unity of the Spirit in the bond of peace" (Eph 4:1–3). So the church is the place in which we reach out to each other, resolve conflicts, and draw those on the fringes into the fellowship. The Holy Spirit equips the church to do all that through the proclamation and application of the gospel.

Given the vital place of the church, it stands to reason that the well-being of the church is of enormous importance and of high priority in the discussions, evaluations, and practice of the different forms of education within the congregation.

In this context it is helpful to revisit briefly John Calvin's striking image of the church as our mother. It is useful for illustrating some relevant biblical truths. In the first place, the Lord our God has used the church as his instrument to give life in Christ and to nourish believers with the critical life-giving instruction in his deeds of salvation and the rule of thankfulness. Through biblical preaching and catechetical instruction the church has, humanly speaking, provided life-giving, foundational, and vital education in the faith which parents can then pass on to their children at home and more formally at school or homeschool.

In the second place, this common source of educational nurture means that members of the church have the same educational basis and goal. This is often reflected in the statement that Christian school education is done in accordance with the Word of God as confessed in the Three Forms of Unity, that is: the Belgic Confession, the Heidelberg Catechism, and the Canons of Dort. There is never any doubt, whether our children are educated in school or in a homeschooling context, that their education must be done on this foundation to the glory of God as taught in the Reformed church. In this way, to use Calvin's words, those gathered by the Father into the bosom of the church "may be nourished by her help and ministry as long as they are infants and children, but also that they may be guided by her motherly care until they mature and at last reach the goal of faith ... so that for those to whom he is Father the church may also be Mother."[39]

In the third place, this common source, basis, and goal provide a far-reaching unity in Christ. This unity is expressed in several ways in Scripture. For our purpose, most apt is the characterization of the church as "the household" or "family" of God (1 Pet 4:17). Christians belong together as brothers and sisters in the Lord—"a spiritual house" (1 Pet 2:5). This unity in the household of God or family of God underlines again that education, especially in what really counts, is family centered! Whether we give formal instruction to our children at home or by means of a parentally-controlled school, we educate as parents with a view to raising our children in the fear of the Lord for a life of service to his praise and glory.

In view of the central place that the church and the communion of saints occupy, this fellowship in the Holy Spirit must be nurtured and protected in every possible way. With respect to educational choices this truth means that supporters of both Christian schools and homeschools are under the holy obligation to give a high priority to the well-being of the communion of saints when making and defending their educational choices. It is good to have holy zeal for what one believes to be the right decision for their family. But if it unnecessarily fractures the fellowship that the Lord is gathering together as his people, then such zeal is misplaced and harmful.

---

39 Calvin, *Institutes*, 4.1.1 (p. 1012).

In Conclusion

The great importance of education for God's children is reflected in the emphasis Scripture places on the responsibility of the parents to give their children a godly education.

The home continues to be the primary place of education for a life of service in the Lord. The Christian school is an extension of the home. Wise parents will regularly pray with their children for the school and the teachers and support their school instruction in every possible way. At the same time they will lovingly instill in their children a sense of the holy privilege they may have in being God's children by reminding them of the glorious baptismal promises. Furthermore, a truly Christian lifestyle in the homes and a strong sense of godly priorities also go a long way to underline the instruction given at home and at school. Educating in the fear of the Lord is a continuing endeavor that requires constant parental love and energy as godly parents seek to be God's instruments to mold their children after the image of their Creator. This task can never be simply relegated as the job of the teachers at school. They are to help in this task, but the primary responsibility for it continues to rest with the parents. Indeed, a Christian school, fully supported and enhanced by the participation of the parents according to their parental duties in their homes truly makes that Christian school an extension of the home—a homeschool, if you like!

Although the practice of homeschooling can cause friction in the church, this need not be the case. Homeschooling and Christian schools are both biblically responsible avenues for educating our children. Each method can be supportive of the other and so maximize the benefits of each. Indeed, this growing movement of taking education back to the home can be a real blessing by underlining the parental responsibilities for education. Another potential blessing is that homeschooling parents can be more flexible and have more choices when considering employment in an area not serviced by a Christian school or for that matter by a Reformed church. Along with others, they could form the nucleus of a

Reformed church plant and eventually, under God's blessing, even be instrumental in establishing a new congregation and a Christian school to serve those unable to homeschool.

Another element to keep in mind is that with increasing government intrusion into what should be taught in schools, a day may come when homeschooling remains the only viable option for Christian parents to give a godly education to their children. May that never happen! But the increasing reach of state control in determining the parameters in which Christian schools can operate is a worrisome trend.[40] We do, after all, live in a western culture that is abandoning its Christian heritage.

Educating God's children is a tremendous task and the responsibilities are daunting. At the same time we know that we do not need to do this task on our own or in a vacuum. We can do it in the power of the Lord as parents at home and as teachers at school and at homeschool. All this can be done within the communion of saints, the household of God. What a blessing!

---

40 An example (2017) is the attempt of an Alberta government to impose conditions on Christian schools that went directly against their parental rights as Christians. Jay Cameron, John Carpay, and James Kitchen, *Parental Rights Are Human Rights: Alberta's Bill 24 Violates Charter Freedoms* (Calgary, AB: Justice Centre for Constitutional Freedoms, 2017); also see for Ontario Ted Postma, "'Legalization' of Education," T*he Messenger* 60, no. 1 & 2 (February 2013): 16–18, 20–22 respectively; for other examples, including the need for Christian schools to follow the curriculum required by the state: Janet Epp Buckingham, *Fighting Over God: A Legal and Political History of Religious Freedom in Canada* (Montreal, QC & Kingston, ON: McGill-Queen's University Press, 2014), 50-69 (passim), 218–19.

CHAPTER 3

The Home as Nurturer for Identity, Worship, and Renewal

In the previous chapters we have seen several aspects of parental responsibility for the education of their children. We will now focus on some other elements which underline the enormous importance of the family and the home during the first years of a child's development before formal education begins. It is impossible to overestimate the influence of a godly parental upbringing on a child during this formative and critical period of its nurture. The old saying, "give us a child until he is five or six, and we'll have him for life," contains much truth. Does God's Word not say: "Train up a child in the way he should go, and when he is old he will not depart from it" (Prov 22:6)?

The traditional family unit with a stay-at-home mother is under enormous stress today. According to a 2015 Pew Research Center report, almost half of two-parent American households (46 percent) with children younger than 18 work full time, with another 17 percent having mothers working part time and only 26 percent of mothers are not employed outside the home. In these last two cases, the fathers have full time work. Canadian statistics are similar.[1] This is a far cry from about forty years ago when the vast majority of mothers with children stayed at home.

---

1 Pew Research Center, *Raising Kids and Running a Household. How Working Parents Share the Load* (November 2015), 2, www.pewresearch.org. An undated Ontario report states: "Nearly 70 percent of mothers with pre-school children and more than three-quarters of mothers with school-aged children are employed or looking actively for work; most of these are employed full-time." Ontario Human Rights Commission, *The Changing Face of Canadian Families*, 2; found at www.ohrc.on.ca.

Although it is difficult to gauge how such a trend has impacted Christian households, anecdotal evidence suggests that it has not completely bypassed them for a variety of reasons.[2] The trend is, however, putting a strain on the functioning of the office and task God has given Christian parents. It is, therefore, appropriate that we pause and reflect on the fact that the home remains the place of first importance for the nurture of our children.

In this chapter we will consider some aspects of the challenge of nurturing young children in the faith, and ways in which the benefits of a Christian home can be maximized under the Lord's blessing. We will consider the need to give them a clear identity, to practice regular family worship, and to encourage the renewal of their lives as a new creation.

Realizing a Clear Identity

What all children need is a clear sense of who they are and how they fit into the world in which they find themselves. For our purposes, two issues stand out for Christian children: their identity as children of God and their gender as a gift of God. Parents need to do their utmost to help their children realize and appreciate these aspects of their identity.

Children of God

Children born to believers are children not only of their earthly parents; they are also children of God. This is an awesome truth that has enormous beneficial consequences as a child comes to terms with this privileged identity. What a thrill for young children when their parents tell them that they have an all-powerful Father in heaven who loves them so much that he has embraced them as his very own children. All this was signified and sealed when they as helpless infants received the sacrament of holy baptism, administered of free grace and entirely of the Father's volition.

---

2   If a mother with children at home needs to find work outside the home because of a genuine financial need, such as the high cost of Christian education, deacons should help to enable the mother to stay at home with her little ones. See on this issue Van Dam, *The Deacon*, 184–85.

Their being children of God, the Father, is the bedrock identity that children of believing parents need to appreciate and cherish. When such a privileged sense of who they are is deep-rooted in young lives growing up, they are given what is essential for them to face many future trials because they will understand that as children of Almighty God, they are also in a covenant with him.

That covenant relationship comes with many rich and encouraging promises.[3] Being baptized into the name of the triune God (Matt 28:19) means that God the Father testifies and seals that he is indeed adopting those receiving baptism as his children and heirs. He will, therefore, provide them with all good and avert all evil or turn it to their benefit (Rom 8:28). Receiving baptism into the name of the Son signifies the promise that he will wash away all their sins with his blood. He furthermore promises to unite with himself in his death and resurrection all those who received this baptism (Rom 6:5). What an encouragement for children as they grow up into adulthood that there is forgiveness for *all* their sins so that they can be counted as righteous before God. But there is more. By being baptized into the name of the Holy Spirit, the Holy Spirit gives the assurance that he will dwell in those baptized and make them living members of Christ, imparting the cleansing from sins and the daily renewal of their lives. All these promises as they are explained to our children in our homes give them an enormous sense of identity and importance in the sight of God. They are children of the living God, their covenant Lord! What an identity!

However, with these promises also comes the obligation to honor the gracious demands of the covenant and to trust and love the Lord God with one's whole heart, soul, and mind and with all one's strength (Matt 22:37). It means not loving the world of sin (1 John 2:15), resisting the inclinations of one's sinful heart (Eph 4:22), and leading a God-fearing life (Col 3:5). There will be obstacles and struggle. But when children of the Lord stumble and fall, they can be assured of a loving God who will graciously forgive any sin that is sincerely confessed. There is never any reason to despair of God's mercy. Baptism is a seal and trustworthy testimony that those baptized have an eternal covenant with God.

---

3   For what follows, see the Form for the Baptism of Infants in *Book of Praise*, 597–99.

As they grasp the implications of their awesome identity, they will be able to face all the problems they will meet in their lives. There will be many difficulties because Satan constantly seeks ways to lead the children of God astray, especially concerning their identity. But, believing parents may tell their children that God's promises are sure and that if they trust in him, accepting his Word and not resisting the work of the Holy Spirit, then the Lord God himself will see them through all life's problems, also those concerning their core identity as children of God. And it is the identity that God gave them that is especially under attack by Satan today. One particularly vicious assault of the evil one on the identity of children is his seeking to have them question whether their God-given gender identity matches their biological sex.

Gender Identity

Satan has been busy assaulting and deconstructing God's creation work and ordinances. He continues to try to destroy the divine institution of marriage. The latest onslaught on this divine gift is the promotion of same-sex marriage which civil authorities throughout the Western world are legalizing. Satan now wants to go one step further and destroy God's gift of sexuality as a biological given. The secular narrative is that people must decide for themselves whether they want to identify as a male or female, regardless of their sex at birth. This is the world that our young children are growing up in. Satan cannot wait to get his identity altering poison into their young minds.

The Gender Ideology Offensive

The official 2015 Ontario curriculum encouraged teachers to expose children in grade three to the notion that being a boy or girl does not necessarily relate to your physical anatomy. Gender identity is described as "a person's sense of self, with respect to being male or female. Gender identity ... may be different from birth-assigned sex."[4] To say that teaching this ideology to eight and nine year olds is confusing is an understatement.

---

4 Ministry of Education, *The Ontario Curriculum Grades 1–8: Health and Physical Education* (Toronto, ON: Queens Printer for Ontario, 2015), 124, 231.

The 2019 curriculum toned down some of the most objectionable material but the new gender ideology remains.[5]

Children can struggle with their identity, also respecting their gender. This is obviously a very sensitive issue for it revolves around one's feelings and the matter goes to the very heart of who they are. Transgender activists have been quite successful in promoting the idea that one's natal sex has little or nothing to do with one's gender identity. As this ideology has been entering public school curricula an increasing number of children are confused and want to change their biological sex. There are even reports of entire peer groups at school identifying themselves as transgender. Governments are bending to the transgender pressures and even facilitating sex change operations. In Canada, for example, most provincial health care plans pay the essential costs of a sex reassignment surgery for those who feel that they are not in the right body. And so male bodies are subjected to hormonal treatments and operated on to look like females and females can become males. Parents faced with a child that wants to change his or her biological sex will often go along with the child's wishes for fear of losing the love of their son or daughter.[6] Christian households are not exempt from these pressures.

The tragedy of the current craze and confusion about gender identity is that the much trumpeted solution of changing one's physical sex organs and characteristics does not solve the problem. Medically speaking, you cannot really transition to becoming a male if you are a biological female or vice versa, no matter how clever the doctors are or how much the "new" body looks like the gender of one's choice. As Quentin Van Meter, a pediatric endocrinologist put it: "You're never changing the sex of the patient. Never. Every cell in the body is programmed to be male or female."[7] A similar message was given by Dr. Paul McHugh, who helped persuade Johns Hopkins Hospital to stop doing sex-change operations

---

5   For the new curriculum see, Ministry of Education, *The Ontario Curriculum Grades 1–8: Health and Physical Education* (Toronto, ON: Queens Printer for Ontario, 2019); for a critique, André Schutten and Ed Hoogerdyk, "Ontario Government Releases Updated 2019 Sex-Ed Curriculum;." available at https://old.arpacanada.ca. My thanks to Keith Sikkema for alerting me to this resource.

6   Nancy R. Pearcey, *Love Thy Body* (Grand Rapids, MI: Baker Books, 2018), 198–99; Leanne Escobal, "Transgender Surgery Costs and Financing." found in https://www.finder.com/ca/pay-for-transgender-surgery-medical-expenses (updated July 9, 2021).

7   As quoted by Jamie Dean, "Suffer the Children," *World Magazine* 32, no. 7 (15 April 2017): 34–35.

in the 1970's when follow-up studies showed that it was impossible to change one's biological sex. He stated that "people who undergo sex reassignment surgery do not change from men to women or vice versa. Rather, they become feminized men or masculinized women."[8] Because it is not a biological problem but one in the mind, surgery is of no help and is actually counterproductive. Those who have undergone sex-change operations experience a far greater risk of mental disorders such as anxiety, depression, and the desire for suicide.[9]

With respect to children, studies have shown that about 85-90 percent of those with gender confusion or gender dysphoria accepted their biological gender as they became older. In other words, they spontaneously outgrew the problem. The fact that some have continuing difficulties indicates they need help to overcome them. But, they should not be encouraged to embrace their gender confusion as normal or to celebrate and reinforce this condition and go for a sex change operation, as the transgender lobby would urge them to do.[10] But the opposition to those who encourage confused children to accept their biological sex is fierce. People have lost jobs for opposing the transgender ideology and in Canada a father has even been put into prison for resisting the transgender thinking in his daughter.[11]

---

8 Paul McHugh, "Transgender Surgery Isn't the Solution," *Wall Street Journal*, 13 May 2016. A startling case is that of Blair Logsdon who, starting at the age of 26, underwent 167 surgeries from 1987 to 2005 in the hope of solving his gender confusion, going from male to female to male to female. Those operations never solved his problem. Walt Heyer, "This Man Received 167 Sex-Change Surgeries. He Lives in a World of Regret." found in https://stream.org (published January 13, 2018).

9 Attempts at suicide for all ages of transgender individuals is about 41 percent compared to under 5 percent for the general American population. Lawrence S. Mayer and Paul R. McHugh, "Sexuality and Gender: Findings from the Biological, Psychological, and Social Sciences," *The New Atlantis* 50 (Fall 2016): 8.

10 Paul McHugh and Gerard V. Bradley, "Uninformed Consent: The Transgender Crisis," *Commentary* 152, no. 2 (September 2021): 38. *National Geographic* glorified transgender children by posting a picture of a nine year old transgender girl on the front cover of their January 2017 issue which celebrated the "Gender Revolution." The issue featured eighty transgender nine-year-olds from around the world.

11 Dr. Kenneth Zucker, a psychologist, has successfully helped young children with gender dysphoria to accept the body they were born with. But under pressure from transgender activists he was dismissed from Toronto's Centre for Addiction and Mental Health at the end of 2015. His good work was not politically correct. Barbara Kay, "Scandal at CAMH—One Entirely of Its Own Making," *National Post*, 3 February 2016. A British Columbia farmer was jailed in 2021 for refusing to use male pronouns for his 14 year old biological daughter. Andrew Weichel, "B.C. Dad Jailed 6 Months After Repeatedly Exposing Transgender Son's Identity, Despite Publication Ban," *CTV News Vancouver*, 16 April 2021.

Christian Parental Response

Christian parents are best equipped to educate and help their children to be comfortable with the gender that God has given them at birth. Already at an early age, parents should reinforce the biological identity of their children and enable them to celebrate their being a boy or girl. One pitfall to avoid is stereotyping or being rigidly outspoken on what is considered appropriate for a boy or girl.

Stereotyping can cause children to worry about their identity. For example, boys are supposed to be self-confident, rough, assertive, and play with guns or trucks, and girls are expected to be more accommodating, gentle, emotional, and play with dolls. If a child does not conform to such gender expectations and parents let that be known, then the seeds of confusion and future trouble about one's true identity can be sown. Stereotyping should be rejected. Each child is a unique creation from God.

It is also difficult to justify gender stereotyping from Scripture. The Bible pictures Esau as the rough outdoors sort, but Jacob as a quiet and stay-at-home type close to his mother (Gen 25:27–28). In Scripture women showed "male" qualities. They were the ones who asserted themselves and challenged Pharaoh's command to kill the male children (Exod 1:15-2:4) and it was a woman, Jehosheba, who defied Queen Athaliah's decree to kill all her grandchildren by hiding her infant nephew Joash (2 Kings 11:1–2). Our Saviour characterized himself as "gentle and lowly in heart" (Matt 11:29). Christian virtues for both male and female include being gentle and meek (Matt 5:5; 2 Cor 10:1). The gifts of the Spirit are not classified for male and female, but both genders need to exhibit "love, joy, peace, patience, kindness, goodness, faithfulness, gentleness, self-control" (Gal 5:22–23).

Parents can remind their children who struggle with their sexual identity that their biological sex is a gift from God who makes no mistakes. They can, therefore, give their children hope that it is possible to overcome any gender dysphoria which they may be struggling with. To reject God's gift of gender and to question one's biological identity is to cast oneself at the mercy of one's feelings and emotions with no sure objective foundation.

In God's grace, godly parents can provide the anchor that their children need, such as a firm and loving hand to guide them to accept their God-given identity. Only with the Creator is there a blessed way out for those struggling with their sexual identity.

It would be appropriate for parents to imprint on any confused child the comfort of Scripture, the sword of the Spirit who can change hearts and minds. For example, the Psalms are full of encouragement and consolation. David, the inspired psalmist, confessed: "O Lord, you have searched me and known me! You know when I sit down and when I rise up; you discern my thoughts from afar. You search out my path and my lying down and are acquainted with all my ways. Even before a word is on my tongue, behold, O Lord, you know it altogether" (Ps 139:1–4). Yes, God knows us through and through. He made us! "You formed my inward parts; you knitted me together in my mother's womb. I praise you, for I am fearfully and wonderfully made. Wonderful are your works; my soul knows it very well. My frame was not hidden from you, when I was being made in secret, intricately woven in the depths of the earth. Your eyes saw my unformed substance" (Ps 139:13–16).

Children can be prepared for the onslaught of transgender thinking before they leave the safety of the parental home. But even if children struggle with gender dysphoria, they can be assured that the God of their baptism loves them and that his promises are sure. Is it not remarkable that the very first convert outside Jerusalem that Scripture mentions was someone with an abnormal sexual identity, an Ethiopian eunuch (Acts 8:26–39)? Yet the Lord called him to himself. We have a Savior who as a human being knows what it is like to be tempted. He is merciful and faithful and able to help, also those struggling with their biological identity (Heb 2:17–18; 4:15).

Parents who emphasize to their children that they belong to Christ build a firm foundation for dealing with feelings of gender dysphoria that may come up. The key to one's identity is not found in one's gender but ultimately it is found in Christ. Our children are in a fallen world, but they receive a new identity in union with their Savior. Parents can equip their young children to struggle in the fight of faith against the sins and the darkness of this world and help them to put to death the old nature and embrace Christ. The education parents give in the home from the earliest years of childhood can be used by the Lord to help children to be transformed so that they too will be enabled to say with the apostle Paul "I have been crucified with Christ. It is no longer I who live, but Christ who lives in me. And the life I now live in the flesh I live by faith in the Son of God, who loved me and gave himself for me" (Gal 2:20). Or as the apostle puts it elsewhere: "for me to live is Christ" (Phil 1:21). Parents must do everything in their power to focus their identity and that of their children on Christ. Only in him is one's true identity to be found.

When children struggle with gender dysphoria and ask "who am I?", we as covenant community may remind them of the riches we have in Christ. As people of God, his congregation, we will do everything in our power to embrace those struggling with these issues and to help usher them into the light and peace that only Christ can give. As parents we prayerfully do our best to make our children realize the privilege and blessing of their unique status as children of God who gave each of them a specific biological gender. Should our children struggle to appropriate this God-given identity, we will continue to be there for them. In the worst case scenario we will continually uphold them before God's throne of grace. An effective way to help give our children a biblical sense of who they are is to give a high priority to practicing regular daily family worship.

Practicing Family Worship

Regular family worship is often a casualty of the fast-paced life many experience today. Christian parents may often wish to practice it, but they simply do not get around to it. The family unit is under great stress and there seems little opportunity to sit down as a family and worship. Yet, it is critically important that such time be set aside, not only because God wants our worship and praise, but also so that we can use this opportunity to teach our children the great deeds of the Lord (cf. Deut 6:7–9, Ps 78:4). The Westminster Confession of Faith underscores the importance of family worship by mentioning it explicitly. "God is to be worshiped everywhere in spirit and truth; as in private families daily, and in secret, each one by himself; so, more solemnly in the public assemblies" (Chapter 21:6).[12] Family worship makes concrete the centrality of God in the Christian life and home. When children experience it, they realize all the more that the focus of the home is on living a life of gratitude to the Lord for his salvation. This daily family time of worship and praise will also provide them with a foundational Christian education that will serve them well for the rest of their lives. When we recognize the great importance of family worship and wish to practice it, inevitably some obvious questions arise. Before discussing family worship it may, therefore, be good to pause for a moment and address some commonly raised practical issues.

Time and Place

Each family will have to decide which time slot is best for their communal worship. In our hurried society with conflicting schedules, it is often difficult for families to find a time when they can all be together on a regular basis. Parents should insist, as much as possible, that at least for one meal in the day everyone should be together around the same table for their food and fellowship. For many families that meal seems to be supper and so after supper is often an ideal time for family worship. The immediate pressures of the day's activities are usually over and some time can be set aside for Bible reading, prayer, and singing. Regularity is obviously very important. Family time together in fellowship and worship should be a time no one wants to miss. It is precious and must not become a casualty of the daily rat race. If one person cannot make it, the family worship should not be cancelled. It is a top priority for a Christian family. A final point to note regarding time is this: family worship should not be long and boring, but to the point and sensitive to the family circumstances.

The best place for family worship and devotions depends on the situation in the home. Doing it after the meal around the kitchen or

---

[12] *The Confession of Faith and Catechisms: The Westminster Confession of Faith and Catechisms Adopted by The Orthodox Presbyterian Church, with Proof Texts* (Willow Grove, PA: The Committee on Christian Education of the Orthodox Presbyterian Church, 2005), 106–7.

dining room table can work. Moving to another room has the advantage of getting away from the dishes and probably being able to focus better on the Bible reading and singing. Wherever one meets, the Bibles and books used for singing should be readily available and be kept in the same place. If possible, everyone should have their own copy of the Bible and songbook.

Having dealt with a couple of practical matters, the next question is: what actually constitutes family worship? The traditional format found in Reformed homes for centuries includes three core elements: reading Scripture, prayer, and singing. Let us briefly consider each in turn.[13]

Scripture Reading

The father as the head of the household has the responsibility of preparing himself for family worship. He should be ready to answer any obvious questions that may come up from the reading he has selected since he has the primary duty to instruct his children in the Lord (Eph 6:4). It is important to be realistic and keep the Bible reading short and manageable. With children, a brief passage properly explained will make more impact than a tedious reading of many verses. The reading of Scripture does not need to be done by only the father. He can delegate the reading to other members of the family, with the possibility of everyone taking a turn, if they are able to do so in a manner in keeping with the seriousness of reading God's Word. Indeed, if the children are capable, it is a thrill for them to participate in the actual reading. It is another indication that they belong! The reading of Holy Scripture is a solemn occasion which warrants appropriate attention and a receptive attitude so that the words of life can be effectively heard and absorbed. The gospel "is the power of God for salvation to everyone who believes" (Rom 1:16). Children should be encouraged to ask questions and the father should not hesitate to inquire of the children if they have understood what was

---

[13] Two excellent brief resources on family worship which have also influenced what follows are Donald S. Whitney, *Family Worship* (Wheaton, IL: Crossway, 2016) and Joel R. Beeke, *Family Worship* (Grand Rapids, MI: Reformation Heritage Books, 2009). An older longer work also remains relevant. James W. Alexander, *Thoughts on Family Worship* (Philadelphia, PA: Presbyterian Board of Publication, 1847). It is available in modern editions.

read. Discussing the message of Scripture is edifying and can help shape the hearts and minds of all. It is, after all, the Word of God of which God promises that it will accomplish its purpose (Isa 55:11).

The Scripture passages chosen should take into consideration the age of the children. The very young will be most edified by narrative passages followed by an explanation and discussion. It may even be appropriate to use a Bible story book for this age group. A classic is Catherine Vos, *The Child's Story Bible* which is still in print.[14] The material read must obviously be meaningful for the children and explanations as needed are the order of the day. In a mixed group of older and younger children, Scripture can be read that is appropriate for the older children with some freedom being made to include the very young. They can be included by clarifying the passage as it is being read as necessary or by reading a separate short passage for them before proceeding to a longer one for the older children. In any case, it is important that everyone feels engaged and also feels able to participate. As soon as they are able to read, children should ideally have their own copy of Scripture.

Over the course of time, there should be some balance between reading from the Old and New Testament. A preplanned program of reading can be very helpful to ensure such balance. The entire counsel of God should be the focus of family worship in one way or another. Special occasions need to be kept in mind. Serious sickness in the family or unexpected challenges that cause great tension or similar circumstances are ideal opportunities to let the Word of God provide comfort, direction, and hope. Such times can also be times to deviate from a preplanned reading schedule. The relevance and importance of family worship are then underlined.

After listening to God's Word and reflecting on it, it is appropriate to respond with prayer.

Prayer

In prayer we come before God's throne of grace. This means that we address him with respect and adoration, thanking him and praising his

---

14 Catherine Vos, *The Child's Story Bible*, 2nd ed. (Edinburgh, UK: Banner of Truth Trust, 2021).

name for his many blessings. Praying to the heavenly Father is a wonderful opportunity to thank him for the many good things received. As the Heidelberg Catechism reminds us, "prayer is the most important part of the thankfulness which God requires of us."[15] A family coming to the throne of grace can remember and thank the Lord for all sorts of blessings they have experienced. This also reminds everyone that these gifts do not come by chance or solely by human endeavor but in God's sovereign care.

Although we are not worthy of ourselves to appear before God, we can come boldly into his presence (Heb 4:16). We do so as his humble children, never flippantly, aware that it is only because of the redeeming work of Christ that we are able to come near to God. Consequently, any family quarrels or sin should be confessed and forgiveness sought from each other prior to asking God for forgiveness (cf. Matt 6:14). It is, therefore, important that the head of the family asks what the prayers to be offered should include.

Besides possible offenses that need confession and the more general petition for forgiveness of sins, family prayer can and should also mention all the needs and cares that are experienced. God also accepts our complaints and questions. We are, after all, his children and as such we can approach our heavenly Father with everything that occupies our minds, including heartfelt sorrow. There may even be times when provocative questions can be directed to God with respect to suffering that is being endured. Listen, for example, to the sorrowful cry of the Sons of Korah when they end their petitions with words such as these: "O LORD, why do you cast my soul away? Why do you hide your face from me … You have caused my beloved and my friend to shun me; my companions have become darkness" (Ps 88:14, 18). It is all gloom, but this is the prayer of a believer who began with: "O LORD, God of my salvation, I cry out day and night before you. Let my prayer come before you; incline your ear to my cry!" (Ps 88:1–2). It is striking how many songs of lament are found in the biblical Psalms, the Word of God (see, e.g., Ps 44, 86, 77). That fact shows that a Christian family should not hesitate to bring their sorrows, questions, and grief to God's throne of grace, knowing that

---

15 Lord's Day 45, QA 116. *Book of Praise*, 559.

he is merciful. "He is near to the brokenhearted and saves the crushed in spirit. Many are the afflictions of the righteous, but the LORD delivers him out of them all" (Ps 34:18). The LORD "heals the brokenhearted and binds up their wounds" (Ps 147:3). Almighty God is also our Father and we can approach him as his children whom he loves and welcomes into his presence, also when we share our distresses and sorrows with him and ask for relief.

In family worship, it is good if not only father and mother but also the children participate in the prayer. Even small children can be prepared to offer a prayer. It is a golden educational opportunity to make them experience their being part of the family and also having the privilege of directly addressing their Father in heaven. It is important that the entire family prays together.

On the whole, family prayers should be kept to the point and not go on and on (cf. Matt 6:7). They should be simple and in language everyone can understand. Since family prayer follows Scripture reading, it is good if that can be reflected, if only briefly, in the prayer as a response to God's Word. This helps make the Bible reading relevant for the family. Variety in the wording and petitions is desirable to avoid formalism and monotony. One way to that end is to have the prayers reflect the events and experiences of the day—prayers from the heart, mentioning specific events and names. Petitions should also include intercession not only for the immediate needs of the family, but also those of others. There can be those for whom spontaneous praying is very difficult. In such a case, one can use the Lord's Prayer, reflect on the Heidelberg Catechism's teaching on prayer (Lord Days 45–52), and make use of edifying educational material and so gradually be equipped to have the confidence to compose one's own petitions from the heart to God.[16]

Prayer can be followed by communal praise.

---

16 For the Heidelberg Catechism, *Book of Praise*, 559–64; Beeke, *Family Worship*, chapter 3 (Kindle); Donald K. McKim, *Everyday Prayer with John Calvin* (Phillipsburg, NJ: P&R Publishing, 2019).

Singing

Singing should be an integral part of the Christian life and certainly of worship, also that taking place in the home. Making music to the Lord in song in the family circle is a practice with a long history in the church.[17] It is also striking how often Scripture exhorts us to sing. Why is that? One reason is the need to praise God because he *is* God! For example:

> Oh come, let us sing to the LORD;
>> Let us make a joyful noise to the rock of our salvation!
>
> Let us come into his presence with thanksgiving;
>> Let us make a joyful noise to him with songs of praise!
>
> For the LORD is a great God,
>> and a great King above all gods. (Ps 95:1–3)

As is already clear from the above, a closely related reason is thanksgiving and gratitude that we may know him as merciful and gracious, as God who saves and redeems his people. For instance:

> Praise the LORD!
>
> For it is good to sing praises to our God;
>> for it is pleasant, and a song of praise is fitting.
>
> The LORD builds up Jerusalem;
>> he gathers the outcasts of Israel.
>
> He heals the brokenhearted
>> and binds up their wounds. (Ps 147:1–3)

Indeed, all our needs can be brought to the throne of grace, also with our singing. Even when we are in the depths of despair, we can go to him.

> Out of the depths I cry to you, O LORD!
>> O Lord, hear my voice!
>
> Let your ears be attentive
>> to the voice of my pleas for mercy! (Ps 130:1–2)

---

17 James W. Alexander, *Thoughts on Family Worship*, 220–31.

Singing the psalms can also vocalize a family's firm trust in the Lord, such as confessing that he is our shepherd and takes care of all our needs.

> Even though I walk through the valley of the shadow of death,
>   I will fear no evil,
> for you are with me;
>   your rod and your staff, they comfort me. (Ps 23:4)

For all these reasons, and more could be mentioned, our singing to our heavenly Father cannot be restricted to the worship services on the Lord's Day. Indeed, it is normal and to be expected that "glad songs of salvation are in the tents of the righteous" (Ps 118:15). Singing is speaking and praying in an intensive manner when vocalizing our thanks and praise to God. What a blessing to be able to thank God and petition him not only with our spoken words, but even with our singing! What better medium is there than song to remember God's saving work? Who can remain unmoved when we sing before God's throne of grace about our sorrows or sickness? How expressive when our soul sings to express our anguish in searching for a way out of the present misery to be with God and enjoy his peace and fellowship (e.g. Ps 42)! As John Calvin noted, the psalms represent all the emotions. "The Holy Spirit has here drawn to the life all the griefs, sorrows, fears, doubts, hopes, cares, perplexities, in short, all the distracting emotions with which the minds of men are wont to be agitated."[18] By singing the words of the Psalms we can express to God all our feelings and desires, from joyous thanksgiving to our sorrowful cries for help.

Another reason for a family to sing in worship together is that in so addressing God in unison, with thanks and prayers, the members of the family experience the unity in the Spirit as children of God and as partners together in covenant with the LORD. It is a tremendous blessing when the Holy Spirit uses the communally sung Word to bind the family members into a beautiful and loving fellowship of faith and hope in God.[19] Furthermore, the Holy Spirit

---

18 John Calvin, *Commentary on the Book of Psalms*, reprint, trans. from the original Latin, and collated with the author's French version, James Anderson (Grand Rapids, MI: Eerdmans, 1963), 1:xxxvii.

19 It is interesting to note that secular research has also found that singing together promotes social integration; e.g., Graham F. Welch, et al., "Singing and Social Inclusion," *Frontiers in Psychology* 5 (July 2014): 1–12.

continues his work of renewal in the family when we honor the biblical command to "be filled with the Spirit, addressing one another in psalms and hymns and spiritual songs, singing and making melody to the Lord with your heart" (Eph 5:18–19). Similarly, "let the word of Christ [and that includes the Psalms][20] dwell in you richly, teaching and admonishing one another in all wisdom, singing psalms and hymns and spiritual songs, with thankfulness in your hearts to God" (Col 3:16).

These apostolic admonitions indicate that when a family sings together, they also speak to each other and instruct each other in God's ways. Family singing is a huge educational asset, for when we vocalize the deeds of God and his mercies in song we not only remind each other of them, but God's great and mighty acts of love and salvation go deep into our memory and consciousness and become difficult to forget or push aside. Singing godly songs from an early age is formative for one's mindset and outlook on life. The Holy Spirit uses such singing to help young and old resist sin. Indeed godly singing is a strong antidote to God-dishonoring worldly music that seeks to captivate young hearts for sinful thinking and worse. Satan and his cohorts are in retreat when songs of the covenant are sung because such singing enables the Spirit to more and more fill and shape human hearts and encourage desires for holy service.

When God uses family singing as a means to continue his work in the lives of his children, he also enables the family to sing new songs of redemption. Indeed, the exhortation rings throughout the book of Psalms. "Sing to the LORD a new song!" (e.g., Ps 33:3; Ps 96:1). As the realization of the greatness of God's saving work deepens, old songs gain new meaning and new songs are composed and sung. When David experienced God's deliverance, he acknowledged that God "put a new song in my mouth, a song of praise to our God" (Ps 40:3). Singing is a beautiful medium for praising God and the Hebrew name for the book of Psalms is "Praises." Not surprisingly, therefore, the biblical collection of Psalms ends in a triumphant crescendo of praise with Psalm 150. Throughout the ages, God's people have composed more songs of praise and new ones will also be sung before God's throne (cf. Rev 5:9; 14:3).

---

20 G.K. Beale, *Colossians and Philemon*, Baker Exegetical Commentary on the New Testament (Grand Rapids, MI: Baker Academic, 2019), 302–6.

We may appropriate such new songs and hymns for our singing and so educate the family on the great priority of God in our life and set the focus for our lives on his saving work and agenda.

Our worship and singing here is only a small beginning of the glorious worship that awaits us. The great family of God, redeemed from sin and all the limitations of a fallen world, will one day be able to worship perfectly! God's Word tells us that singing new songs will be part of that reality (e.g. Rev 14:1–3). Our lives today, and therefore also our family worship, can focus on that glorious reality that is coming!

As children get older, besides participating in family worship, they should be taught and encouraged to have their own private devotions at set times including Bible reading and prayer. Early morning before school or before going to sleep at night seem appropriate. The learning of psalms and other biblical songs from memory is an enormous educational asset and can help children through difficult times as they grow up. Edifying songs sung and learned can quicken the spirit. They can be of great encouragement when they are recalled in challenging circumstances and so in effect function as prayers to God.

Family Nurturing the New Creation

The early childhood years are critical for the development of a biblical outlook on life. The home education which children receive in their pre-school years can impact them for the rest of their days. We have considered the great importance of parents enabling their children to develop a clear sense of their identity as children of God who has embraced them in his covenant and who has also endowed them with their gender. The great importance of family worship has also been considered. In chapters 1 and 2, we saw that life-producing discipline and meaningful interaction in the family circle are critical components for godly nurture. When all these different elements are realized, then under the Lord's blessing, a family develops a clear focus and identity that sets it off from worldly norms and goals. In closing, let us consider the overall focus of a Christian family to be a nursery that promotes regeneration and the new creation.

Parents are God's first means to begin the realization of the baptismal promises given to their children. Godly parents may begin the process of molding their children in God's ways with the knowledge that these children have been claimed by God and given the promise of the forgiveness of all their sins because of Christ's sacrifice. Although children are born and conceived in sin, parents may be assured that the renewal of their lives is possible through the promised work of the Holy Spirit. As agents for that renewal of life, parents need to be very intentional in raising and nurturing the children whom God has entrusted to them.

Heart and Mind

From birth God has graciously endowed all children with an innate knowledge of himself. As Calvin put it: "this conviction, namely, that there is some God, is naturally inborn in all, and is fixed deep within, as it were in the very marrow." This "sense of divinity which can never be effaced is engraved upon men's minds." Calvin concluded: "it is not a doctrine that must first be learned in school, but one of which each of us is master from his mother's womb and which nature itself permits no one to forget, although many strive with every nerve to this end" (cf. Rom 1:19–21).[21] If young children have a knowledge of God, be it rudimentary, they also intuitively know the difference between good and evil. What we call conscience is a gift of God. "The spirit of man is the lamp of the LORD, searching all his innermost parts" (Prov 20:27). As Calvin wrote: "Each one undoubtedly feels within the heavenly grace that quickens him." Even children are, therefore, able to show God's glory (Ps 8:2).[22]

The fact that small children are already graciously equipped by God with a sense of his existence is of great encouragement to Christian parents to work as instruments of the Holy Spirit who is able to renew their children to be a new creation. Since the heart is the center of our existence, it is the heart of the child that needs to be molded by the Spirit and Word of God. The child must have the mind of Christ (cf. 1 Cor 2:12–16). Humanly speaking, without the instruction and nurture

---

21 Calvin, *Institutes*, 1.3.3 (p. 46).
22 Calvin, *Institutes*, 1.5.3 (pp. 54–55).

of Christian parents, children, though born with a sense of the reality of God, will embrace the way of their sinful hearts (Eph 2:23). So parents need to consciously work towards shaping the minds of their children to be godly.

The prayer of David can be that of parents for their children. "Give me an undivided heart" (Ps 86:11 NIV84). As the context of this psalm makes clear, an undivided heart can only be achieved by way of instruction. "Teach me your way, O LORD, and I will walk in your truth; give me an undivided heart, that I may fear your name" (Ps 86:11 NIV84). One can also translate "give me an undivided heart" as "unite my heart" (ESV) or "make my heart one." The human heart can go into different directions and lead a divided existence. But then one cannot be wholeheartedly committed to the Lord. An important goal of parental instruction is to help children develop a single minded focus on the Lord and his will amidst all the competing wants of the sinful heart. As children mature, they will experience the centrifugal forces of conflicting desires that can divide their hearts. They need to learn discernment, to reject sin, to prioritize, and to make decisions that are pleasing to the Lord. If our children love their heavenly Father and Savior, then God will give them singleness of heart and action (Jer 32:39; Ezek 11:19). When parents focus their children on pleasing God then, under his blessing, his wishes become theirs and their mind becomes the mind of Christ. Their heart will be undivided for the Lord and they will desire "whatever is honorable, whatever is just, whatever is pure, whatever is lovely, whatever is commendable" (Phil 4:8).

Such a development is a lifelong process of transformation that begins from infancy. The apostolic command is relevant for all ages. "Be transformed by the renewing of your mind" (Rom 12:2). Our minds are precious. But they need to be renewed, regenerated by the Holy Spirit (Col 3:9–10). As research in the working of the brain continues, we can use a modern metaphor and speak of the need for the brain to be rewired. The old wiring of our sinful nature needs to be replaced with the new. Research has shown that our physical brain is critically related to our mind. Theologian N. T. Wright highlighted the amazing scientific fact that "every thought we think, every act we perform, and especially every habit we adopt and develop creates pathways in our brains. That's why a habit is what it is: something that, initially difficult or even impossible (think of learning a foreign language or a musical instrument), gradually becomes as we say, 'second nature.'"[23] The fact that neural brain pathways can be formed by outside influences underlines the importance of godly parental upbringing from infancy. After all, sinful habits can wire the brain with circuitry promoting sinful thinking and behavior. Studies into the influence of exposure to pornography on the brain have made this clear.[24]

And so as parents help their children to shape their minds in a manner pleasing to God, they are also in the process of helping them to offer their bodies to the Lord in holy service because there is a certain physicality to training the brain to godly obedience. The brain is part of the body, a temple of the Holy Spirit, and its neural pathways need to be conditioned to be pure so that the mind of a child can be transformed and be in sync with the mind of Christ. Learning biblical songs and Scripture passages are obvious means for young children to develop godly circuitry in their brains that will help them to develop in a manner pleasing to the Lord. Christian parents will do everything possible to keep the corrupting influences of the world at bay during the formative years of their children and to train them to fear God so that they may have undivided hearts focussed on their Savior. When parents do that, they can also emphasize to their children by their loving everyday example that the new life in Christ is a life of joy.

Joy in the Lord

The Heidelberg Catechism describes the coming to life of the new nature as "a heartfelt joy in God through Christ, and a love and a delight to live according to the will of God in all good works" (QA 90).[25] This reality means that a Christian home should reflect much joy in Christ. Christians have every reason to be optimistic about the future. We live in God's world. He is sovereign and all-powerful and so we know the

---

23 N. T. Wright, *The Case for the Psalms. Why They Are Essential* (New York, NY: HarperOne, 2013), 157.
24 William M. Struthers, *Wired for Intimacy: How Pornography Hijacks the Male Brain* (Downers Grove, IL: InterVarsity Press, 2009).
25 *Book of Praise*, 549.

eventual renewal of all creation is on schedule. We can look forward to the return of our Savior who promised that he is coming as quickly as possible (Rev 22:20).

The nurturing joy of a Christian family reinforces in children their identity as belonging to God and that their life is ultimately a journey to him. Establishing that kind of atmosphere in the home requires dedicated parental leadership and discipline to create an environment that is joyful and not oppressive. It also means that the family functions as a unit and does not automatically disperse and disappear in different bedrooms where the children are glued to their electronic devices. There needs to be time for family activities and discussion that encourages the flourishing of Christian virtues where God and his Word are central. The family unit then provides a safe haven and a strong bulwark for the attacks of the evil one, an oasis of joy and peace in a world that is both unhappy and in upheaval. Children will truly feel at home in such a family environment in which they are constantly re-orientated to the true purpose and goal of life. Parents who provide such a family setting will equip their children with discernment on what the world offers in the media, literature, and the arts. Such parents will also enable them to work for renewal in different areas of life, as the Lord gives opportunity. But the renewal starts in the home and with the children!

A family that experiences the joy in Christ is also a family best able to keep the lines of communication open between the generations. After all, when you share your joy in singing and family worship, you also more easily open up to each other about the challenges and struggles of the faith. The transforming power of God's work of renewal in singing means that the so-called generation gap disappears and parents and children know that they are all sons and daughters of God in heaven and therefore brothers and sisters of each other. When parents and children relate to each other as one in Christ, as siblings in Father's Family, then what joy can be experienced! In such a family it is possible to truly share burdens and joys and to mutually encourage each other in the challenges of being believers in a world not yet redeemed. Then all are fortified with the inextinguishable joy in Christ that conquers satanic attacks of temptation and doubt and that overcomes the decadent world of sin. It even becomes possible in faith to rejoice in all circumstances of life and so to obey the apostolic word: "Rejoice in the Lord always; again I will say rejoice. … The Lord is at hand" (Phil 4:4). We live in anticipation of his coming (cf. Phil 3:20). A Christian family can, therefore, benefit from the biblical injunction and experience God's comfort: "Do not be anxious about anything, but in everything by prayer and supplication with thanksgiving let your requests be made known to God. And the peace of God which surpasses all understanding, will guard your hearts and your minds in Christ Jesus" (Phil 4:5–7).

The Christian family is an enormous gift of God. It must be treasured, protected, and enjoyed as the first place of nurture for the next generation. Children who have been blessed with parents who provided such a family environment during their formative years are enormously helped to face the challenges of life and the corrosive effects of sin. Buoyed by the knowledge imprinted in their minds at an early age that a loving heavenly covenantal Lord has given them rich baptismal promises, such children will know their true identity and that their God is able see them through life's journey to Father's house and the new world that is coming.[26]

---

26 For more on the importance of the Christian family for nurture, see Herman Bavinck, *The Christian Family*, ed. Stephen J. Grabill, trans. Nelson D. Kloosterman, intro. James Eglinton, reprint, 1912 (Grand Rapids, MI: Christian's Library Press, 2012), 105–8; more generally, W. Meijer, *Christ in the Family*, ed. Debbie Lodder and Teresa Metzlar, trans. G. Ravensbergen, rev. J. Moesker (London, ON: ILPB, 1985).

CHAPTER 4

The Privilege and Challenge of Educating Children with Disabilities

---

It is an enormous challenge to raise and educate children with disabilities.[1] I have no expertise in this area and I recognize that only those who have been entrusted with such children have any real idea of what is involved. The purpose of this chapter is, however, not to relate life experiences, but to consult Scripture and to seek guidance from God's Word on the place and task of these children, as well as the challenges and privileges inherent in their upbringing and education. God's Word is a light on life's path, also when we are confronted as parents, teachers, and a faith community with children who have special needs. His Word gives direction, encouragement, and instruction also when confronted with these realities.

Scripture makes it clear that the LORD our God has a special concern for those who are often regarded as being on the fringes of society because they are not like the majority of people (cf. Ps 146:8). He instructed his people not to curse the deaf or put stumbling blocks before the blind (Lev 19:14). The Lord Jesus showed mercy and healed the deaf and speech-impaired (Mark 7:32–35), the blind (Matt 20:30–34), and the paralytic (Luke 5:18–25). It is a telling and touching truth that those specifically invited to the wedding feast in the kingdom of God include the disabled: the "crippled and blind and lame" (Luke 14:21).

---

1   "Persons with disabilities include those who have long-term physical, mental, intellectual or sensory impairments which in interaction with various barriers may hinder their full and effective participation in society on an equal basis with others." Article 1 of the *UN Convention on the Protection and Promotion of the Rights and Dignity of Persons with Disabilities* (2006) as quoted in Terry A. DeYoung, et al., *Everybody Belongs, Serving Together: Inclusive Church Ministry with People with Disabilities* (n.p.: Reformed Church Press, 2021), 18.

If the Lord has a special concern for those with special needs, so should the community of believers. Also those who have disabilities are part of the body of Christ. They belong. We are, therefore, to have equal concern for each other. If one member of the church suffers, we suffer together (1 Cor 12:25–26).

In looking for illumination from God's Word, we will seek foundational guidance by looking at some basic principles. We will first consider why the LORD would entrust parents with children with disabilities, both mild and severe. What could his purpose be? What office or task do these children have? Next we will consider the educational responsibilities of the parents and the faith community. Finally, we will consider the goal of educating these children.

What is the Sense of Living with Disabilities?

What is the sense of living with disabilities, even severe ones?[2] A common answer our secular society gives is that there is no point in raising such a child. If an expectant mother knows that the child she is carrying has disabilities, it is best to have an abortion as soon as you know the child to be born is not normal. Get it over with. With euthanasia more and more becoming acceptable, newborn infants with severe disabilities are no longer assured of life. The Netherlands appears to lead the way. Doctors there can legally end the lives of infants who have a "hopeless prognosis" and face "unbearable suffering" although they are not in intensive care. Canada is not far behind in legalizing the killing of those with a serious illness or disability.[3] The Nazi euthanasia program of the 1930's reminds us that the legal and often enforced killing of children with disabilities is not outside the realm of the possible in the sinful

---

2   What follows in this section are some thoughts triggered by having the privilege of conducting a funeral for a member of the congregation to which I belong who had developmental disabilities.
3   For a summary of the current (2021) situation, see ARPA Canada, *Assisted Suicide and Euthanasia,* Respectfully Submitted (2021 Fall), available at arpacanada.ca.

world in which we live.[4] So, the question is urgent. Is there any sense in having a child with disabilities?

As Christians we can be very thankful that the Lord our God enables us to give a positive answer. Parents of such children will testify that it is far from easy to raise a child with significant disabilities. There are all kinds of frustrations, challenges, and questions. There seems to be no end to lugging the child in and out of a wheelchair, ongoing diaper changes, and the need to always be there for the child, so that there is less opportunity to go out. The list goes on. Those without children with disabilities actually have little notion of what it takes to raise such a child. Those who have a child with special needs can even feel lonely and abandoned by the church community. However, in faith these same parents will also testify that in spite of all the difficulties there is much reason for gratitude and joy in the Lord in receiving and raising children with disabilities.[5] Such children are a precious gift from God's fatherly hand. This reality does not undo the troubles or answer all the questions, but it does enable the parents to carry on in the strength of God's promises. "Cast all your anxiety on him because he cares for you" and "he is the one who gives power and strength to his people" (Ps 68:35).

Uncertainty and Certainty

Receiving a special needs child raises all kinds of questions, especially "why?" Does the Lord not love us? Have we done something to deserve this? Is God punishing us? The good element of such questions is that they are directed to God. He, after all, is the Giver of life. In his hands is all our existence. He is sovereign and, therefore, he indeed is the one who gives such children to whomever he pleases. God is the Creator and Giver of life and he is not accountable to us.

---

4   Peter Singer, *Ethics in the Real World: 82 Brief Essays on Things That Matter*, with a new afterword by the author (Princeton and Oxford, NJ: Princeton University Press, 2017), 81; Jonathon Van Maren, "Child Euthanasia Comes to the Netherlands," *First Things* October 15, 2020 can be found at www.firstthings.com; for eugenics and eliminating "undesirables" in Nazi Germany and as still being very much with us today, Deborah Ummel, "Dream or Nightmare? The Impact of American Eugenics, Past and Present," *Cross Currents* 66 (2016): 389–98.
5   See, e.g., Frame, *The Doctrine of the Christian Life*, 738; Donna De Boer, as told to Lil Grissen, "A Very Special Child," *The Banner* 113 (20 January 1978): 7; W. Pouwelse, "Special Children," *Clarion* 35 (1986): 101.

We may never get the answers we would like to have during this earthly life. But, with all the questions and doubts that come up, believing parents may have the comfort of knowing for a certainty that such a child comes from the hand of God and is a member of the covenant community. That reality is signified and sealed at baptism when the triune God himself claimed that child as his own precious possession. The One who embraces that child as his very own will also provide in every way. He will use the parents to that end and parents can be sure that God will give them what is necessary. His grace is sufficient and his power is made perfect in weakness (2 Cor 12:9). God will also provide by means of the church community, Christian organizations, as well as by society's support services. But he will provide. And all things will work out for good for all the promises of the covenant are also for those with disabilities (Rom 8:28). His Word is true and his promises are sure. All this is a source of great encouragement to the parents.

In this context it is also instructive to remember what happened in Jerusalem about two thousand years ago. When passing by a man with a disability—he was blind from birth—the disciples asked Jesus: "Rabbi, who sinned, this man or his parents, that he was born blind?" (John 9:2). The answer Jesus gave was memorable. "It was not that this man sinned, or his parents, but that the works of God might be displayed in him" (John 9:3). Jesus healed the man and so displayed God's power; but, the point our Savior made also holds true for people with disabilities today who are not healed. In unexpected ways, God's work is displayed through these children. Many a parent can testify to that reality in the way they experienced God's power and mercy in giving them such children. Also a church community cannot remain unaffected by the opportunity to accept and to minister to those with disabilities in their midst. These members too have a task and office to perform, often in surprising ways, ways in which God's love and mercy are also displayed.

An Office to Perform

The office of those with disabilities varies depending on how the Lord has endowed them. But some elements are common to all who are developmentally or otherwise significantly challenged. For one thing, their very presence testifies to the brokenness of this creation. The results of original sin in Adam are very much with us in this present life and this reality is underlined by the special needs children God gives. Their presence reminds us that we can never underestimate the devastation which the fall into sin has caused and it keeps us mindful of the need for redemption and renewal through the work of the Savior. Having a child with disabilities can help in keeping our focus on what's truly important in life. Ultimately this world is a passing stage (1 John 2:15-17) and we need to live close to the Lord in expectation of the full deliverance from all the misery that sin has brought into the world. And the Lord will grant that deliverance! We can now already see how he is restoring life in a fallen world. This is often especially visible in children with special needs.

God makes no mistakes when he entrusts parents with a child with significant disabilities. He himself has designed that child in the womb of its mother (Ps 139:13) and he has designed it in such a way that it could fulfill its office and calling (cf. Eph 4:7). Such children are often endowed with limitations that enable them to be untouched and unencumbered by many of the concerns that can burden people today. Most of us go through life with many responsibilities and cares. Worries can gnaw away at the joy of life and even rob people of happiness. But this is not the case with many people with special needs. Because of the way God has made them, these particular members of the church have few of the responsibilities that can weigh others down. As a result they can reflect something of the happiness that should be part of everyone's life before God. Those with disabilities may not even be able to speak, but they can communicate a tremendous joy that shines from their life. Parents have testified to the fact that they have been so enriched by the joy that their special child or children have given them. In giving and showing this joy, these children carry out their office according to God's design for their life. In showing this joy, they give hope for the full joy and redemption that is coming. After all, if such happiness is possible in a broken world, how wonderful it must be on the new earth that is coming! Such a joy exuding from the life of a person with special needs can even affect an entire congregation in which such a child of God is a member.

Another aspect of the office of those with disabilities is that they often put others to shame by exhibiting a firm and unwavering child-like faith. There is no doubt in their minds that God loves them and will provide for them. With no hesitation whatsoever they will entrust themselves completely to the Lord knowing that he cares for them. Many a parent has said that they were put to shame by the simple and complete confidence in the Lord and his promises that their child with disabilities demonstrated. Also in this respect, God shows his work of the renewal of life through the testimony of those with developmental or other issues. In this way he also encourages us to emulate their faith. In this respect, we all need to be like children (cf. Matt 18:3).

And finally, although more could be said, special children can also teach us gratitude. It is so easy to become dissatisfied with life and the lot that God has given, until one stands before a developmentally challenged person who is happy and firmly believes in God's good provision for his or her life. Such people can put those endowed with so many of God's gifts to shame for their ungratefulness. If a person with severe developmental restrictions can be happy with the Lord's provision, should others not be even more grateful and joyous?

And when in God's sovereign disposition, such a developmentally challenged person has completed his or her task, then the Lord calls him or her home to himself. The vacuum that is often left by such a death underlines the vital role that such a person played in the family and often within the congregation. These special members of the church leave a real legacy, a legacy of reminding God's people of what is truly important in life and of what unencumbered joy can be like, regardless of the outward circumstances of life. Those challenged in all sorts of ways, physically and mentally, are therefore at the end of the day a great blessing for others. They can stimulate us to be of good courage as we all move along life's path toward the perfection that will one day characterize the new world.

In It Together for Blessing

Since God himself designed each one of his children for their specific calling and office, it is a privilege and duty to support those with disabilities and their parents. After all, a church community is a covenant fellowship of believers and we bear each other's burdens and share each other's joys. Those with special needs are precious to all of us for they are children with whom God has made his covenant.

In this context it is good to be aware of what can be involved when someone who has not previously been exposed to special needs children begins to relate to them. Dan Vander Plaats of Elim Christian Services in greater Chicago has helpfully noted five stages that people typically can go through when they begin to interact with people with disabilities: ignorance, pity, care, friendship, and co-laborers.[6] After an initial disinterest in those with special needs, people who are newly exposed to children with disabilities become aware of their situation and feel sorry for them because they see no meaning or purpose for their disabilities. However, when the realization sinks in that those with special needs are also created in God's image and therefore have value, the need to help them becomes important. Friendships then develop with both sides of the relationship experiencing blessings. This process leads to integrating those with special needs more fully into the fellowship of the church so that they are truly engaged in the Christian service of love to the neighbor. Consequently, both those with disabilities and those without them work side by side for the benefit of all by encouraging and equipping each other to do the good works which God has prepared for them to do (cf. Eph 2:10) and so show their thankfulness to him.

When working together within the communion of saints one does need to be aware of the limitations and the need for boundaries. Jay Pathak and Dave Runyon have underlined the difference between being responsible *to* a person and being responsible *for* a person.[7] Keeping this distinction in mind makes a huge difference in how we relate, also to people with special needs. We are responsible to others to love, serve, encourage, and to pray for them. But to be responsible for someone means taking responsibility for their well-being, both in terms of finances and their happiness and success.

---

[6] For what follows, see Dan Vander Plaats, "Changing Attitudes Toward People with Disabilities in the Church," in *Everybody Belongs, Serving Together*, eds. Terry A. DeYoung, et al. (n.p.: Reformed Church Press, 2021), 39–40 (also see www.the5stages.com).

[7] For what follows, see Jay Pathak and Dave Runyon, *The Art of Neighboring: Building Genuine Relationships Right Outside Your Door* (Grand Rapids, MI: Baker Books, 2012), 133–34.

To be responsible for someone else's outcomes and choices is unhealthy and leads to problems. One must do everything possible for those with special needs. But it is unsustainable to be responsible for the choices they make. It leads to people trying to help those with disabilities to be overwhelmed and discouraged. "How much better to remain responsible *to* the people God has entrusted to our care and give the burdens to him."[8]

In conclusion, it is very important that those with special needs experience the blessed reality of being part of the communion of saints. It is absolutely vital to understanding their true identity and task as God's children and a crucial foundation on which to educate them for a life of godly service.

Home and School Responsibilities

As noted in the first chapters, parents have the first responsibility to educate their children in the fear of the Lord and to prepare them for life in its fullness; that is, to give them true wisdom and understanding. As those who gave their children physical life, parents pray that they may also be God's instruments to give their offspring life in the Lord, eternal life. This parental task and agenda is ultimately that of the school teacher as well. Not surprisingly, Scripture can refer to the teacher as the father of his sons, the pupils. The school parents carry on the work of the biological home parents. It is therefore very important that there be good communication between the school and the home. One way this can be done is through a support group with a mandate such as that of the Assisting the Special Child (ASC) Committee which "researches and assists parents and staff" of the schools associated with the League of Canadian Reformed School Societies "in the preparation of programs for the benefit of children with exceptionalities." Other examples of such support can be given as well.[9]

---

8 Bert VanGoolen in an email dated October 25, 2021 to the author.
9 *ASC Newsletter for Fall 2021*, 1; www.lcrss.ca. Other examples include the following. Within the Edvance Christian School Association, Sara Pot networks "with and for Christian schools and their families in support of students with special needs and a vision of belonging for all." See www.edvance.ca/about/person/sara-pot. For the Association of Christian Schools International, see Charlotte A. Marshall, *By the Numbers: How Christian Schools Serve Students with Special Needs*; (2020), found at blog.acsi.org.

The Teaching Task

But how do we give children who are challenged with disabilities true wisdom in the Lord and what they need for life now and forever? This teaching needs to be given with consistent life-producing loving discipline within the realm of what can be expected of them. Such firm instruction in love must in the first place have as constant goal to give our children a very clear sense of their identity, not only as children of their earthly father and mother, but also of God in heaven. They may not be able to learn as quickly or as in depth as their peers, but they need to know to the full extent of their capability that there is a God in heaven who is for real, who loves them and cares for them, and who has come down from heaven and claimed him or her as his very own. Our children with disabilities need to know that they have a God who has attached his name and promises to their persons. This God will go through life with them, moment by moment. They need to know that as they have loving parents, they also have a Father in heaven who has embraced them.

Now all this can seem very daunting and difficult. How to tell that God so loved the world that he gave his only Son to die for sinners so that we may have life? Can a child with special needs understand this? Probably more than we may realize. But, let us take a step back for a moment. Can we truly understand the gospel? Do we not need to take all this in faith ourselves? Who is able to comprehend the unsearchable love of God in Christ? Often a child, also those who are challenged with disabilities and have special needs, will simply accept things because mother or father or teacher has said so. Their faith can be so strong that they can put adults to shame. By giving these special children such faith, the Lord also equips them to know the comfort of the gospel. He gives them a clearly defined sense of identity and belonging. If they are taught, they will know for a certainty that they do not just belong to an earthly father and mother, but to God himself and his family! This is of enormous encouragement for a child and lays the foundation for any instruction that goes beyond that.

As God's representatives, parents and teacher-parents will do everything possible to underline that basic message of their special identity by the way they deal with these children entrusted to them. Because they belong, parents and teachers also need to spend time with them, to talk to them, to try to understand them, and to communicate with them. A child with special needs must know that their parents are there for them; within reason, of course, as other children have a right to the same expectations.

Those with disabilities also need to be taught to remember the basic truths of Scripture and the essential facts which they require to function for life here on earth. Memory work and routine is extremely important. Children love regularity and memorizing. One should not become discouraged if their children take a long time to learn something. They learn very little on their own and we must keep at it. For example, one can teach them a simple Psalm by singing it with him or her over and over again at set times such as before going to bed. They will eventually learn and make it their own. As a pastor, I once served a congregation which had children with special needs. I was asked to remember them from time to time by having psalms and hymns which they were learning sung in public worship. Of course, I gladly complied. That gave those children such a thrill! They belonged. The worship service is for them too! And so, patient, constant instruction to get the truths across, in song or otherwise, is very important. It is a disciplined instruction and such a routine in teaching and memory work gives them a sense of their real identity. This sense of identity as part of the congregation can be reinforced by having their names mentioned as appropriate in the church's bulletin and in public prayer, such as on the occasion of their birthdays.

Other ways of getting the truths of the gospel across is by making the most of story time before a child goes to bed and using the special feast days in the Christian calendar to underline the main truths of the gospel and how it impacts their lives. Also the faith of children needs to be reinforced according to their ability with regularly hearing the key contents of the gospel and how the Good News applies to their lives.

Of course, parents and teachers also teach the consequences of the gospel by their own example, attitude, and body language. One's actions and lifestyle must match one's words. Indeed, what special children see may be the only way they can be taught, especially those who have great difficulty learning concepts. Such children will be able to imitate a godly lifestyle and attitude. It is, for example, important that they learn to be friendly and polite and not nasty to others. They must also learn from their parents to watch their tongue and to be careful with what passes over their lips. I remember being told of a person with special needs at work hearing someone using the name of the Lord in vain. He protested and said that swearing should not take place. That simple testimony eventually resulted in no one using God's name in vain when he was around. The one with developmental disabilities had embraced in faith the example and teaching of his parents and produced godly fruit. More examples could undoubtedly be mentioned of the enormous positive impact in the lives of people with special needs of a godly teaching by word and deed on the part of parents and teachers.

The life wisdom that God wants us to pass on to our children also includes everything that pertains to the practical everyday work world. Where possible our special children and adults should learn social and technical skills and be integrated as much as possible in family life, in the classrooms of the schools, and in the work places of society. With respect to the working world, it is sometimes amazing how God has gifted people with disabilities to function very well in the work place when their skills are matched with the needs of the company hiring them. Progress in including people with disabilities in the working world continues to be made and this ongoing development is to be applauded.[10]

Experiencing Joy

Another important element needs to be mentioned. The Lord wants all his people to experience joy—the joy of redemption, the exhilaration of forgiveness, the happiness of belonging to Jesus Christ. Negatively that means that we must not burden special needs children with expectations and obligations that are beyond their capacity. It is important to know and stay within their limits. Otherwise, such children will feel like failures and there will be little of the joy left or experienced.

---

10 On how God can use those with disabilities in the work place, see, e.g., E. Vander Weij, "Fully Capable Work Force, Valuable Employees," *Clarion* 32 (1983): 125–26; for hiring in Canada and the United States respectively see https://www.canada.ca/en/employment-social-development/campaigns/hiring-persons-disabilities.html and https://adata.org/learn-about-ada.

Positively, recognizing the key element of joy means that we can reinforce and bring about the feeling of true happiness in the life of children with disabilities by reminding them of their special status as God's children in his world. There are different ways of doing that. If such children have done something wrong and can be held responsible, they should be told and shown the seriousness of their guilt. But then also the joy of forgiveness and how Christ makes this possible can be explained and reinforced. There can be many ways to underline this basic message and so give reason to the children to be happy in the Lord.

Another way to encourage and promote joy is to integrate the children with special needs as much as possible into family life and elsewhere. They should be treated as normally as possible, as part of the family or class at school. Then they can participate with a sense of belonging and experience the joy of singing, family fun, and outings. Such integration is also good for the rest of the family, because the other children should not think that only their special brother or sister gets the attention. All belong to the family! And so treating all the same as much as possible is important. Sometimes Christian schools do not have the resources to include some children with disabilities, who then go to a public school. But such children should not be forgotten. They can, for example, share the Christian joy of their church community by participating in some way in part of a Christmas or Easter program of the Christian school. They belong, also with the other children of the church, and that should be evident as much as possible.

Having these children share the Christian joy also means that when children with a developmental disability struggle with questions around their condition with its limitations that we take the time to listen and respond with the gospel. For instance, such a child may ask, if God is all-powerful and good, why did he make me the way I am? I want to be like the ones who do not have special needs and who are not limited the way I am. Also school teachers who deal with such special individuals must be prepared to offer a listening ear and give biblical emotional support for those with these types of questions. After all, home and school are in this together and also school teachers are "parents" in a real way to their student "children." We should not be afraid to confide that we too do not understand everything, but that like little children we too have to learn to trust in God who does work all things for our well-being and salvation (Rom 8:28). Our God is not mean and nasty. He is our Father and seeks our good (cf. Matt 7:9–11)! Also by our life example, they should see that we leave our problems and difficulties with the Lord and live in faith and trust. That will be of great encouragement to those with special needs and to all our children.

Concluding Comments

The Lord our God has a purpose in placing each one of us in this world at a particular time of history. He has given us all a task in his service. As parents and as parent-teachers we have the responsibility to give true life to the children entrusted to us, also those challenged with disabilities and special needs. To that end wisdom needs to be passed on by disciplined instruction and example. The heart of what we are to impart to those in our care is a sense of the true fear and love of God. That is essential for living life in its fullness.

Since God is the one who has entrusted our children to us, including those with disabilities, we can also be sure that he equips us to do the task he expects of us. This does not mean it will always be easy. We will need to go to the throne of grace often. But it does mean that God is behind us all the way and will strengthen and encourage us in this task. We can count on him! According to the testimony of those who have children with special needs, one way he encourages us is by the openness, honesty, thankfulness, and happiness often exhibited by such children.

A key task is to make sure that those with disabilities and challenges also feel included in the family and church of God. They belong and they too must know the joy of redemption.

Knowing this identity and joy means that those with special needs will also be able to fulfill their life calling and task. Ultimately that life calling and task is to praise God and thank him for his goodness. We are here on earth to glorify our heavenly Father (cf. 1 Cor 10:31). Our children with special needs have that task as well and the Father equips them for that obligation, also through the work of both the natural and teaching parents. We need never doubt that. Even the most severely disabled or challenged child is used by God to bring glory to him. After all, such a child will still leave a tremendous mark on our life and give our life a joy and a meaning we may never have known could exist.

A child with disabilities, even one that is only able to respond very little verbally, can change our life in a way a normal child never can. Parents of such a child have told me that a child with special needs drove them closer and closer to the Lord than they otherwise would have been. Such experiences make life rich and beautiful beyond measure. The heartaches, sleepless nights, and worries about that child can result in a walk with God that is the envy of our brothers and sisters in the faith. And let us face it, if the purpose of life is to glorify God, could anything more beautiful than a close walk with God be imagined? Such parents can daily thank God for that particular child he has put in their life path for it has made their life so unbelievably rich, a richness surpassing the treasures of this world. And when we tire and grow weary in raising such children, he will sustain us by his grace, just as he does with the so-called "normal" children who can also cause us much anguish and worries. If we only go to him, he will show us the way, also with our special children.

May all those parents with special needs children experience God's nearness and grace as they deal with the challenges God has put on their path. The same can be said for teachers, members of the congregation, and those who interact in different areas of life with our brothers and sisters with disabilities. It is a challenge. But for Christians that challenge also includes the very rich privilege of having the opportunity to be an instrument for good from God for such children. The consequences can have eternal blessed significance.

PART B

THE IMPORTANCE OF LANGUAGE

CHAPTER 5

The Gift of Language: Corrupted and Redeemed

Educating would be impossible without the gift of language. Indeed, life as human beings would be unthinkable without being able to speak. Language is truly a marvelous gift which the Creator gave only to the crown of his creation, human beings. There is nothing like this means of communicating anywhere in the world of mammals. As noted linguist Noam Chomsky observed: "human language appears to be a unique phenomenon, without significant analogue in the animal world."[1] Elsewhere he noted that "when we study human language, we are approaching what some might call the 'human essence,' the distinctive qualities of mind that are, so far as we know, unique to man." To be able to express oneself and communicate using different and new expressions according to the occasion is truly a marvel and "a creative activity."[2] No human society has ever been known to be without this ability.

Every time we speak, we use this gift of God. Through articulated words we can express and pass on our thoughts, feelings, plans, and also the gospel, along with the joy it brings to our lives. With the gift of language, we can train our children to think logically and creatively, and equip them for holy service to the Lord. Seeing its indispensable place in educating, it is beneficial to consider some aspects of language; namely, the origin

---

[1] Noam Chomsky, *Language and Mind*, 3rd ed. (Cambridge, UK: Cambridge University Press, 2006), 59, also see 61–62. Animals do communicate in some ways of course, but that sort of communication is completely different from the versatility and productivity of human speech and language. Moisés Silva, *God, Language and Scripture: Reading the Bible in the Light of General Linguistics*, Foundations of Contemporary Interpretation (Grand Rapids, MI: Zondervan, 1990), 24, note 7.

[2] For these two quotes, see Chomsky, *Language and Mind*, 88; also see 89–90.

and power of language, its corruption by sin, and the redemption of language in Christ.

The Origin and Power of Language

God, the Creator, is the one who gave humans the gift of language. He made Adam and Eve unique among all his handiwork and an important part of that uniqueness was their God-given ability to formulate thoughts and to communicate them by audible speech. This is a powerful way of transmitting information very precisely and clearly and, in the case of a command, even starting a whole series of events as the instructions are carried out.

It is telling that Scripture begins with God using the spoken word to create. In the account of creation, we repeatedly hear the words: "And God said," followed by the results of his commands that brought all creation into being (Gen 1). God's use of language underlines the enormous power of the spoken word. As the psalmist described the Creator's work: "He spoke, and it came to be; he commanded, and it stood firm" (Ps 33:9; similarly 148:5). By speaking, God also assigned to his creation their names and identity. "God called the light Day and the darkness he called Night" (Gen 1:5). Similarly he named the expanse heaven, the dry land earth, and the waters seas (Gen 1:8, 10).

God created humans in his own image and he also gave them the power and ability to speak. Although humans are only creatures and not divine, God did give them a very potent tool with the gift of language. Just as God could by speaking assign to his creation their names and identity, so he gave that same capability to humankind. The LORD God brought the creatures he had made to Adam. "And whatever the man called every living creature, that was its name" (Gen 2:19). Thus Adam honored God's command to have dominion over creation as his representative, made in his image (Gen 1:26).

It needs to be realized that the ability to speak, and then employing language to name parts of creation, presupposes that God gave humans the intelligence, wisdom, and insight needed. There is a close relationship of language to one's mind and the ability to rationally order one's thoughts.[3] To formulate words and sentences so that ideas or commands can be communicated is a God-given faculty that is truly miraculous. The book of Genesis has come down to us in God's providential care. This means that through the gift of language, God was able to communicate to Adam his deeds of creation. These works of God were subsequently handed down through the generations and ultimately came to Israel in written form. Although Adam as a mere creature could not understand how God was able to create, yet with the use of language, God was able to inform him truly of his work in a way that was meaningful for Adam and Eve. They in turn could remember and pass this information on to posterity.[4]

Verbal language remains an instrument of communication between God and us and it also makes meaningful interaction among humans possible. It is a marvel of God's grace that he has given us his Word in written form in Holy Scripture. This Word of God is a powerful tool of the Holy Spirit to work faith and to facilitate fellowship with God (Rom 10:17). The Word is like a hammer that breaks the rock to pieces (Jer 23:29) and accomplishes its purpose (Isa 55:11). In educating our children, passing on this Word must therefore have a foundational role and central place as we seek to raise them in the fear of the LORD. In our teaching we will also tell them that God most powerfully communicated his love to us with the Word made flesh (John 1:14; 3:16). Indeed, it was through the eternal Word, the Son, that God created all things and continues to uphold creation (Col 1:16–17; Heb 1:3).

The gift of language enabled Adam and Eve to have fellowship with God and with each other in Eden in an intimate and precise way that was unknown in the rest of creation. The very thoughts of their heart could be vocalized and shared. But we no longer possess the ability to use this gift perfectly as originally intended. It has been corrupted by sin.

---

3   See also Silva, *God, Language and Scripture*, 25–26.
4   J. C. Sikkel, *Het boek der geboorten: verklaring van het boek Genesis* (Amsterdam, NL: Van Bottenburg, 1923), 73; see also Van Dam, *In the Beginning*, 26.

The Corruption of Language

The serpent abused the gift of language by using it to create doubt in Eve's mind about what the LORD had said to Adam. "Did God actually say, 'You shall not eat of any tree in the garden?'" (Gen 3:1). This crafty animal was used by Satan (cf. Rev 12:9) not only to create doubt, but also to confuse Eve and to insinuate that she could determine whether God really meant to say what he had clearly commanded. Eve corrected Satan's suggestion that God had forbidden them to eat from any tree in the garden. "We may eat of the fruit of the trees of the garden, but God said, 'You shall not eat of the fruit of the tree that is in the midst of the garden.'" But then she went beyond what God had said by adding: "neither shall you touch it, lest you die" (Gen 3:2–3). Satan then used the marvel of language to lie and to oppose God by saying: "You will not surely die. For God knows that when you eat of it your eyes will be opened, and you will be like God, knowing good and evil" (Gen 3:4–5). Eve then fell into sin and enticed her husband to eat of the forbidden fruit as well.

Then in his mercy the LORD God used the gift of language to call Adam and Eve into his presence and confront them with their sin. The horror of sin affecting language became evident when Adam and Eve used their speech to shift the blame for their actions to someone else (Gen 3:9–12). Instead of being an instrument of communication and fellowship, their use of language now set up barriers between them. The impact of sin on language was devastating. The apostle James would later write that "the tongue is a fire, a world of unrighteousness. The tongue is set among our members, staining the whole body, setting on fire the entire course of life, and set on fire by hell" (James 3:6). When sin has the upper hand, the tongue is destructive to the extreme. "It is a restless evil, full of deadly poison" (James 3:8). Rather than drawing people together in harmony, such a tongue slanders, lies, creates discord, incites hate, and causes much sin.

Adam and Eve were expelled from the garden, but only after God had graciously used the miracle of language to announce that he would put enmity between the serpent and the woman and that the serpent would eventually be crushed (Gen 3:15). With the fall of humanity into sin, the positive use of language became very difficult. Nevertheless, this medium of communication retained its power and the greatness of this gift was not to be underestimated. It could be used for public worship in calling upon the name of the LORD (Gen 4:26), but it also forcefully exalted sin (Gen 4:23–24). Language also enabled the human race to find some sort of unity in their rebellion against God. In spite of the disruptions of sin caused by the tongue, the fact that there was but one language with everyone using the same words enabled the building of the tower of Babel. This was done to enhance their security and to prevent their dispersion in a direct challenge to God's will that they fill the earth (Gen 1:28). This misuse of language prompted the LORD to come down in judgment and confuse their language so that they could no longer understand each other. In this way, the LORD dispersed them over the earth and so also graciously restrained their sin in opposing God's design for humankind (Gen 11:1–9). With the unity of language broken, communication became difficult. Tempers must have flared and created discord resulting in humanity's dispersal over the entire globe. We can assume that after this miracle of confusing their language, the different language groups developed into ever more complexity along with actual physical changes resulting in the different races we are familiar with today (cf. Acts 17:26). The disunity within the human race resulting from God's judgment at the tower of Babel is still with us today.[5]

"As Were the Days of Noah ..."

Although there is no longer one language, making the transmission of ideas more difficult worldwide, yet, even within one language, it is hard to overestimate the ongoing destruction caused by the sin of the tongue today. When the Lord Jesus instructed his disciples about what Christians can expect in the last days, that is the final post-Pentecost time period before Christ's return, he said, among other things, that it would be like

---

5   See further, G. Ch. Aalders, *Genesis*, trans. William Heynen, Bible Student's Commentary (Grand Rapids, MI: Zondervan, 1981), 1:253–55; Carl J. Lawrenz and John C. Jeske, *A Commentary on Genesis 1–11* (Milwaukee, WI: Northwestern Publishing House, 2004), 330; also see Charles V. Taylor, "The Origin of Language," *Journal of Creation* 11, no. 1 (1997): 76–81.

the days of Noah, with humanity unperturbed by their disobedience and not believing in God's coming judgment (Matt 24:37–39). What were those days like? Scripture informs us that "the LORD saw that the wickedness of man was great in the earth, and that every intention of the thoughts of his heart was only evil continually" (Gen 6:5). That means that everything shaped by the thoughts of the human heart was exclusively wicked all the time. Whatever came up in the human mind was evil. Language expressing what was in the mind was thus also evil. Mainstream Western culture today regrettably shares much of this characterization. As in the days of Noah, when "the earth was corrupt in God's sight" (Gen 6:11), thus it is largely so today.

When God and his norms, such as the ninth commandment forbidding false testimony (Exod 20:16), are eliminated from one's mind and thinking, then language is easily abused and goes counter to God's design and intent for this gift. Language then no longer serves to communicate truth and righteousness. The modern secular mindset shows an evil aptitude for expressing wicked thoughts with pleasant sounding words that nevertheless seek to exclude all distinctions between right and wrong. This is especially the case when sensitive ethical issues are discussed. As a result, much present day speech lacks moral overtones. As the late professor Allan Bloom correctly observed in his critique of the intellectual and moral confusion of our age: "there is now an entirely new language of good and evil, originating in an attempt to get 'beyond good and evil' and preventing us from talking with any conviction about good and evil anymore."[6] Bloom went on to note that this change of language is as great as when Christianity replaced paganism. Indeed, we are changing as a civilization into a new paganism. "A new language always reflects a new point of view, and the gradual, unconscious polarization of new words, or of old words used in new ways, is a sure sign of a profound change in people's articulation of the world."[7]

Examples of this profound change at the cost of Christian truth come to mind. The phrase "mercy killing" which describes what really happens, namely killing, is generally avoided in favor of the word euthanasia. This

---

[6] Allan Bloom, *The Closing of the American Mind: How Higher Education Has Failed Democracy and Impoverished the Souls of Today's Students* (New York, NY: Simon and Schuster, 1987), 141.

[7] Bloom, *The Closing of the American Mind*, 141.

term masks the basic issue with a euphemism. By avoiding the mention of killing, it shifts the point of contention away from whether it is morally justified to kill to whether it is a human right to be able to die "with dignity."[8] The moral corruptness of our society is evident from the fact that killing someone for virtually any reason is now legally codified in law. In Canada, for example, the act of being put to death, either with a medically administered lethal injection or by helping a person to die, is legally available for anyone facing unbearable suffering or coping with disabilities or mental health concerns.[9] All this killing is covered with terms least likely to give offense, such as euthanasia and medical assistance in dying.

A similar masking of evil in ending life contrary to God's will is evident from the way those in favor of killing preborn children are called pro-choice rather than pro-abortion. The word abortion does still carry negative connotations of death, but to say you are pro-choice sounds more positive. It means you are for something, namely, the freedom to choose, which is enshrined as a positive value. Furthermore, the label of pro-choice makes it easy for politicians to evade the issue of life and death for the preborn and say something like: "Personally I am not for abortion, but I cannot impose my views on others." Also the term pro-choice takes the attention away from the preborn child who is to be murdered.[10]

Both mercy killing and the killing of preborn children used to be criminal offenses in most Western nations in agreement with the biblical sixth commandment: "you shall not murder" (Exod 20:13). But that is no longer the state of affairs. The change in society's morals has also been reflected in the transformation of the language used. Language has a powerful molding force. It can easily alter one's outlook on ethical issues unless one is strongly grounded in biblical values.

---

8   Since the early seventeenth century, the word euthanasia meant "a gentle and easy death." It was not until about 1869 that the term denoted "the action of inducing a gentle and easy death." *The Compact Edition of the Oxford English Dictionary: Complete Text Reproduced Micrographically* (Oxford, UK: Oxford University Press, 1971), 904; cf. L.L. de Veber, "Mercy Killing: History and Medicine," *Life and Learning* 8 (1998): 469–79.

9   See, e.g., ARPA Canada, *Assisted Suicide and Euthanasia*.

10 For more examples regarding abortion, see John Jalsevac, "Abortionists as Euphemists: The Curious Case of Shifting Language," *Reformed Perspective* 38, no. 4 (2009): 15–16.

Such molding power of language is also evident in the changed meaning of the word gay. For centuries that word simply meant merry, carefree, happy, and being full of joy. But by the 1960's the word gay was used by homosexuals to identify themselves with respect to their sexual orientation. The word gay "is now the standard accepted term throughout the English-speaking world." As a result the older meanings "have more or less dropped out of natural use."[11] Homosexuals have not only been influential in changing the meaning of the word gay, but they have also to a large extent hijacked the symbol of the rainbow for their purpose. The Bible speaks of the rainbow as a sign of God's covenant with humanity and all living beings that he would never again destroy all flesh with a flood (Gen 9:12–17). The gay rights movement has made the rainbow flag a symbol of the diversity and unity of the LGBTQ community. The language of the rainbow in our secularized culture does not communicate biblical truths but only the aspirations of the homosexual movement.[12]

The homosexual movement pushes hard to be accepted and uses language to achieve its goals. An example is its use of the word homophobia with far reaching and evil consequences. The saga of Dr. Chris Kempling illustrates this point. He was convicted of conduct unbecoming a member of the British Columbia College of Teachers for expressing his Christian belief that homosexual behavior is immoral. If you take that position, the homosexual movement, and consequently much of society that has been influenced by it, will consider you to be homophobic; that is, you are suffering from homophobia. A phobia is an irrational fear, a mental illness. But, as Kempling, a mental health professional, explained: "I have never encountered anyone with an irrational fear of homosexuals. But the concept of homophobia, as defined by gay activists, is the unwillingness to approve of homosexuality. Even toleration without approval is defined as 'homophobic.' So, if you have a moral objection to homosexuality, you are 'mentally ill.'" Dr. Kempling lost his appeals and eventually left the public education system.[13]

---

11 The quotes are from the definition of the word gay in the online edition of the Oxford English dictionary available at www.lexico.com/en/definition/gay.
12 Nora Gonzalez, "How Did the Rainbow Flag Become a Symbol of LGBTQ Pride?" *Encyclopedia Britannica*, found in www.britannica.com.
13 For the quotation, see Chris Kempling, "A New Dictionary? Redefining the English Language," *Reformed Perspective* 24, no. 9/10 (2005): 5; for his ordeal, Chris Kempling, "Holding Hands with Gomorrah," *Reformed Perspective* 24, no. 9/10 (2005): 4–5 and Chris Kempling, *Update: Chris Kempling's Defence* (2009), found in old.arpacanada.ca/news/2009/02/04/.

Another area of conflict where the language used plays an important role is the transgender debate. The word gender is key for the so-called progressives to create the right linguistic environment for discussing this issue. Although historically the term gender has denoted biological sex, the word's connotations have changed since the 1960's.[14] The term sex refers to biological male and female. There is no ambiguity. But as the online Oxford English Dictionary notes: "Although the words gender and sex are often used interchangeably, they have slightly different connotations; sex tends to refer to biological differences, while gender more often refers to cultural and social differences and sometimes encompasses a broader range of identities than the binary of male and female."[15] By using the word gender, one is using a word that in today's context implicitly acknowledges that there could be more than simply male and female. The transgender movement makes much of these new meanings of the term gender as it pushes the notion that one's sex is not biologically determined but is a social and cultural construct. More examples of the changed use of language from the current cultural war can be mentioned.[16]

Even innocent sounding words like weekend can change one's perception and thinking, in this case, of what constitutes a biblical week. You would think that technically, the word weekend means the end of the week, namely Saturday. But that is not how it is used. According to lexical authorities, the first use of the word weekend occurred in 1879 in Britain and included the Sunday. This was a time when the process of secularization was ongoing in that country and in Europe generally.[17] It is of interest to note that this term did not appear in the expanded Webster's International Dictionary produced in America in 1895. A week was defined as "a period of seven days, usually that reckoned from one Sabbath or Sunday to the next."[18] That definition has changed. Calendars,

---

14 Bruce Thornton, "Culture Wars and the Degradation of Language" (FrontPage Magazine, 16 November 2021), found at www.frontpagemag.com.
15 Quoted from www.lexico.com/en/definition/gender.
16 For more on the word gender and other examples, see Thornton, "Culture Wars".
17 *The Compact Edition of the Oxford English Dictionary,* 3727; for secularization, Owen Chadwick, T*he Secularization of the European Mind in the Nineteenth Century* (Cambridge, UK: Cambridge University Press, 1975), 88–106.
18 *Webster's International Dictionary of the English Language*, revised and enlarged under the supervision of Noah Porter (Springfield, MA: G. & C. Merriam Company, 1895), 2:1639.

especially those coming from Europe, regularly start the week with Monday, a day which the International Organization for Standardization also accepts as the first day of the week.[19] The weekend then indeed refers to Saturday and Sunday as the last two days of the week. But with this understanding, the Christian heritage of a week beginning with Sunday, the day of Christ's resurrection, is completely lost and we have abandoned another aspect of biblical thinking. Christians, therefore, need to be very cognizant of how they use the word weekend. It should not be used to include the Sunday since that is, biblically speaking, the first day of the week, a day when we begin the week with worship.

The growing popularity of trying to avoid a reference to Christ in referring to dates is another indication of the waning influence of Christianity on our culture. Dionysius Exiguus (c. 470–540) was the first one to date events using the year of the birth of Christ as the base point. His method was adopted all over the Christian world and dates were defined by "Before Christ" (BC) or "in the year of our Lord," Anno Domini (AD). Today, more and more scholars are now using the designations "before the Common Era" (BCE) or "Common Era" (CE) to avoid referring directly to Christ. This religiously more neutral manner of dating, cannot, however, get around the fact that even these designations pivot around the date of the birth of Christ. The growing popularity of these more neutral references is, nevertheless, another sign of how secularism continues to exert its influence on current language.[20]

The above examples are sufficient to illustrate how language reflects current culture, also when that culture is hostile to biblical values. Much more could be said. In summarizing the destructive nature of our secular culture's influence on language, it is beneficial to listen to some of the results of Harry Blamires's study. He investigated the devastating influence

---

19 "A week starts with Monday (day 1) and ends with Sunday (day 7)." Markus Kuhn, *A Summary of the International Standard Time and Time Notation*, found at www.cl.cam.ac.uk/~mgk25/iso-time.html.

20 Alden A. Mosshammer, "Dionysius Exiguus," in *Religion Past and Present*, eds. Hans Dieter Betz, et al. (Leiden, NL / Boston, MA: Brill, 2008), 4:74; the default use of BCE and CE even in mainstream biblical scholarship is evident throughout the standard work of Patrick H. Alexander, et al., *The SBL Handbook of Style for Ancient Near Eastern, Biblical, and Early Christian Studies* (Peabody, MA: Hendrickson, 1999).

of post-Christian thinking in changing the connotations of key words such as freedom, value, rights, and discrimination in order to destabilize and decompose the Christian social and intellectual frameworks on which our civilization has been built. In his conclusions he presents his "Decalogue of Decomposition."

> Where there are objective values, let them be subjectivized.
> Where there are absolutes, let them be relativized.
> Where there are intimations of transcendence, let them be dismissed.
> Where there are structures, moral or social, let them be fragmented.
> Where there are foundations, let them be destablized.
> Where there are traditions, let them be discredited.
> Where there are distinctions, let them be whittled away.
> Where there are boundaries, let them be abolished.
> Where there are contrasts, let them be intermingled.
> Where there are contradictions, let them be amalgamated.[21]

Although the opposition seems rather overwhelming, Christians should resist as much as possible unbiblical cultural forces on language. At the same time we need to be able to communicate meaningfully to those who are opposed to Christian norms. The pervasive secularization of society can make it very difficult to make effective use of terms familiar to Christians when speaking to non-Christians. The future does not look bright for the use of such biblically-influenced terminology. In America, less than a quarter of the population are practicing Christians and fewer and fewer attend church regularly.[22] All of this translates into a diminished positive Christian impact on current language. As Christian influence wanes, the Ten Commandments and biblical terms such as righteousness and even love as the Bible teaches them are, generally speaking, no longer comprehended by our secular society. Unfortunately, they are not even as well understood as they used to be, even among those who identify

---

21 Blamires, *The Post Christian Mind: Exposing Its Destructive Agenda,* 205–6.
22 See, e.g., the research findings of The Barna Group and the Pew Research Center in, respectively, Barna, *Signs of Decline and Hope Among Key Metrics of Faith* (4 March 2020), found at www.barna.com/research/changing-state-of-the-church/ and Pew Research Center, In *U.S., Decline of Christianity Continues at Rapid Pace* (17 October 2019), found in www.pewresearch.org.

as Christians.[23] These factors often make communicating the gospel and Christian values an uphill battle.

Since we live in a world that shows many of the ungodly characteristics of society as it was in the days of Noah, this reality presents parents and teachers with challenges for educating God's children.

The Need for Discernment in Educating in a Corrupt Culture

The challenges with which our secularized culture presents us must be recognized and dealt with. Parents and teachers need to be very careful not to mimic the practices of a sinful culture but have their own Christian style of communicating to those in their charge. This demands much godly discernment. The pressures are everywhere to conform to the messaging of our times by using terms loaded with new meaning. When we speak, for example, of God's ordinance of marriage, we will not use ambiguous neutral terms such as "partner" to describe one's husband or wife. We will prefer "killing" to "euthanasia," avoid the use of "weekend," and call "sin" what Scripture characterizes as such. And should it happen, due to ungodly pressures, that children come to the conclusion that their perceived gender does not match their biological sex, we should not give in by using their preferred pronouns that deny their God-given anatomy. Instead parents and teachers should lovingly try to understand their predicament and counsel them with the necessary wisdom and discernment.[24] Many more examples of the need to assert Christian values in the face of language usage that is hostile to Christian values in all areas of life could be given, but that is beyond the scope of this chapter. An excellent work in this regard is Blamires's book, *The Post-Christian Mind* as referenced above.

On another level, with respect to the use of language in educating,

---

23 See, e.g., Collin Hansen, "Why Johnny Can't Read the Bible," *Christianity Today* 54, no. 5 (2010): 38–41 and Justin Dillehay and Ivan Mesa, *Bible Literacy Crisis! (and What We Can Do About It in 2020)* (14 January 2020), found at www.thegospelcoalition.org/.
24 See, e.g., Nancy R. Pearcey, *Love Thy Body*, 193–227.

there should be zero tolerance for children and students using language that is abusive, bullying, crude, and inappropriate. It hardly needs to be noted that this applies to parents and teachers as well! The harmful consequences of the sinful use of the tongue can be far-reaching. Bullying can negatively impact a person's psychological health and well-being.[25] Crude and inappropriate talk lowers the standards of social interchange and results in an undesirable toxic and coarse environment that is very unedifying and unchristian. The apostolic admonitions remain relevant: "Let no corrupting talk come out of your mouths" (Eph 4:29); "Let there be no filthiness nor foolish talk nor crude joking, which are out of place" (Eph 5:4). The consequences of the wrong use of language are simply devastating. The sinful tongue "is a fire, a world of unrighteousness … It is a restless evil, full of deadly poison" (James 3:6, 8).

An important part of Christian education is making children aware of the ungodly aspects of the culture in which we live and how they should use their tongues so that their language corresponds to God's norms rather those of our mainstream secular society. The prayer of David must be also be that of our students. "Let the words of my mouth and the meditation of my heart be acceptable in your sight, O LORD, my rock and my redeemer" (Ps 19:14). To instill such a desire as an educational goal is quite a challenging endeavor. Every means available to equip ourselves, including professional development opportunities for teachers, should be used.[26] Ultimately, however, we of our sinful selves are unable to do this and the current trend is certainly not in our favor. We and our language need to be redeemed. And thank God, this is possible in Christ. As Christians, those redeemed by Christ, we can meet the challenges enabled by the Word and Holy Spirit. Let us take a closer look at God's work of redemption in this context.

---

25 Ken Rigby, "Consequences of Bullying in Schools," *Canadian Journal of Psychiatry* 48 (2003): 583–90.

26 An example of a document created to help with curriculum development is John Wynia, et al., *Conceptual Framework for the Language Arts* (Hamilton, ON: League of the Canadian Reformed School Societies, Inc., 2019), available via Curriculum Assistance for Reformed Education (CARE), email: coordinator@lcrsss.ca.

The Redemption of Language

God had broken up humanity's single language at the tower of Babel in order to counter sin. But in the LORD's gracious plan of redemption, he did not want to leave language fragmented. He promised to redeem the tongue and make language new and unified again. God was determined that this creational gift would be restored to its rightful purpose, which was to enable humans to communicate rightly with God and with each other with a view to fulfilling their God-given office and calling. However, if language is to be redeemed and renewed so that it is pleasing to God, then a new heart is an absolute necessity. The fall into sin has corrupted the human heart so that it "is deceitful above all things, and is desperately sick" (Jer 17:9). Consequently the thoughts of the heart and mind are by nature only evil, resulting in sinful language (Mark 7:21–22).

God therefore exhorted his wayward people to repent and get a new heart. "Make yourselves a new heart and a new spirit!" (Ezek 18:31). That is an absolute necessity. At the same time, although God's people had the responsibility to get a new heart, they were unable due to their sinful condition. Only God can renew and give a new heart. In great compassion he therefore promised: "I will give you a new heart, and a new spirit I will put within you. And I will remove the heart of stone from your flesh and give you a heart of flesh. And I will put my Spirit within you, and cause you to walk in my statutes and be careful to obey my rules" (Ezek 36:26–27; cf. 11:19).

Since "out of the abundance of the heart, the mouth speaks" (Matt 12:34), a new heart comes with a new language. Indeed, God promised that the redeemed would speak a new language. Isaiah prophesied that in the future: "there will be five cities in the land of Egypt that speak the language of Canaan," that is, the language in which God was worshipped. They will, therefore, use the same language as Israel and, as the prophet continued, "swear allegiance to the LORD of hosts" (Isa 19:18). Thus, having one language with God's people involves conversion to the true faith. In a similar vein, God said through the prophet Zephaniah that "At that time I will change the speech of the peoples to a pure speech, that all of them may call upon the name of the LORD and serve him with one accord" (Zeph 3:9).

It is noteworthy how nations and peoples other than Israel are involved in these prophesies. A unity of language will at some point in the future emerge from the Babel confusion of speech. It will be a unity worked by God. A unity which speaks of the oneness of the new creation, the new humanity, that God raises up in this world. The initial fulfillment of the prophesies of the nations learning the "language of Canaan," the language of those who worship God, occurred at the outpouring of the Holy Spirit on the day of Pentecost. The believers "were all filled with the Holy Spirit and began to speak in other tongues as the Spirit gave them utterance. ... The multitude came together, and they were bewildered, because each one was hearing them speak in his own language" (Acts 2:4, 6). In other words, as S. G. De Graaf put it: "Probably the Holy Spirit caused the disciples to speak one language, the language of the Spirit, but at the same time caused the listeners to hear it as their own. It was a miracle of the Spirit who gave forceful expression to the fact that the Holy Spirit created a unity among peoples."[27] In this way the confusion of languages which started at Babel was overcome. The miracle of Pentecost was also a powerful indicator of how God was raising up a new human race, recreated by the Spirit, and experiencing the unity of faith. At Pentecost this unity included the overcoming of all language barriers. Even though different languages still present obstacles to Christian unity today, it is amazing how that unity can still be experienced when meeting foreign believers in spite of language and cultural barriers. One day, all those barriers will be gone.

So what characterizes the language of Christians, as those raised as a new creation in Christ? In short, it is language cleansed and molded by the working of the Holy Spirit in our hearts. A purified heart yields corresponding language. "Out of the abundance of the heart, the mouth speaks" (Matt 12:34). All this has implications for Christian education.

---

[27] S. G. de Graaf, *Christ and the Nations*, vol. 4 of *Promise and Deliverance*, trans. H. Evan Runner and Elisabeth Wichers Runner (St. Catharines, ON: Paideia Press, 1981), 133; similarly, e.g., Simon J. Kistemaker, *Exposition of the Acts of the Apostles,* New Testament Commentary (Grand Rapids, MI: Baker, 1990), 79; D. G. Peterson, *The Acts of the Apostles*, Pillar New Testament Commentary (Grand Rapids, MI: Eerdmans, 2009), 136.

The Need to Prepare the Heart

If the heart is key to what words come from our mouths, then for truly Christian language to be possible, we must protect the heart—our own and those of our children and students. Scripture admonishes: "Keep your heart with all vigilance, for from it flow the springs of life. Put away from you crooked speech, and put devious talk far from you" (Prov 4:23–24). Scripture pictures the heart as the center of our consciousness and this we must protect from influences that endanger the work of the Word and Spirit in our lives. Although we are not of the unbelieving world, Christ has placed us in the middle of it (John 17:15–16). In our Western culture there is so much that competes for the attention of our heart and tries to influence our thinking and speaking. We need to be aware of how easily the media can subtly change how we view developments in our society and articulate our thoughts. Especially the minds of children need to be safeguarded to the best of our ability since they are quite pliant as they become aware of the world around them. Watching what they are exposed to, also by way of electronic media, is critically important.

Positively we need to enable and encourage the work of the Spirit as he seeks to mold the hearts and thinking of parents, teachers, and students in harmony with God's will so we all can reflect his image in our life. Simply put, God says: "Give me your heart!" (Prov 23:26). It is precisely our heart and mind that "our sworn enemies—the devil, the world, and our own flesh—do not cease to attack."[28] But we are to be entirely for God's service. This is only possible if we use his means to shape our thinking; that is, by letting his Word rule our thoughts. The psalmist therefore confessed: "I have stored up your word in my heart, that I might not sin against you" (Ps 119:11). Scripture affirms that the one who has God's law in his heart, "his steps do not slip" (Ps 37:31). Our hearts are, so to speak, to be drenched with the instruction and knowledge of God as he speaks in his Word. In this way we are enabled to "take every thought captive to obey Christ" (2 Cor 10:5). That is the challenge and struggle, also in teaching our children: to bring everything, including our thoughts and speech, in subjection to Christ. We need to face that challenge with integrity

---

28 Heidelberg Catechism, Q. & A. 127. *Book of Praise*, 563.

and pray the prayer of David: "Search me, O God, and know my heart! Try me and know my thoughts! And see if there be any grievous way in me, and lead me in the way everlasting" (Ps 139:23–24).

How can we help our children and students to open their hearts to the work of the Spirit and have their hearts filled with his Word for life direction and encouragement? Obviously, we need to teach them the will of God for their lives and share the gospel with them. As noted in chapter 1 and elsewhere in this book, such teaching is an ongoing effort making use of every available opportunity, at home, at school, the preaching on the Lord's Day, and literally wherever the occasion for teaching the saving acts and ways of the LORD presents itself. The Spirit works through the Word and we can use the means available to convey and imprint the Word in their hearts and minds. The practice of having students memorize Scripture passages is, for example, to be commended. One way to strengthen the impact of the language of Scripture is to put it to song. Indeed, the LORD himself showed us the way by giving us the Psalter.

The Use of Songs

The Psalms are an important resource for teaching. After all, singing is an intensified form of speaking and therefore a very powerful medium for communicating. Some examples to illustrate this fact come to mind. After the LORD delivered Israel from Egypt, the nation expressed their thankfulness in the most intense and powerful way possible—by singing (Exod 15). When Moses wanted to teach Israel God's great deeds, he composed a song (Deut 32). Deborah used a song to express her gratitude for God's victory (Judg 5). Music and song intensify the spoken word and impact the heart more profoundly than simply speaking. It is therefore not surprising that from ancient times, language coupled with music has been used to ingrain in young minds the wonderful works of God.

God's people from biblical times have sung the biblical Psalms and the LORD has used that intensified musical and sung language to recount and teach his people his great deeds of salvation. Psalm 78, for example, even presents itself specifically as a teaching song. "Give ear, O my people, to my teaching; incline your ears to the words of my mouth!" (Ps 78:1). The psalm then goes on to recount important historical events that showed why the LORD had chosen Judah and not Ephraim for his dwelling place and David as his king. All this had to be taught to the children (Ps 78:4). Other psalms recounting and so teaching God's saving works include Psalms 104–106. God also used the psalms to teach people his law and will. "I will instruct you and teach you in the way you should go" (Ps 32:8). The Psalter appropriately begins with contrasting the way of the righteous and the wicked (Ps 1) and Psalm 119 is an extended expression of joy and devotion for the enormous gift of God's law, with repeated requests that the LORD teach the poet the divine law. The LORD also used the psalms to teach his people and give them the assurance of the forgiveness of all their sins which were brought to the throne of grace, as we see for instance in Psalms 32 and 103 (cf. Ps 51:13). The psalms also teach by way of example that there is always hope for God's people (Ps 130). Even those who feel most abandoned, and whose only friend is darkness, can bring their needs to God. The fact that Psalm 88 is included in God's Word underlines that fact. More examples could be given, but in short, the psalms are an enormous teaching tool in which language is strengthened by singing and so the knowledge and fear of the LORD is imprinted on his people, both young and old. "Come, O children, listen to me; I will teach you the fear of the LORD" (Ps 34:11).

The use of intensified language in song or communal enthusiastic praise continues in the New Testament. Mary rejoiced in God for his mighty work in her life using the medium of a song (Luke 1:46–55) and the angels announcing the birth of Jesus did so with exuberant praise which may or may not have been in song (Luke 2:14). These formats made it easy for the church to adapt these expressions of praise to music and so teach countless generations the great deeds of God of which they speak. The teaching function of the intensified language of song is also evident in the apostolic admonition. "Let the word of Christ dwell in you richly, teaching and admonishing one another in all wisdom, singing psalms and hymns and spiritual songs, with thankfulness in your hearts to God" (Col 3:16). It is this Word of God that we also seek to imprint in the minds and hearts of our children and students. One very good way to do this is to teach them songs and hymns at a young age. The great deeds of God and his praise learned and memorized in those early years will remain with them throughout their life.

When the Lord blesses this type of education using the intensified language of song and singing, the Word of God is more easily fixed in their hearts. The Holy Spirit will be able to use the Word internalized in their minds as a sword to ward off the attacks of the evil one which are directed at God's children. The sword of the Spirit is a key component of God's equipping us against the assaults of the evil one (Eph 6:17). As the apostle Paul noted: "The weapons of our warfare are not of the flesh but have divine power to destroy strongholds. We destroy arguments and every lofty opinion raised against the knowledge of God, and take every thought captive to obey Christ" (2 Cor 10:4–5).

With the spiritual weapon of the Word available in their hearts and minds, children can be taught to bring their thoughts and speech in subjection to God's norms in opposition to Satan's use of speech and language. Secular humanity lives in unrighteousness and uses the language of falsehood, dishonor, injustice, filth, ugliness, and mediocrity to exercise its enormous and destructive influence on today's civic culture. In contrast, Christians are to live and speak reflecting divine standards. We may do so joyfully without being anxious in spite of the pushback from secularism. When we make our requests known to God, then his peace, which surpasses all understanding, will guard our hearts and minds in Christ Jesus (Phil 4:7). That is, God's peace will prevent our hearts and minds from being overwhelmed by the sinful use of language. In faith, we will see our way clear to use the gift of speech properly in accord with the divine norms that the apostle Paul enumerated. "Whatever is true, whatever is honorable, whatever is just, whatever is pure, whatever is lovely, whatever is commendable, if there is any excellence, if there is anything worthy of praise, think about these things" and "practice these things and the God of peace will be with you" (Phil 3:8, 9).

These are the criteria that we need to impart to our children and students in their use of language. To make that possible the ancient command to impress a love for God and his will on the hearts of our children, teaching them diligently at every occasion (Deut 6:5–8) is absolutely necessary. Instilling a love for God and his norms is key to shaping the thoughts of their hearts and minds for godly language and conversation. One can have all kinds of gifts and evidences of dedication to God's will for life, but if one does not have love, it is meaningless. "Love is patient and kind; love does not envy or boast; it is not arrogant or rude. It does not insist on its own way; it is not irritable or resentful; it does not rejoice at wrongdoing, but rejoices with the truth. Love bears all things, believes all things, hopes all things, endures all things. Love never ends" (I Cor 13:4–8). These words deserve a place on the walls of our homes and schools. Parents and teachers are to teach and by example exhibit such conversation and speaking that is informed and molded by their love for God and their children and students. When the Spirit uses such instruction to change the hearts and minds of children, unseemly talk and bullying will cease. The hearts and mouths of the young will be a fountain of life (Prov 10:11; cf. 15:4). Language molded by the Spirit will also promote truth and counter lies and so oppose Satan, the father of lies (John 8:44).

We live in a culture that is toxic with sin, and God's gift of language and speaking is used to further the evil agenda of the Devil. Teaching our children and students to use language molded by the norms of God's Word is a task made easier with the use of music and song, psalms and hymns. The sung Word of God, when imbedded in the hearts and minds of children, is a powerful weapon of the Holy Spirit to help them discern the deceptive spirits and sins of our age and to counter with thoughts and language pleasing to God.

We must, however, not simply be on the defensive. Scripture exhorts God's people to sing new songs in response to his salvation. "Sing to him a new song!" (Ps 33:2). "Sing to the LORD a new song!" (Ps 149:1). The keynotes are thanks and praise for his mercies. It is inevitable that those whom God has redeemed are moved to use the gift of language to praise him anew every day. The command and urge to sing new songs in response to God's works of redemption also apply to the New Testament church. Mary, the mother of Jesus, composed her new song (Luke 1:46–55) and many Christians have done so since. These new songs are part and parcel of the new language which we have received from God. With them we go on the offensive and spread the good news of salvation. David's sentiments still ring true today. He sang that the LORD "put a new song in my mouth, a song of praise to our God. Many will see and fear, and put their trust in the LORD" (Ps 40:3). That missionary enthusiasm for the great works of God can also be instilled in our children and students as the Lord graciously uses the godly education they receive to prepare their hearts for his service.

Seen in the grand scope of God's sovereign guiding of history to the final goal of a new heaven and a new earth, our singing new songs of our redemption now is but a beginning of participating with an innumerable multitude in glory "singing a new song before the throne" (Rev 14:3; cf. 5:9). The intensified language of song will characterize our worship and praise to God for eternity. What a privilege to tell and teach children such songs, and be used by God to imbed in their hearts and minds an enduring love for God and the ability to use language to his praise and glory.

In Conclusion

God's gift of language, though corrupted by sin, still retains enormous power to shape minds, to influence culture, and to determine future actions. When sin dominates a culture that has jettisoned divine norms, then even words take on a different nuance, connotation, and even meaning. This presents an enormous challenge to Christians who need much discernment in order to communicate without adopting the sinful presuppositions that have become imbedded in some current vocabulary. On another level, as the apostle James noted, the sinful tongue is a destructive fire full of deadly poison.

Within this context, parents and teachers need to fully appreciate the challenges they face in teaching children to use the gift of language in accordance with God's norms. In a culture where society's parlance is being shaped by powerful forces of secularization, it is difficult to teach the use of language molded by the Spirit while using current terminology and conventions to communicate. For such teaching to be effective, the hearts of children need to be prepared by protecting their minds as much as possible from sin and encouraging the work of the Spirit in their life with appropriate teaching. Since Christ's redemptive work is also able to restore language to its proper godly function, parents and teachers can work with confidence knowing that in the Lord their work is not in vain in seeking to train children to use language according to biblical norms. The use of intensified language in the form of memorized psalms and hymns that recount God's work of salvation and praise him can be effective in internalizing much of God's Word and the gospel into young hearts and minds. Psalms and hymns embedded in young hearts and minds will benefit them for their entire life.

Within a broader framework, we must never forget that although the curse of the confusion of tongues at the tower of Babel is still with us today so that people no longer speak a single language, yet for children of God who have been raised a new creation, this curse has in principle been undone. The outpouring of the Holy Spirit on the day of Pentecost marked another stage in God's plan of redemption in raising up a new humanity with the second Adam as the head. This people of God which encompasses persons from all nations and languages experience a unity in Christ that transcends language barriers.

Parents, teachers, and children can all be encouraged by the fact that the day will come when all the redeemed will speak in one tongue to the praise of God.

CHAPTER 6

Education in the Word in an Age of the Picture

We live in a society that is becoming more and more conditioned by images. Pictures take precedence everywhere, be it on our television, computer screen, or smart phone. Images and icons communicate. As the old saying puts it: "a picture is worth a thousand words" and advertisers have taken heed as well. The widespread use of images and accompanying sound bites generally results in a swift, but also a much more superficial understanding. Rapid sequences of images do not allow for meaningful reflection. It also does not engender patience in seeking to understand what is being communicated. As Jacques Ellul noted: the "visionary reality of connected images cannot tolerate critical discourse, explanation, duplication, or reflection." We become passive in the face of images. Verbal communication, however, can stimulate critical thinking. "Nothing is worse for the image's influence than to be taken apart and analyzed by language. The word produces disenchantment with the image; the word strips it of its hypnotic and magical power."[1]

The fact that images are literally everywhere does mean that the written word no longer has the uncontested primary place it once had for the purpose of communicating and passing on information. This demotion of the use of words to inform and instruct has implications for teaching. What exactly is the role of verbal language and listening at school, as opposed to the use of images? If pictures have a paramount place in the life of our children so that they are conditioned by them, how are we to effectively teach them using words? Above all, how are we to pass

---

1 Jacques Ellul, *The Humiliation of the Word*, trans. from the French (Grand Rapids, MI: Eerdmans, 1985), 142; see also pp. 204–27.

on to them *the* Word of life and the full implications of the gospel in all subject areas? How can we teach our children to listen patiently to verbal communication and to God's written revelation when much of society today impatiently and selectively grasps what matters to them from pictures and sound bites they see and hear? These questions are important. Children need to able to benefit from teaching using words and so also learn to appropriate God's Word and make it their own. Otherwise, their outlook on life will be shaped by suggestive images.

What does Scripture, and specifically the Old Testament, tell us about the place and function of word communication and pictures in the teaching process? How can God's Word help us in providing direction in our own educational endeavors? How did God teach his people? Does the second commandment prohibiting images have anything to say to Reformed teachers? This chapter will consider these issues.

The Priority of Verbal Communication both Oral and Written

When God related to his people, he spoke to them. Thus he uttered words of blessing for Adam and Eve after their creation (Gen 1:28–30); he commanded Adam not to eat from the tree of the knowledge of good and evil (Gen 2:17) and after the fall into sin, he called Adam and spoke to him (Gen 3:9). By speaking, he informed Adam and Eve of the way of life and of the promise of the coming salvation (Gen 3:15). It was by speaking that God communicated to many more since he addressed the earth's first couple. When prophets spoke on God's behalf, as his mouthpiece (cf. Exod 4:15–16; Jer 1:9), then their message was prefaced either by the phrase "the word of the LORD that came to … " (e.g., Jer 1:4; Hos 1:1; Joel 1:1) or by "thus says the LORD" (e.g. Exod 4:22; 5:1; 1 Sam 2:27; Jer 33:2).

So important was God's verbal communication that he made sure that what was important for his people then and in the future was put down in written form. God himself inscribed with his own fingers the

Ten Words of the covenant on tablets of stone which he gave to Moses (Exod 24:12; 31:18). And when those stones were broken, he himself wrote those words out again in permanent form (Exod 32:19; 34:28). In his providence, God made sure that any revelation that needed to be handed down in written form was duly put in writing. Sometimes Scripture records God's express commands that his words be put in writing. He told Jeremiah: "Write in a book all the words that I have spoken to you" (Jer 30:2; similarly Isa 30:8; Hab 2:2). The apostles also committed God's word to writing so that it would be remembered (2 Pet 3:1–2; cf. 1:13–15). The apostle John was repeatedly told to put in writing the content of the visions which he saw on the island of Patmos (e.g., Rev 1:11; 14:13; 21:5). God's written word is just as authoritative as his spoken word. "All Scripture is breathed out by God" (2 Tim 3:16).

When the promised Messiah, the chief prophet and teacher from God, came in the fullness of time, he came as the Word incarnate (John 1:1, 14). He, therefore, did not need to say: "thus says the LORD," but he could speak on his own divine authority: "truly, I say to you" (e.g., Matt 5:18, 26). In this way they heard the very "word of God" (Luke 5:1; John 3:34; 14:24). Clearly the manner in which revelation was given, by the use of words, spoken or written down, was of paramount importance. This is a consistent theme throughout Scripture. The first emphasis is on what is heard and not on what is seen.

This emphasis on the spoken and written word does not mean that the visual was lacking in God's relationship with his people and in his revelation of himself to them and his teaching them. We will come back to this point. For now we can note that we often read that the LORD or God "appeared," for example, to Abraham in the form of a man (Gen 17:1–2; 18:1–2), to Moses in a burning bush (Exod 3:2–6), and to Solomon in a dream (1 Kgs 3:5). The term "appeared" literally means "be seen" or "become visible." It is striking how God's glory appeared to Israel in the pillar of cloud and fire during the Exodus and wilderness wandering (Exod 16:10; cf. 13:21–22) so that Israel could actually see God's presence and know that he was with them. In this way God met the human need to see and not only to hear. However, there is no doubt about the fact that the high point in God's self-revelation came when the LORD spoke directly to his people from Mount Sinai. So awestruck were the people that they asked Moses to speak on God's behalf to them, "but do not let God speak to us, lest we die" (Exod 20:19).

Another example that comes to mind on the priority of the verbal is God's response to Moses's request "Please show me your glory" (Exod 33:18). Moses wanted a visible guarantee that God would be going with them to Canaan. God obliged by showing Moses as much of his glory as possible (Exod 33:19, 21–23). However, the emphasis in God's self-revelation clearly came when God spoke and explained his name Yahweh, the LORD. When the actual revelation took place, we do not even read of the visible revelation of God's glory, but we are informed of what God said in explaining the significance of his name Yahweh, the LORD. "The LORD, the LORD, a God merciful and gracious, slow to anger, and abounding in steadfast love and faithfulness, keeping steadfast love for thousands, forgiving iniquity and transgression and sin, but who will by no means clear the guilty, visiting the iniquity of the fathers on the children and the children's children, to the third and fourth generation" (Exod 34:6–7). What Moses heard was of more significance than what Moses saw in perceiving the true glory of God.[2]

The primary stress on verbal communication, rather than on something visual, must be placed within the wider context of how Scripture informs us of the place and function of the word of God. God's word is effective. By his word, creation came into being (Gen 1; Ps 33:6). The word of God continues to accomplish that for which he spoke it. As the LORD communicated to the prophet Isaiah: "For as the rain and the snow come down from heaven, and do not return there but water the earth, making it bring forth and sprout, giving seed to the sower and bread to the eater, so shall my word be that goes out from my mouth; it shall not return to me empty, but it shall accomplish that which I purpose, and succeed in the thing for which I sent it" (Isa 55:10–11; cf. Heb 4:12). Because the word is God's word, therefore, it brings about the new creation and works faith. As Romans 10:17 puts it: "So faith comes from hearing, and hearing through the word of Christ." What the eye sees does not as such work

---

2 Apart from God's revealing himself in these special ways, he, of course, also reveals his glory and majesty, his power and divine nature from his work of creation (cf., e.g., Rom 1:20 and Ps 19:1).

faith. In the parable of the rich man and the poor man named Lazarus, the rich man died and was in torment, but the poor man was carried by the angels to Abraham's side. The rich man pleaded to Abraham that Lazarus be sent to warn his brothers lest they also end up in such anguish. Abraham's answer is telling. "If they do not hear Moses and the Prophets, neither will they be convinced if someone should rise from the dead" (Luke 16:31). Signs and wonders do not as such convince and work faith. God's verbal revelation as communicated through Moses, the Prophets, and the apostles does.

Under his sovereign guidance, this divine self-revelation has been written down and resulted in what we call Holy Scripture, the Word of God. While fallen humankind may trust their eyes more than their ears, Holy Scripture demands our first trust. It is the truth (John 17:17). It sets the standard for reliability and trustworthiness. It is divinely inspired. Indeed, "all Scripture is breathed out by God and profitable for teaching, for reproof, for correction, and for training in righteousness, that the man of God may be complete, equipped for every good work" (2 Tim 3:16–17).

The Teaching Task

What are the implications of God's communicating verbally to reveal himself and his will and his eventually giving the Word in written form for the task of teaching? There are at least three major implications.

The First Place of the Spoken and Written Word

The first implication is that teachers today should also prioritize the spoken and written word in giving instruction. Scripture points in this direction as well when God told parents to train their children by speaking to them. The well-known words of divine exhortation come to mind. "These words that I command you today shall be on your heart. You shall teach them diligently to your children, and shall talk to them when you sit in your house, and when you walk by the way, and when you lie down, and when you rise. You shall bind them as a sign on your hand, and they shall be as frontlets between your eyes. You shall write them on the doorposts of your house and on your gates" (Deut 6:6–9). Whenever and wherever possible the sustained verbal teaching had to continue.

Such instruction would allow for reflection on the part of the children. Unlike a quick succession of images on an electronic device which is to be grasped intuitively and does not allow for thoughtful consideration, the spoken word requires it. It is one of the challenges of our current culture that children need to be taught patience in comprehending what is being verbally communicated because so much of the information they are interested in is transmitted visually. E.W. Schaeffer-de Wal, who was a secondary school teacher in Rotterdam, has noted that in her experience students often lacked the ability to have the patience to concentrate so that they could comprehend what they were being taught. They were so accustomed to quickly and superficially pick up random information from visuals. They would typically, without being fully aware of it, select from the images the message which they could immediately understand and discard the rest before it even entered their consciousness.[3] This habit hindered them from receiving the full benefit of spoken and written instruction.

If parents in Israel heeded God's instructions for teaching their children, their offspring would have time for reflection and be taught patience to come to a full understanding. God therefore expected the children to ask questions. Parental instruction was not to be a long, uninterrupted, and difficult monologue. Furthermore, parents needed to speak to their children and not at them so that they truly listened and were engaged. Children could and were expected to inquire further. After all, the teaching had to be understandable so that children could use it and benefit from it in their daily life. So questions were encouraged. The LORD therefore told the parents: "when your son asks you in time to come, 'What is the meaning of the testimonies and statues and the rules that the LORD our God has commanded you?' then you shall say to your son, 'We were Pharaoh's slaves in Egypt. And the LORD brought us out of Egypt with

---

3 E. W. Schaeffer-de Wal, "Christelijke opvoeding als vertaling III," *De Reformatie* 62, no. 2 (1986): 31.

a mighty hand.'" Parents were subsequently to relate the great deeds of the LORD (Deut 6:20–25). God thus demanded that the questions of children be taken seriously.

Obviously the parental answers had to be clear so that the children could comprehend and be encouraged to further listening. Their answers were also to be practical, showing the relevance of God's salvation in their lives so that they would live a life of gratitude to God and enjoy true life with him.

These considerations bring us to the second major implication of verbal instruction.

The Clarity of Verbal Communication

Unlike communicating through signs alone, the spoken word can be clear and unambiguous, just as God's verbal revelation was. When God spoke from Mount Sinai, Israel understood. Although God came from heaven, he spoke their language. This practice is also evident from the languages that Scripture is written in. God used the languages current at the time in which the revelation was given, whether it was Hebrew, Aramaic, or Greek. Similarly, the Lord Jesus used the everyday language of the people, Aramaic, in his ministry at a time when Hebrew was considered a holy language to be used in the Temple and synagogue.[4] Likewise at Pentecost the Holy Spirit enabled all those assembled to hear the gospel in their native tongues, no matter from what language group they came (Acts 2:6–11).

Parents and teachers today likewise need to be clear in their speaking and use language that is current so that the children can relate to it and understand it. That means, among other things, that we must never in any way encourage or promote a special religious or church language over against the so-called ordinary language of everyday. It is for this reason that "church language" such as the use of "Thee" and "Thou" in singing

---

4   Aramaic phrases attributed to Jesus are found in, e.g., Mark 5:4; 7:34; 14:36; 15:34. For Hebrew as the official religious language, Emil Schürer, *The History of the Jewish People in the Age of Jesus Christ (175 B.C. - A.D. 135)*, vol. 2, ed. & rev. Geza Vermes, et al. (Edinburgh, UK: T. & T. Clark, 1979), 22.

psalms and hymns should be avoided as much as possible. Children or students must not get the idea that life is divided into the religious and the secular. Life is a unit and the use of our language must reflect that unity. The words which we use to express our Christian faith are as much as possible to be words that we use in everyday life.[5]

That last qualification, as much as possible, is important for ultimately what needs to be taught is the Word of God, the gospel in its fullness. That should be at the core of all teaching. Consequently, when it comes to language, terms like love and justice need to be explained from a biblical perspective. Such an exercise is helpful for it sensitizes students to the fact that there is a difference between the worldview taught in Scripture and that which is dominant in our secular culture. The gospel has ramifications for all of life, also for how we understand concepts like love and justice. Parents and teachers need to make those in their charge aware that there is an antithesis, a conflict, between biblical and worldly notions of reality and salvation. When the riches of Scripture are taught, those being educated receive what is critical for them to be equipped to live and work to God's praise and glory. Then under God's blessing they begin to see reality through the lens of Scripture. Biblical presuppositions then start to form the basis of their thinking, norms, and priorities in life. The fruits of teaching God's Word then become evident and students realize that the Word is relevant for all their life.

These observations bring us to the third major implication of prioritizing the use of words and the Word of God.

The Word and Faith

Parents and teachers are dealing with covenant children whom God has claimed for himself as signified and sealed in holy baptism. These children

---

[5] See also on the need to use contemporary language, K. Schilder, "Kerktaal en leven," in *Om woord en kerk: preeken, lezingen, studien en kerkbode-artikelen*, comp. C. Veenhof (Goes, NL: Oosterbaan & Le Cointre, 1948–53), 3:169–88. In this connection one can also think of the notion of "heart language." The language we use needs to resonate with us to be as meaningful as possible. See Josh Panos, "The Heart Language in a Globalizing World." https://www.thegospelcoalition.org/article/heart-language-globalizing-world/ (December 18, 2018). My thanks to Keith Sikkema for this reference.

will one day have to consciously respond to the gracious embrace of their heavenly Father by committing their lives in faith to him. The means that God uses to evoke that response includes parents and teachers speaking to children of his saving work in Christ. God has given us his own record of that salvation in his Word. As we noted earlier, the Word of God is a powerful instrument. Faith is not worked by signs and wonders but comes from hearing the Word (Rom 10:17) and results in a new creation (2 Cor 5:17). Without faith the Word cannot be truly discerned (1 Cor 2:14). Parents and teachers are to be agents of God to work faith in the lives of those whom they teach. Being God's instruments is a high calling and an enormous responsibility which provides those who instruct the necessary motivation they need to do their utmost in making use of God's first means of communication which is by the spoken and written word. In this way those who teach can ultimately pass on the message of the Word of God and be used by him to work faith in the hearts and minds of those listening.

God has, however, done more than simply use verbal communication. He has helped his children in the past to really listen and be confronted by the wide scope and great depth of the Word of God with the use of images and visual aids. And so, visual media can be used, not for their own sake but in a serving and supportive relationship to verbal communication and in teaching the implications of the Word.

The Place of the Visual

If I understand E. W. Schaeffer-de Wal correctly, she may be going too far when she writes: "The language of the relationship between God and us is definitely *not* the language of imagery (or the language of images) but it is a verbal language."[6] Much as I affirm that God speaks to us through the use of words and that he cannot be understood without the Word, yet, it is not purely an "either-or" dilemma when it comes to teaching.

---

6   Schaeffer-de Wal, "Christelijke opvoeding," 32 (emphasis is in the original Dutch).

THE IMPORTANCE OF LANGUAGE

When we speak of the Word of God, we speak of God's revelation of himself. Without doubt there is the priority of the use of language; however, images and visual aids were not neglected.[7] God recognized them as necessary so that the Word might be as effective as possible. Signs served the Word, and helped in communicating, understanding, and remembering it.

This point can be illustrated: first of all, with reference to God himself and his self-revelation with respect to his very person. God made visible before the eyes of Israel something of his glory so that it became real and perceptible to them. We have already touched on the following example. The LORD went before Israel "by day in a pillar of cloud to lead them along the way, and by night in a pillar of fire to give them light, that they might travel by day and by night. The pillar of cloud by day and the pillar of fire by night did not depart from before the people" (Exod 13:21–22; cf. 14:19, 24) so that the LORD was described as being "in plain view"[8] of the Israelites (Num 14:14). In this way the LORD very concretely showed his presence. Through this cloud the LORD also effected a type of non-verbal communication. When God caused the cloud to go up from the tabernacle, Israel knew they had to travel. If the cloud was not taken up, Israel did not need to travel that day (Exod 40:35–38; Num 9:15–23). In such instances God communicated his commands without using words to his people.[9]

God also made himself visible at Mount Sinai where he used Israel's perception, not just by the ear, but also by the eye to impress upon them his presence and greatness. We read in Exodus 19:18 that "Mount Sinai was wrapped in smoke, because the LORD had descended on it in fire. The smoke of it went up like the smoke of a kiln, and the whole mountain trembled greatly" (cf. Deut 5:4). At a later date, a select number from Israel went up Mount Sinai to have a meal of covenant fellowship with

---

7   For Calvin's view of signs as divine aids for God's self-revelation, Ronald S. Wallace, *Calvin's Doctrine of the Word and Sacrament* (Grand Rapids, MI: Eerdmans, 1957), 78–81.

8   Lit. "eye to eye." The phrase is used elsewhere only in Isa 52:8. A similar translation "in plain sight" is found in *Tanakh - The Holy Scriptures: The New JPS Translation According to the Traditional Hebrew Text* (Philadelphia, PA: Jewish Publication Society, 1985), 230.

9   See W. H. Gispen, *Het boek Numeri,* Commentaar op het Oude Testament (Kampen, NL: Kok, 1959–64), 1:147.

God. They went up "and they saw the God of Israel. There was under his feet as it were a pavement of sapphire stone, like the very heaven for clearness. ... they beheld God and ate and drank" (Exod 24:9–11; cf. Ezek 1). Also, as covenant mediator, Moses spoke to God "face to face as a man speaks to his friend" (Exod 33:11; cf. Deut 34:10). This event included that he beheld "the form of the LORD" (Num 12:8). This perception was more than seeing God in a vision or dream (cf. Ps 17:15; 1 John 3:2; Rev 22:4).

God also passed on the gospel of his redemption with the use of a wide array of images that appeal to the eye rather than the ear. Think of the tabernacle and later the temple, as well as the elaborate rituals and feasts connected with the service of God. The visual realities associated with the sanctuary as a holy dwelling place of God to which only the priests had access and the bloody sacrifices for reconciliation were not incidental, but of great importance in picturing the gospel! They were crucial for Father's teaching the covenant children in the old dispensation. The LORD did not want his children to be brought up only by hearing about his holiness and the gospel of reconciliation. He also wanted them to see it and to perceive it by means of their physical eyes to further impress on them what was all involved in saving his people from their sins and reconciling them to God who is holy. And so their whole way of life was immersed with sacrifices, festivals, and memorials.[10] All these visual stimuli, along with the associated smells and sounds, not only helped integrate the faith into the fullness of life, but also prompted questions from the children. Consider these specific examples.

When the LORD instituted the Passover sacrifice, he said through Moses: "When your children say to you, 'What do you mean by this service?' you shall say, 'It is the sacrifice of the LORD's Passover, for he passed over the houses of the people of Israel in Egypt, when he struck the Egyptians but spared our houses'" (Exod 12:26–27). A clear answer had to be given and a historical consciousness of the great deeds of God was to be imprinted in the children. Even if there was no question, the opportunity had to be seized to tell the children the meaning of what they saw. For example, regarding the eating of unleavened bread, the

---

10 See further, e.g., J. V. Fesko, *Christ and the Desert Tabernacle* (Darlington, UK: EP Books, 2012).

LORD demanded that the parents relate its significance to their children (Exod 13:8). Sometimes the LORD commanded that a memorial be erected so that children would see and ask about their meaning. Think of the twelve stones that were erected beside the Jordan as a memorial of the miraculous crossing in the time of Joshua. They were to be erected "that this may be a sign among you. When your children ask in time to come, 'What do those stones mean to you?' then you shall tell them …" (Josh 4:6).[11] Note how all these visual helps served the passing on of the Word and the great deeds of God as well as the remembering of the contents of the Word.

Similarly, prophets made use of visual aids. When the prophet Ahijah was about to tell Jeroboam that the LORD would tear most of the kingdom from Solomon and give him ten tribes, then he took off his new garment and tore it into twelve pieces, with ten going to Jeroboam (1 Kgs 11:29–31). The prophet Isaiah had to go naked and barefoot through Jerusalem to reinforce this message from the LORD. "As my servant Isaiah has walked naked and barefoot for three years as a sign and a portent against Egypt and Cush, so shall the king of Assyria lead away the Egyptian captives and the Cushite exiles, both the young and the old, naked and barefoot." In this way the LORD showed the futility of Judah hoping for help from these nations (Isa 20:3–6).[12] More examples could be mentioned. It should be pointed out that the use of "visual aids" sometimes went to quite some length. For example, the prophet Hosea's marriage was to be a picture of what was taking place between God and his adulterous people. The LORD accordingly commanded Hosea: "Go, take to yourself a wife of whoredom and have children of whoredom, for the land commits great whoredom by forsaking the LORD" (Hos 1:2). The prophet Ezekiel was told that his wife would die and he was not to mourn because Ezekiel was to be a sign to the people. God's people were also not to mourn when their precious temple would be desecrated. It was

---

11   There was only one memorial; cf. Josh 4:9 (NIV84, cf. ESV) and see Richard S. Hess, *Joshua*, Tyndale Old Testament Commentaries (Downers Grove, IL: InterVarsity Press, 1996), 108–9.

12   It is doubtful whether total nudity is in view. "The outer garment and the inner tunic would have been removed, leaving only the loin cloth." John N. Oswalt, *The Book of Isaiah, Chapters 1–39*, The New International Commentary on the Old Testament (Grand Rapids, MI: Eerdmans, 1986), 385; similarly Edward J. Young, *The Book of Isaiah,* New International Commentary of the Old Testament (Grand Rapids, MI: Eerdmans, 1965–72), 2:54–55.

God's just judgment (Ezek 24:15–27). It is important to notice that these signs and pictures which were given could not be understood without the Word. They were there for the Word and were not independent of it. They were to serve the better understanding and remembering of what God had said.

Although we no longer live in the old dispensation, yet the principle of "illustrating" the Word of God and his great deeds of salvation is still relevant. To this very day our heavenly Father continues to speak to his children also through certain images as explained in his Word. One can think in this context of the rainbow which communicates as a visible sign that God will never again destroy all life as he did in the days of Noah and that he will ensure that day and night and the seasons will not cease (Gen 8:8–17). God has also pictured in a visible way his salvation in the sacraments. In this way he uses visual aids to reinforce the message of salvation by reassuring us by these visible tokens of his faithfulness to his covenant promises. Finally, in a more general context we confess that God makes himself known to us "by the creation, preservation, and government of the universe; which is before our eyes as a most beautiful book" (Belgic Confession, Art. 2).[13] It is important to note that in all these examples, the prior instruction of the Word of God and the accompanying patience to understand their significance properly is needed in order to appreciate the information that these signs are intended to transmit. The images illustrated the Word.

In light of the above, we cannot discount the use of visual aids in supporting the communicating of God's Word. The rigid distinction of saying that the language of the relationship between God and us is only a verbal language and is not the language of imagery cannot be maintained. Insofar as we can use visual aids to reinforce the transmission of the Word to those in our care, it is justified. One can think in this context of the effective use that can be made of pictures in so-called children's Bible story books (although we must be very careful here!). The imaginative use by teachers of visual aids can only be applauded and encouraged. Positive use can be made of the technological advances in this area. The key thing is that it

---

13 *Book of Praise*, 499.

must all ultimately serve the transmission of the Word and its implications for all of life. That is the crucial thing! An important precaution is therefore that our pictures and images be very carefully chosen so that they are not burdened by secular or heretical connotations and truly help to get across the verbal message that accompanies them.[14]

But what about the prohibition of images in the second commandment? Does this law have any relevance here?

The Second Commandment

In the first part of this commandment, the LORD enjoined his people: "You shall not make for yourself a carved image, or any likeness of anything that is in heaven above, or that is in the earth beneath, or that is in the water under the earth. You shall not bow down to them or serve them" (Exod 20:4–5). To understand this commandment as well as possible, we must realize that image-making had a very specific function in the ancient world in which Israel lived. An image was not just considered to be a picture of the god in question. No, it was the dwelling place of the divine reality. A decisive moment was when the image that had been made was animated so that the god's presence was presumed to have entered the statue. If the priests did their duties to that image then such a god was in their power so to speak. At bottom the essence of image-making was to have the deity under your control.[15] In this way pagan peoples sought security, imagining that the gods were at their beck and call.

When we keep this background in mind, we can better understand Israel's decision to make a golden calf as an image of the LORD who led

---

14 These are factors that also need to be carefully considered before preachers contemplating the use of visuals with a sermon. Cf. the study of Henry David Schuringa, "Hearing the Word in a Visual Age: A Practical Theological Consideration of Preaching within the Contemporary Urge to Visualization" (Ph.D. diss., Kampen, NL: Theologische Universiteit at Kampen, 1995), 220–235.
15 Cornelis Van Dam, *The Urim and Thummim: A Means of Revelation in Ancient Israel* (Winona Lake, IN: Eisenbrauns, 1997), 119–21.

them out of Egypt. Israel had grown restless because Moses delayed to come down from Mount Sinai. God seemed to have left them. In such a situation of feeling abandoned, there rose a demand for an image. Israel wanted to have God close by, yes, when it came down to it, under their control according to the pagan way of thinking of their day. And therefore, when the calf of gold was made, Aaron said, "This is your god O Israel, who brought you out of the land of Egypt! ... Tomorrow shall be a feast to the LORD" (Exod 32:4, 5).[16] They had their image. God was now with them. No more worries! The Heidelberg Catechism, therefore, rightly places the second commandment in the context of the correct worship of God, as well as stressing the point that no image of God can be made (Q. & A. 96–97).

The second commandment is relevant for the task of teaching. It makes clear the absolute necessity that those who teach make known to their students the true God as he has revealed himself in his Word so that he can be rightly worshipped by us. There are many images of God today by which people try to conceptualize God into someone that will be useful to them and serve their purpose. In this way they seek to control God and make him to be what they want him to be. Some examples of modern images of God come to mind. God is love. Emphasizing this attribute of God, while negating others, implies in the modern secular mind that there is no hell. Others image God as a grand old man. This translates into God and his Word being out of touch with reality. He is simply out of date. You may want to pay lip service to him but he can basically be ignored. More false images of God could be mentioned.[17] With many misconceptions about God currently circulating, parents and teachers must be careful to portray only the God of Scripture who cannot be manipulated or controlled. God is sovereign and transcendent. He cannot be fully grasped, be it literally or mentally. God is God! We are in awe of him. He is the Creator and we are but creatures. As the prophet Isaiah put it: "To whom then will you liken God, or what likeness compare with him? ... To whom then will you

---

16 For the translation of Exod 32:4, see NIV84 footnote and Cornelis Van Dam, "Golden Calf," in *Dictionary of the Old Testament: Pentateuch*, ed. T. Desmond Alexander and David W. Baker (Downers Grove, IL: InterVarsity Press, 2003), 368–69.

17 See, e.g., J.B. Phillips, *Your God is Too Small* (London, UK: Epworth, 1952), 11–60. Although this is an older work, it continues to be very relevant and has become a classic on the issue.

compare me, that I should be like him? says the Holy One. ... Have you not known? Have you not heard? The LORD is the everlasting God, the Creator of the ends of the earth" (Isa 40:18, 25, 28). God is more than we can ever imagine!

It is for this reason that the revelation of God through his Word is such a miracle. There we see God revealed as we are to perceive him. There he has disclosed himself as he wants to be known to his people. There his glory, his love, his righteousness, and his wrath are pictured for us. And therefore, when his Word revelation is faithfully passed on to children and students, they will have the means to have a true image of God. For through the Word, God reveals himself and shows his identity. But more is needed to enable children to see who God really is.

Parents and teachers should not restrict their teaching to merely verbal communication. Students must also see the biblical message. Within this context that means that parents and teachers themselves are to be visual aids. Not only by speaking, but also in their attitudes and actions, they need to show something of the greatness of God and his holiness and sovereignty. After all, Christian parents and teachers are children of Father above, re-created in his image (Eph 4:22–24; Col 3:9–10; cf. Rom 8:29). That image they must show for students to imitate (cf. 1 Cor 11:1; Phil 3:17). Students must be able to *see* something of the new creation in their teachers and so perceive something of the greatness of their heavenly Father. One of the motivations for students to listen can be their desire to emulate or be like the teacher. If a teacher projects a true and loving image of what it means to be a joyful child of God, students will take note and desire the same and also experience the peace, joy, and surety of the new life that they see in their teachers. If teachers are a picture of the new life with all the positive features, then the students will have less difficulty in listening to their instruction. What a teacher stands for and speaks about then becomes attractive (cf. 1 Pet 3:15). When teacher "fathers" or "mothers" so do their calling with their student "children," they may be God's instruments to beget children after their godly image. Or to put it differently, God may use them to renew their students after his image.

God does not want us to make an image of himself; but, he does want to make us new after his image. Students need to be molded by the Word and Spirit after the image of God. Parents and teachers may be instruments of God in that divine molding process. The old creation must give way to the new. Again the priority of the Word is unmistakable, although the student "children" cannot do without seeing their parent or teacher modeling God's image. But verbal communication and the Word are indeed in first place in teaching. Students as well as their teachers must more and more be molded by Holy Scripture. Their thoughts must follow the patterns set by God. Their goals and desires must be in conformity with his will. The Word of God must be integrated into their hearts and lives. This brings us to the importance of memory work.[18]

Memorizing Scripture

If important parts of Scripture are committed to memory, the Word of God will more effectively accomplish its purpose. When God renewed his covenant with Israel, he reminded his people through Moses of the gift of his revelation. "The word is very near you. It is in your mouth and in your heart, so that you can do it" (Deut 30:14). The implication is that Israel should retain in their hearts and memory God's word which they recently heard so that they can live in covenant obedience. In a similar vein, David said of the righteous: "The law of his God is in his heart; his steps do not slip" (Ps 37:31). The believer can, therefore, be characterized as someone who says: "I have stored up your word in my heart, that I might not sin against you" (Ps 119:11). God's Word must abide in us (cf. John 15:7). "Let the word of Christ dwell in you richly" (Col. 3:16). Memorizing Scripture is one way to make this possible.

In our day, memory work is generally not regarded too favorably. It should, however, be realized that this resistance to memory work is a relatively recent phenomenon. The notion that truth can exist meaningfully in a book or on the internet (for reference purposes, to be consulted when needed), rather than in a person's mind, is a comparatively new

---

18 On the importance of memory work, also see chapter 1.

idea.[19] This notion certainly has no support in Scripture. Of course the material to be memorized must be meaningful and relate to the life and environment of the students. They must be able to understand and appreciate what they learn. Then the material functions and has value for their faith, and the Word of God is integrated into real life.[20] It is obvious that for this relevance to be real and meaningful, students must not only hear but also see this integration. In this respect, parents and teachers must be good visual aids for showing students how helpful memorized Scripture is in the daily experiences of life. One can imagine how devastating it would be for children to notice that their parents or teachers do not even know the passages assigned to them for memory work. If those who teach do not know the memory work, why should the student? The adults seem to have made out alright without memory work, so why should the students do this work?

The importance of memorizing Scripture as a tool for integrating God's Word into life cannot be overestimated. Our students are constantly bombarded by worldly language and images in so much of life, including the pervasive influence of the internet and social media on their own phones. How can we expect them to stand if they have not stored in their hearts the demands and promises of the LORD? The world seeks our heart, our very life. But God says, "Give me your heart!" (cf. Prov 23:26). The Word is used by the Spirit to bring about the new life and to nurture it. But we need to have the Word as a vital part of our life and being so we can say: "I have stored up your Word in my heart that I might not sin against you" (Ps 119:11).

The Enduring Task

As parents and teachers seek to sow the good seed of the Word of God into the lives of those in their charge, the struggle against the attraction of worldly images and superficial messaging continues. The secular visual

---

19 Marion Snapper, "The Dethronement of Memory in Church Education," 42–46.
20 See on these criteria, J. Marion Snapper, "Memorization in Church Education," 41–45.

culture is of great concern. However, the corruption and secularization of language should alarm us at least as much, as we saw in the previous chapter. As a result there appears to be a growing gap between the language we hear in church and in the public square. There seem to be two interrelated reasons for this. The first reason is that Christianity is waning in influence and much of life no longer has a Christian frame of reference. Secularism has triumphed and molded much language and discourse. Consequently Christians find it more and more difficult to be heard, especially in discussions on morals and education. Their language no longer fits the secular context.[21] A second related reason is the degeneration of language as we saw in the previous chapter. Today the forces of darkness have more and more claimed language for their purposes so that much discourse today either carries sinful innuendo or relativizes morals. As a result many secularists can truly no longer really understand what Christians are talking about when they express themselves on issues dear to them. They consequently have little appreciation for what Christians stand for (cf. 2 Thess 2:11–12). In this sense the antithesis between light and darkness comes out more clearly now than it has in recent Western history and our students should be aware of this and be prepared to meet the challenges.

Parents and teachers are to be God's instruments to help them meet those challenges. For that reason it is critically important that the Word of life be impressed on the lives and hearts of our children and students. It is a matter of life and death. Our children and students are not immune to the words and images of this world, and for that matter neither are we as parents and teachers so long as that struggle against our old nature is ongoing. The Word is needed to protect and nurture the life of all God's children, young and old. The heart, the center of our consciousness, needs to be guarded. God's Word commands: "Keep your heart with all vigilance, for from it flow the springs of life" (Prov 4:23). As another translation renders: "Above all else, guard your heart" (NIV84).[22]

---

21 Cf. Blamires, *The Christian Mind*, Blamires, *Recovering the Christian Mind: Meeting the Challenge of Secularism*, and Blamires, *The Post Christian Mind: Exposing Its Destructive Agenda*.

22 Helpful resources include: Tedd Tripp, Shepherding a Child's Heart, 2nd ed., rev. and updated (Wapwallopen, PA: Shepherd Press, 2005), Starr Meade, *Comforting Hearts, Teaching Minds: Family Devotions Based on the Heidelberg Catechism* (Phillipsburg, NJ: P&R Publishing, 2013), and Starr Meade, *Training Hearts, Teaching Minds: Family Devotions Based on the Shorter Catechism* (Phillipsburg, NJ: P&R Publishing, 2000).

We, therefore, need to continue to expose the words and pictures the world presents for what they are and impress upon our children and students the great significance of the Word of God for all of life. It is of utmost importance that they learn to distinguish and discriminate between the holy and the unholy, between good and evil. Such an ability is possible if one is armed with the Word of God and a correct understanding of it. We are in the world, but not of it. Enabled by the Word and Spirit, discernment is possible. As part of equipping the next generation, illustrations can be helpful to support the message of the Word. The very best visual help that children and students can receive is the example of a godly life of their parents and teachers. That is of tremendous help. Teaching must never be done in a theoretical vacuum but it should be practical and demonstrate that it is a necessary condition for a future life of service. We have the Word. It relates to life and it is the Word of life! And to our encouragement, it is also an effective Word, also in the lives of children and students. It will accomplish the purpose for which God sent it (Isa 55:11).

One final point. Since we train students for a life of service in God's kingdom, the exposure of darkness for what it is should at the same time serve as a challenge to advance the claims of the light of the gospel as the Lord gives opportunity and provides time before his glorious return. There is a task, both for parents and teachers as well as for children and students, also in the fundamental issue of language and image, of communicating through words and visuals. Christians should go forth as able communicators of the Word in all of life, by speaking and applying it and reinforcing the message by being pictures of Christ's redemptive work. They will be able if God's Word is written on their hearts (cf. Jer 31:33). Then they will be letters from Christ, inscribed "not with ink but with the Spirit of the living God, not on tablets of stone but on tablets of human hearts" (cf. 2 Cor 3:3).

PART C

SCIENCE AND EDUCATION

CHAPTER 7

The Bible and Science: God's Revelation in His Word and Creation

The Issue

In our day and age, the controversy about the relationship of the Bible and natural science shows no signs of letting up. How does the authority of the Bible relate to that of science when the latter draws conclusions from its research that conflict with Scripture? In an effort to break through the apparent deadlock, the suggestion has been made that the present dilemma would be solved if it be realized more fully and adequately that the created world is also God's revelation. The implication is that science, properly done, therefore passes on not only human insights but also God's revelation.[1] Those supporting this position appeal to Article 2 of the Belgic Confession which speaks of revelation, not only from Scripture but also from creation.

Perhaps an illustration will make clear what is at stake and the dilemmas one faces. A geologist says that to the best of his knowledge, based on scientific research of the earth's crust, the earth must be billions of years old. He considers this to be a fact. The Bible reader says, I do not find any evidence for this number of years in Genesis or anywhere else in Scripture, which indicates that the earth is thousands of years old, not billions. So who is right? If one treats both general and special revelation as equals, one could argue that the geologist must be right because he is especially

---

[1] See, e.g., A. Wolters, et al., "Report 28 Committee on Creation and Science," in *Agenda for Synod 1991* (Grand Rapids, MI: Christian Reformed Church in North America, 1991), 404, 407.

equipped to study the data of creation, which according to this view is also revelation. We must trust God's revelation also in the rock formations and the data they yield. Such a conclusion would be in line with the Christian Reformed Church Report on Creation and Science which was adopted in 1991. It stated that "the authority of general revelation, no less than that of special revelation, is a divine authority, which must be acknowledged without reservation."[2]

What we see happening with such a statement is that creation, or what is called general revelation, in effect and in practice is separated from Scripture and becomes an authority of itself, even though it is denied that this is the intent. But, if there is a dispute between what is considered to be a scientific fact and the Bible, science is generally given the greater weight for it virtually functions as the interpreter of revelation in creation. But what about the authority of Scripture when it appears to disagree with scientific theory (e.g. on evolution or the age of the earth)? God cannot contradict himself. How can God say one thing in Scripture and another in his so-called general revelation? How do we get out of this dilemma?

To answer this and related questions, we first need to determine precisely what the place of general revelation is; namely what general revelation reveals and how it can benefit scientific work. Next, to help appreciate the work of science, we will consider the significance of what is generally called laws of nature which function so prominently in scientific research and in the postulating of new theories. In the third place, in light of the above, we will consider further the use of Scripture in the scientific enterprise.

What does General Revelation Reveal?

What does general revelation reveal? If one studies passages dealing with general revelation, one must come to the conclusion that general revelation reveals God, his glory, and his handiwork. Let us look at some important examples. David exclaimed: "O LORD, our Lord, how majestic

---

[2] Wolters, et al., "Report on Creation and Science," 407; cf. Van Dam, *In the Beginning*, 37–38.

is your name in all the earth! You have set your glory above the heavens" (Ps 8:1, 9). Similarly, he affirmed elsewhere: "The heavens declare the glory of God, and the sky above proclaims his handiwork" (Ps 19:1). The apostle Paul spoke of the wrath of God being revealed from heaven against all ungodliness and then continued by stating: "For what can be known about God is plain to them, because God has shown it to them. For his invisible attributes, namely, his eternal power and divine nature, have been clearly perceived, ever since the creation of the world, in the things that have been made. So they are without excuse" (Rom 1:19–20). One can also think of Paul's witness to Lystra that God's goodness is evident from his provision of rains and food (Acts 14:17). In all these instances, the object of the revelation is God, be it his glory or his wrath or his goodness.

The Belgic Confession summarizes biblical truth by stating that God makes himself known by two means.

> First, by the creation, preservation, and government of the universe; which is before our eyes as a most beautiful book, wherein all creatures, great and small, are as so many letters leading us to perceive clearly God's *invisible attributes, namely, his eternal power and divine nature*, as the apostle Paul says in Romans 1:20. All these things are sufficient to convict men and leave them without excuse. Second, he makes himself more clearly and fully known to us by his holy and divine Word as far as is necessary for us in this life, to his glory and our salvation.[3]

One can, therefore, say that both Scripture and general revelation reveal God. *Formally* speaking, one could conclude that science, which is the study of general revelation, should as a result be accorded as much respect as theology which studies God's special revelation. But here we run into a major problem with the way current science is conducted. If general revelation reveals God and if science studies general revelation, then the first conclusion science should come to is the reality and characteristics of God who reveals himself in creation! But mainstream science as conducted today ignores God and gives him no place in their

---

3 Belgic Confession, Art. 2. *Book of Praise*, 499–500 (italics are original).

work. Indeed, the influential and prestigious American National Academy of Sciences defines as the most basic characteristic of science its "reliance upon naturalistic explanations."[4]

The Need for Special Revelation

How can such a science that ignores the Creator and his attributes be considered to be a consistent valid authority by Christians to inform us concerning what God is saying in his general revelation? By not honoring God, they are futile in their thinking and their foolish hearts are darkened (Rom 1:21). Christian scientists will not only see God revealed in creation; but they will also take his written revelation into consideration when theorizing and trying to come to an integrated understanding of our present world.

Consider the following example taken from the science of biology to illustrate the points just made. Some scientists have concluded on the basis of extensive research that one's genetic identity significantly impacts whether you become a homosexual. According to Professor Bill Sullivan: "Sex is not just male or female. Rather it is a continuum that emerges from a person's genetic makeup." He also concluded: "While there is no single 'gay gene,' there is overwhelming evidence of a biological basis for sexual orientation that is programmed into the brain before birth based on a mix of genetics and prenatal conditions, none of which the fetus chooses."[5] According to this examination of general revelation, people cannot be held responsible for their genetic condition and their being homo-sexual. They must be accepted as they are and accommodated in whatever way necessary. All this is considered to be factual information and such an acceptance of its veracity has considerable consequences. As a result our secular society goes to great lengths to meet

---

[4] See Phillip E. Johnson, *Darwin on Trial*, 20th anniversary ed., intro. Michael Behe (Downers Grove, IL: InterVarsity Press, 2010), 26.

[5] Bill Sullivan, "Stop Calling It a Choice: Biological Factors Drive Homosexuality," *The Conversation*, 3 September 2019, found at https://theconversation.com/stop-calling-it-a-choice-biological-factors-drive-homosexuality-122764.

the demands of homosexuals. However, as often happens when general revelation or God's creation is studied, other scientists dispute this analysis as factual and hold another interpretation of the available evidence. They refute the notion that "being gay is an innate condition that is controlled or largely compelled by one's genetic makeup."[6] So, who is closest to the truth? A similar situation exists with the question whether, and to what extent, genetics play a role in gender dysphoria.[7]

In such a situation, special revelation can show the way because it speaks clearly to this issue. Scripture says that God created "male and female" (Gen 1:27). This simple statement excludes the notion that male and female are on a genetic continuum. Male and female are two distinct identities which should not be confused. Scripture, however, also informs us that Adam and Eve sinned and consequently all creation fell from the state of perfection (Rom 5:12; 8:20). We no longer live in a sinless world. This reality has consequences, also for human genetic makeup. Variations from the perfect norm occur, also in genes, resulting in deviations from the perfect creation God made in the beginning. Any influence that genes may have on a person having homosexual temptation would be another indication of such deviation from God's intended norm when he created Adam after his image. The Creator, however, maintains the biological distinction of male and female and condemns homosexual practice as sinful—"an abomination" (Lev 18:22; 1 Cor 6:9). Another affliction is gender dysphoria. This is the diagnosis which mental health professionals give to people who experience psychological distress because of incongruence between their sex at birth and the gender they identify with.[8] Christians who desire to be of a different gender can experience enormous pain and struggle not to fall into sin, to resist mutilating their body, and to live according to divine norms because they realize that God is the one who assigned their sex at birth.

---

6 Paul Sullins, "'Born That Way' No More: The New Science of Sexual Orientation," *Public Discourse: The Journal of the Witherspoon Institute* (2019): found at https://www.thepublicdiscourse.com/2019/09/57342/; also, e.g., Mayer and McHugh, "Sexuality and Gender," 7.

7 E.g., Madeleine Foreman, et al., "Genetic Link between Gender Dysphoria and Sex Hormone Signaling," *The Journal of Clinical Endocrinology and Metabolism* 104, no. 2 (2019): 390–96, found at https://doi.org/10.1210/jc.2018–01105.

8 Karl Bryant, "Gender Dysphoria," in *Encyclopedia Britannica*, Logos ed., Encyclopaedia Britannica staff (Chicago, IL: Encyclopaedia Britannica, 2016).

It should be obvious from the above that those struggling with and suffering from homosexual desire or gender dysphoria need to find biblical support and solace in a welcoming church environment (cf. Gal 6:1). All Christians share in the brokenness of creation and struggle against temptations and sins of some sort in our fallen world with imperfect genetics. For many there can be a lasting and real "thorn in the flesh" (cf. 2 Cor 12:7–8).[9]

In sum, the point of these examples of scientific conclusions on the basis of what is considered general revelation is to indicate that taking Scripture into account helps to discard scientific theories that come into conflict with its teaching; in this case, the theory that male and female are on a genetic continuum. Furthermore, Scripture does not exclude the possibility that genetics may be involved in homosexual desire and gender dysphoria since creation has fallen from its state of perfection. The Lord Jesus himself acknowledged that some males are eunuchs from birth (Matt 19:12). These are boys born with a congenital defect.[10]

Other examples of what Scripture reveals and science needs to take into account can be given. Biblical truths that are relevant for scientific theorizing and need to be factored in include: God's calling creation into existence from nothing (Heb 11:3; Rev 4:11), the creation of light before the light bearers (Gen 1:3, 14–18), the fall into sin (Gen 3), the worldwide flood (Gen 7), the confusion of tongues at the tower of Babel (Gen 11:1–9), the sun standing still in Joshua's day (Josh 10:12–14), the shadow returning in the days of Hezekiah (Isa 38:8), and of course the reality of the ongoing providence of God whereby he upholds and sustains creation.

As a general comment, it should also be emphasized that scientific theories are not facts, in spite of them often being presented as such. Theories are but human attempts to explain a variety of data and cannot be called divine revelation. When Scripture speaks clearly on an issue that

---

9   Helpful books on sex and gender issues include: Ryan T. Anderson, *When Harry Became Sally: Responding to the Transgender Movement* (New York, NY: Encounter Books, 2018); Sam Allberry, *What God Has to Say About Our Bodies: How the Gospel is Good News for Our Physical Selves*, foreword by Paul David Tripp (Wheaton, IL: Crossway, 2021).

10 So, e.g., William Hendriksen, *Exposition of the Gospel According to Matthew*, New Testament Commentary (Grand Rapids, MI: Baker, 1973), 718.

science is dealing with, the relevant scientific theories need to be weighed and evaluated in the light of God's Word.[11]

Scientists need to remember that God does not contradict himself. He does not speak with one voice by the means of his creation, preservation, and government of the universe, that is, general revelation, and with another voice by means of Scripture, that is special revelation. There is one truth. What a scientist can perceive or discover in the created world must always be seen in the light of Scripture. Whenever possible, God's Word must accompany human efforts to understand his work of creation. The testimony of Scripture itself underlines this need for the explanatory assistance of the Word. It is striking how right from the beginning, in Paradise, Adam not only saw God's handiwork, he also heard God's voice (cf. Gen 3:9). God did not leave man with only natural revelation, but he also revealed the purpose of what he made. He, for instance, said that Eve was created to be a helper suitable for Adam (Gen 2:18) and that male and female had specific mandates from him (Gen 1:27–30). After the fall into sin, God's spoken word often preceded and accompanied his mighty acts whereby the LORD God explained the miracles and upheavals which he worked in creation. For example, the Israelites would not have understood the Red Sea crossing correctly if they had simply assumed that a strong east wind came along just at the right time. God's spoken word had preceded and accompanied this event and God's people could respond accordingly (Exod 3:7–10; 14:16–18; 15:1–21). In the New Testament, we find the same pattern. Christ's miracles could not be understood apart from his teaching (e.g., Matt 9:1–8, 18–38.) It may be of interest to pause at one event to illustrate the absolute necessity of needing special revelation to understand extraordinary events in creation. Such an event is the appearance of the star announcing Christ's birth.

The Wise Men from the East and the Star

Matthew recounts how wise men from the east came to Jerusalem looking for the king of the Jews because they had seen his star and had

---

[11] See further on God's Word and science, Van Dam, *In the Beginning*, 48–58.

come to worship him (Matt 2:2). There have been many theories on the identity of this star.[12] But whatever its precise identity, the point that interests us is that God used a phenomenon in creation, a star, to draw the Magi from the east to Bethlehem.

How did these wise men make the connection between this star and Christ's birth? Scripture does not directly tell us. But there is enough evidence to allow for some reasonable speculation of why this star alerted these learned men to the birth of Christ. The term used to describe these scholars (*magoi*) indicates that they were astrologers, experts in interpreting the significance of the position of stars on human affairs. Ancient Mesopotamian civilizations were famous for the detailed records of whatever was relevant to help them understand unusual celestial phenomena.[13] The wise men would take care of such record taking. A prominent seer from Mesopotamia whose writings may be assumed to be part of any well-stocked astrological library was Balaam (Num 22:5). God used him to prophesy the coming of the messianic king when he said: "I see him, but not now; I behold him, but not near; a star shall come out of Jacob, and a scepter shall rise out of Israel" (Num 24:17). This person will crush all Israel's foes (Num 24:17–19). It is not impossible that the interest of the wise men in special stars and a future messianic king may have been due to this prophesy, especially considering that Daniel was a prominent wise man in Babylon whom Nebuchadnezzar had put in charge of all of them (Dan 2:48). Daniel would have had great interest in this prophecy and could have made other magi aware of it.[14] Indeed, Daniel himself also prophesied the coming of the great King (Dan 2:44; 7:13–14).

---

12 For a history of the different theories, see Aaron Adair, "The Star of Christ in the Light of Astronomy," *Zygon* 47, no. 1 (2012): 7–29.

13 A. Leo Oppenheim, *Ancient Mesopotamia*, revised edition completed by Erica Reiner, reprint, 1964 (Chicago: University of Chicago Press, 1977), 224–25; for more detail, see A. J. Sachs and C. B. F. Walker, "Kepler's View of the Star of Bethlehem and the Babylonian Almanac for 7/6 B.C." *Iraq* 46, no. 1 (1984): 43–55.

14 Those entertaining the possibility that the wise men knew of Balaam's prophecy include Eusebius of Caesarea (about AD 265–339), trans. and ed. W. J. Ferrar, *The Proof of the Gospel Being the Demonstratio Evangelica of Eusebius of Caesarea*, Translations of Christian Literature. Series 1 Greek Texts (London, UK; New York, NY: Society for Promoting Christian Knowledge; Macmillan Company, 1920), 2:150 (§ 9.1); Clinton E. Arnold, *Zondervan Illustrated Bible Backgrounds Commentary: Matthew, Mark, Luke* (Grand Rapids, MI: Zondervan, 2002), 14–15; Gispen, *Het Boek Numeri*, 2:131.

In any case, it is clear that God was at work with the Magi, using the language of the stars along with their astrological resources to call these men from the east to see the king of the Jews. Since Jerusalem was the royal city, this was the obvious place for them to go to. After arriving at the royal capital, Jerusalem, special revelation from God's Word was necessary for the Magi to find the newborn king. They asked: "Where is he who has been born king of the Jews? For we saw his star when it rose and have come to worship him" (Matt 2:3). Those who knew the Scriptures were called in and they answered from the Word of God that Bethlehem was the place where they would find him (Matt 2:6). With that biblical directive, they went their way. The star then reappeared and God graciously guided them to the very spot. "Behold, the star that they had seen when it rose went before them until it came to rest over the place where the child was" (Matt 2:9).[15] How that star served as a special sign (cf. Gen 1:14)! The heavens were telling the glory of God in the coming of the Messiah (cf. Ps 19:1).

What is true of extraordinary events in creation and the natural world is also true of what we consider perfectly normal and routine. Phenomena in creation cannot be correctly understood without the special revelation of the Word of God. His creation work cannot be properly understood and interpreted apart from any consideration of the Creator. General revelation needs to be seen in the light of special revelation. An appreciation of an important part of the message of Psalm 19 helps us to grasp the significance of the ongoing relationship between special and general revelation.

Psalm 19 and the Laws of Nature

Psalm 19 has two major parts.[16] Verses 1–6 inform us of the revelation of God's glory in creation. Verses 7–14 tell us of the glory of the LORD

---

15 This passage can best be understood as indicating that the star they had seen in the east and that prompted their journey to Jerusalem now reappeared for the first time. See, e.g., Hendriksen, *Matthew*, 168; D. L. Turner, *Matthew*, Baker Exegetical Commentary on the New Testament (Grand Rapids, MI: Baker Academic, 2008), 85.
16 For what follows, also see Van Dam, *In the Beginning*, 43–46.

revealed in his Word. In this arrangement there is a movement towards a climax. One can marvel at the night sky and see something of the greatness and glory of God in his general revelation. But, when one reads the written Word, God's glory and power is seen in a much richer way. It is striking that in the first half of the Psalm, God is referred to only once and the name used is El, generally interchangeable with Elohim which is the Hebrew word used of the Creator in Genesis 1. In the second half of the Psalm, however, God is referred to seven times and the name used is Yahweh, the covenant God, rendered into English as the LORD. The message is clear. Nature and creation (general revelation) cannot reveal the God of the covenant. That fact is only known through special revelation. At the same time, it is evident that one cannot understand the created world properly without knowing about this covenant God, because his salvation work not only concerns his people, but also all of creation. This is his world and he is busy with it and will renew it on that great day of Jesus Christ (2 Pet 3:13).

These observations bring us to the next question. How does God reveal himself in his creation and why can one not understand creation properly if one does not know the God of creation and re-creation? In order to make the answers to these questions as concrete as possible we will focus on the issue of the laws of nature which are a key element in the modern quest for understanding the world in which we live and see how Scripture deals with them.

David said that "the heavens declare the glory of God, and the sky above proclaims his handiwork" (Ps 19:1). How is this done? It is done without words. In quiet majesty the heavens proclaim the glory of God. "There is no speech, nor are there words, whose voice is not heard" (Ps 19:3). But how do the heavens and the firmament then declare the glory of God? The answer is by doing the task God has given them to do. What is that task? The firmament was created to separate the waters which are under the firmament and the waters which are above the firmament (Gen 1:6-8; cf. Job 38:8–11). The heavenly bodies, the sun, moon, and stars determine the separation of day from night and are there for signs, for fixed times, and for days and years (Gen 1:14). By doing these things so faithfully according to God's will, the heavens and the heavenly bodies basically function as a measuring line and rule, and indeed function as the norm. "Their line has gone out through all the earth" (Ps 19:4 NASB).[17] By determining the separation of day and night and doing other functions, the heavens control certain things without saying a word. This measuring line of control goes out over the whole earth and their unspoken words to the end of the earth (Ps 19:4). So God's glory is shown by the heavens and the heavenly bodies throughout the whole world by their doing their task.[18] Psalm 19 then goes into detail and gives the sun as an example of what was mentioned. The sun follows God's decree for it without wavering. It obeys with joy the will of God by coming

> Out like a bridegroom leaving his chamber,
> and, like a strong man, runs its course with joy.
> Its rising is from the end of the heavens,
>   and its circuit to the end of them,
>   And there is nothing hidden from its heat. (Ps 19:5–6)

Thus, by obeying God, it shows God's glory and majesty by fulfilling the designs of the Creator for its place and function.

Everything in creation is established and runs by God's commands. What we call laws of nature are, therefore, in reality nature obeying God's commands and decrees. This is an important aspect of the comparison in the two parts in Psalm 19. As the sun obeys God's law to creation, so the believer also is to be God's servant. The glory of God is seen in creation and specifically in creation's obedience to God's decrees; but in a far richer way the glory of God is evident in the written law and specifically in the obedience to that law.[19] For that reason the Psalm ends with the prayer of David that he may be able to keep the law and be acceptable in God's sight. Although the law is perfect, his obedience to it is not. Forgiveness is needed.

---

17 The ESV does not follow the Hebrew ("line") here and like the ancient Greek translation renders "voice." "Their voice goes out through all the earth." On this issue, see Cornelis van Dam, "Duidelijke taal. De boodschap van de hemelen volgens Psalm 19:5a," in *Een sprekend begin: opstellen aangeboden aan Prof. Drs. H. M. Ohmann*, eds. R. ter Beek, et al. (Kampen, NL: Van den Berg, 1993), 86–93.

18 Nic. H. Ridderbos, *De Psalmen*, Korte Verklaring (Kampen, NL: Kok, 1962), 1:210. For more detail, see Van Dam, *In the Beginning*, 44–45.

19 The words used for law in this psalm are those emphasizing the notion of commands of God. See further Ridderbos, *De Psalmen*, 1:212. Cf. on creation's and man's being servants, Ps 119:89–96.

SCIENCE AND EDUCATION

Creation obeys God's commands. Because these commands are good, we have a stable universe and we can speak of laws of nature. But these are not autonomous laws. What we experience is creation obeying the will of God as he directs his handiwork. Scripture even speaks of God having a covenant with creation. Jeremiah 33 speaks of the LORD's covenant with the day and with the night so that day and night come at the appointed time (Jer 33:20). This covenant is placed in parallel with "the fixed order of heaven and earth" (Jer 33:25). However, the words "fixed order" translate the Hebrew *ḥuqqôt* which in the singular literally means "statute, ordinance, law, decree, issued by God."[20] In other words, we observe a fixed order in creation because heaven and earth are consistently obeying the decrees which they have received from God. We find a similar thought elsewhere in Jeremiah where the LORD's giving the sun for light by day and the fixed order of the moon and the stars for light by night, as well as God's stirring up the sea, are all called his statutes and ordinances (*ḥuqqôt*, Jer 31:35–36). God continues to be involved in the world he has made. His "word is firmly fixed in the heavens" and by his ordinances everything stands "for all things are his servants" (Ps 119:89, 91).[21]

The Creator gives his orders to the sun, moon, stars, seas and all creation (e.g., Job 38:31–35; Ps 148:5, 6; Prov 8:29; Jer 5:24; cf. also Ps 65:5–10). He makes the winds his messengers, fire and flame his ministers (Ps 104:4). God does not give these orders haphazardly. No. He does so as God who is faithful to the promise spoken to Noah. "While the earth remains, seedtime and harvest, cold and heat, summer and winter, day and night, shall not cease" (Gen 8:22). There is, therefore, a certain regularity and predictability in nature. But, and this must be clear, it is only predictable because God is faithful and is consistent in his wishes for his creation. What we consider to be recurring and predictable from a study of nature is strictly speaking not laws of nature, but evidence of the faithfulness of God to what he has made. He is still involved moment by moment with his work of creation, seeing to it that it carries out what he has

---

20 Clines, *The Dictionary of Classical Hebrew*, 3:302.
21 In Ps 119:91 "appointment" (ESV) and "ordinances" (NASB) translate Hebrew *mišpāṭîm* which can usually be taken as synonymous with *ḥuqqôt* in the Psalms. Helmer Ringgren, "*ḥāqaq* ," in *Theological Dictionary of the Old Testament*, eds. G. Johannes Botterweck, Helmer Ringgren, and Heinz-Josef Fabry (Grand Rapids, MI: Eerdmans, 1986), 5:146.

ordained and commanded. Because God is in total control at all times, therefore, what we call the laws of nature cannot be treated as autonomous and unchanging. Phenomena of creation are God's servants (Ps 119:91; 148:7–8). Consequently, God has used the heavens in order to have them serve his people in special ways. Examples come to mind. The LORD threw great stones, possibly hailstones, down from heaven on the Amorites and caused the sun to stand still in the sky so that Joshua could achieve a full victory (Josh 10).[22] The stars were involved in the battle against Sisera. "From heaven the stars fought, from their courses they fought against Sisera" (Judg 5:20).[23] The LORD used thunder to confuse the Philistines so that they were defeated (1 Sam 7:10; cf. 2 Sam 8–16). God also used the heavens to punish his people. Thus, for example, God kept the rain from falling in Israel for three and a half years in the days of Ahab and Jezebel (1 Kings 17:1; James 5:17).

These examples indicate that we should not look at the created world as running more or less independently like a clock that has been wound up and is now ticking its time away. There are no autonomous laws of creation. God is actively involved in the day to day functioning of his handiwork. The order and regularity that we daily experience in the natural phenomena do not reside in creation but in God who commands the regularity, but who can also command irregularity! This fact means that miracles are not a transgression of God's laws for creation because these do not exist independent of God. They are an expression of his will, which can include judgment. God who ordered the seas to stay within their bounds (Ps 104:6–9) can also call on them to cover the land (Amos 5:8). The Creator even destroyed and cleansed the world with a great flood. The separation between land and water set at creation was erased while the deluge lasted. God made a covenant with Noah and every living creature that this type of destruction would never happen again (Gen 9:8–11). But, we do know that God will one day make all things new by the judgment of fire (cf. Hos 2:18; 2 Pet 3:5–10).[24]

---

22 For the possibility that these stones were meteorites, see Marten H. Woudstra, *The Book of Joshua*, NICOT (Grand Rapids, MI: Eerdmans, 1981), 173, note 23.

23 How this was done we are not told. Was a comet or eclipse or stars leaving their orbits involved? See for possibilities Daniel I. Block, *Judges, Ruth*, The New American Commentary (Nashville, TN: Broadman & Holman, 1999), 236–37.

24 See further, e.g., Weeks, *The Christian School: An Introduction*, 126–27, also 123–37.

God can and has also acted in less momentous ways. For example, we are all familiar with wear and tear. Things get older, not newer. Books get tattered, clothes get worn, and shoes get holes. But this is not an absolute law, operating independently. As Creator, God can also command otherwise and not allow for wear and tear. He did that when Israel wandered in the wilderness for forty years. After those wanderings, God could say to his people, "your clothes have not worn out on you, and your sandals have not worn off your feet" (Deut 29:5). The fact that God can alter what we call the laws of nature must be taken into consideration by present-day science. One can never assume that processes as they are today have always been the same in the past. For instance, if a river bed erodes at a certain rate today, this does not mean it has always done so. There may have been droughts and there may have been much more water. For this reason, to take geology as an example, one can never simply measure layers of sediment on the basis of present rates of deposit and come up with an age. God and his Word must also be reckoned with and it could very well be that the great deluge of Noachian times may be relevant for the particular geological problem that is being studied. Furthermore, dating methods are not free of problems and are informed by presuppositions that may or may not be accurate in light of the biblical testimony on earth's history.[25]

At this point one could raise an objection. But the Bible is not a scientific textbook, is it? Can we really use the Bible in a scientific study of creation? There are several issues here that need to be distinguished. It is true that the Bible was not written to serve as a handbook for geology or chemistry. However, does that fact mean that the Bible has nothing to say that is relevant for these scientific disciplines? Can we exclude his Word when dealing with scientific issues and rely only on what he has to tell us in his book of creation? Excluding any possibly relevant information found in Scripture from scientific research would be a bad mistake.

---

[25] There have been obvious errors of dating when material known to be mere decades old has been dated to be millions and even billions years of age. For such errors as well as dating methods, see John D. Morris, *The Young Earth* (Colorado Springs, CO: Master Books, 1994), 51–67, 93–117; also see Andrew A. Snelling, *Earth's Catastrophic Past: Geology, Creation, and the Flood* (Green Forest, AR; Petersburg, KY: Master Books; Answers in Genesis, 2014), 797–864; Daniel Aloi, "New Radiocarbon Cycle Research May Alter History," Artifax 24, no. 2 (2018): 12–13.

God reveals crucial information to us in his Word. Only from Scripture do we, for example, know that a personal God sustains and governs this world. Not natural autonomous laws, but God makes creation function according to his design and purpose.

The Bible is normative and authoritative for all of life. It is also profitable for equipping scientists for their task (cf. 2 Tim 3:16–17). Furthermore, only the Bible can tell us with authority and truth what happened at the beginning of time and what will happen in the future. Only the Bible can inform us that God created a perfect world and universe, that there was a fall into sin and a terrible flood, and that there will be a restoration one day after a judgment of fire. This framework is relevant for science. Scientists cannot be sure of what happened at the beginning, or what will happen in the future. Science can only be certain of what God is doing now and even that knowledge is very limited, for scientists are finite human creatures.

This finiteness is clearly revealed in Scripture. It is, for example, demonstrated by God's response to Job's questions concerning God's government of the world and in particular his life.[26] God reminded Job that he is only a creature. He is not God. In the course of God's answer to Job, the LORD spoke of the stars and the weather and said:

> Can you bind the chains of the Pleiades
> or loose the cords of Orion?
> Can you lead forth the Mazzaroth in their season,
> or can you guide the Bear with its children?
> Do you know the ordinances of the heavens?
> Can you establish their rule on the earth?
> Can you lift up your voice to the clouds,
> that a flood of waters may cover you?
> Can you send forth lightnings, that they may go
> and say to you, "here we are"? (Job 38:31–35)

---

26 For what follows, I am indebted to Noel Weeks, *The Sufficiency of Scripture* (Carlisle, PA: The Banner of Truth Trust, 1988), 22–25.

All these questions expect "no!" as an answer. A key question is: "Do you know the ordinances [*ḥuqqôt*] of the heavens? Can you establish their rule on the earth?" (Job 38:33). As noted earlier, "ordinances" refers to God's law and rule over creation. Man may be able to deduce all kinds of laws of nature and draw up all manner of working hypotheses. But, he will never be able to give *the* answer to the secret of the workings of creation. For behind creation, behind this book of natural revelation, is God's inscrutable command and ordinance. He is in charge and man will never be in that position. For if scientists were to be able to reproduce these ordinances of God so that he could make the stars leave their courses, well then they would be as God. But how finite humans are! They cannot even be absolutely certain about tomorrow's weather, how much less can they control it. Scientists are able to come up with all kinds of formulas and it is part of their cultural mandate to do so. They are able to grow in understanding of the world and the universe. They can analyze and deduce laws, but they cannot rule as God.

It may be helpful at this point to briefly discuss four basic truths or principles that should be kept in mind when using the Bible, also regarding scientific topics.[27]

Some Principles in Using Scripture

In the first place, the Word of God is clear or perspicuous. This means that believers who read the Bible are not dependent on specialists, be they in science or theology, in order to understand the basic message that comes to them in Scripture. When children of God read and study the Bible, humbly submitting themselves to the Word and asking for the guidance of the Holy Spirit, then the Word *is* a light on their path, a lamp before their feet (Ps 119:105). Believers are able to judge, and are called upon to evaluate any interpretations of Scripture that are suspect (cf. 1 Cor 2:15; 1 John 2:20). This clarity of Scripture does not mean that there are no difficult passages which may require detailed investigation. It

---

[27] Also see on the clarity of Scripture, as well as creationism, Van Dam, *In the Beginning*, 12–13, 30–35.

therefore also does not deny the need for the scholarly study of Scripture.[28] On the other hand, children of God do not need to feel that they are at the mercy of science to inform them of how and what happened, for example at the beginning of history. The Bible is clear on what it says and demands it be taken seriously.

In the second place, God's Word is self-sufficient and self-authenticating. It does not need our reasoning and proofs to show that it is trustworthy and true. As we confess in Article 5 of our Belgic Confession:

> We believe without any doubt all things contained in them [i.e. the Holy Scriptures], not so much because the Church receives and approves them as such, but especially because the Holy Spirit witnesses in our hearts that they are from God, and also because they contain the evidence of this in themselves; for even the blind are able to perceive that the things foretold in them are being fulfilled.[29]

One must, therefore, resist attempting to prove the Bible scientifically on contested points, like creation, the flood, and the sun's standing still. Such proof is not necessary.

Thirdly, God's Word explains itself and is its own interpreter. Behind the many books of Scripture is the one Author, namely God (2 Tim 3:16; 2 Pet 1:21). This means that there is a basic unity underlying all of Scripture. One part of the Bible can, therefore, be used to explain another part. If there are difficulties in understanding particular areas of Genesis, then relevant information found elsewhere in the Old Testament or New Testament can and should be used.

Finally, God's Word has the last say. If there is a real contradiction between what humans say and what God reveals in his Word, God's Word must be maintained and the word of man must be put aside. The clear teachings of Scripture never conflict with facts. God does not contradict himself in his revelation in creation and in the Bible. In order to understand rightly, we need to read the data of creation through the lens of Scripture. The one means of revelation, the book of creation, is not adequately

---

[28] For more on the clarity of Scripture, Herman Bavinck, *Reformed Dogmatics*, 4 vols., ed. John Bolt, trans. John Vriend (Grand Rapids, MI: Baker Academic, 2003–8), 1:475–81.

[29] *Book of Praise*, 500.

understood without the other, the book of special revelation. Our finite sinful minds cannot truly understand creation without the Bible.

Although there cannot be a disagreement between divine revelation in creation and God's written Word, conflict does arise when either form of revelation is not properly understood or considered. For example, scientific theorizing that is influenced by a denial of the Word of God, such as the theory of evolution, creates conflict with Scripture. The biblical account of origins needs to be taken into account to prevent a scientific theory from contradicting God's Word.[30] Conflict can also arise if Scripture is not understood correctly or more is deduced from Scripture than is warranted. For example, if one insists that Scripture teaches either that the earth revolves around the sun or that the sun revolves around the earth, then one goes further than Scripture which uses geocentric language and does not address this larger cosmological issue. Any interpretation of Scripture must be careful not to go beyond what God clearly reveals in his Word. Christian scientific endeavors done on the basis of biblical presuppositions and within a Scriptural worldview are best positioned to avoid coming into conflict with Scripture. When secularized science propounds theories that are clearly not in agreement with biblical facts, the conflict is not between science and faith, but between unbelief and faith.

This last observation brings us to a brief consideration of the place of science in understanding Scripture.

The Place of Science in Understanding Scripture

Scientists investigate and explore God's handiwork and systematize their knowledge of the natural world. This human enterprise is part of the divine mandate to exercise dominion over creation (Gen 1:28). As God's complex creation yields more and more of its secrets to human investigation, we are astounded by the greatness of God, namely his power, wisdom, and faithfulness as seen in his creation work. We marvel

---

30 For a detailed investigation of the historicity of the Genesis creation account which leaves no room for theistic evolution, see Van Dam, *In the Beginning*.

at what the Creator has included in his handiwork and praise him for it. We are also thankful for the many benefits which scientific inventions and technological advances have brought us in fields as diverse as medicine, energy, digital technology, and computers. Scientific work is rightly honored and admired for its achievements. However, there are areas beyond the capability of scientific investigation. The origin of this world, for example, is one of those areas. Science has no way of reconstructing how creation came into existence.[31] One can theorize how this might have happened, but any past event that one seeks to reconstruct can never attain any surety beyond the status of a hypothesis. Such is the nature of what has been called historical science. Such science is different from operational science that deals with current reality and repeatable events and which yields the many discoveries and inventions we enjoy today.[32]

When we are considering issues like the creation of the world or miracles recorded in Scripture, we are dealing with matters beyond the competence of operational science with its experimental models and empirical testing. We need to rely on God's account in Scripture. When it comes to creation, God was there and he alone. He created the heavens and the earth and he has informed us in his Word what we need to know and we accept his account in faith. "By faith we understand that the universe was created by the word of God, so that what is seen was not made out of things that are visible" (Heb 11:3). The latest scientific theory on the origins of this world should not determine one's exegesis. These theories come and go, but the Word remains forever (Isa 40:8). That Word must be understood in the first place, not on the basis of what science is proposing, but on the basis of what Scripture itself says about the issue under discussion. One's understanding of Scripture may never be subjected to the condition that it needs to fit current scientific theory. Proof from science is not needed. We accept God's Word as true in faith.

In sum, the place of science in understanding Scripture is modest, but its contribution to revealing something of God's greatness is substantial! The

---

31 See, e.g., Peter Medawar, *The Limits of Science* (Oxford, UK: Oxford University Press, 1987), 66, 88.
32 A helpful brief description of historical and operational science can be found in an excellent resource, John Byl and Tom Goss, *How Should Christians Approach Origins?* (Winnipeg, MB: Word Alive Press, 2015), 5–6, freely available at reformedperspective.ca.

current fruits of scientific research have demonstrated the greatness and glory of the Creator who made all things in such a way that even today with our advanced technology we only keep discovering more and more of the complex workings of his handiwork, from the smallest molecule and cell, to the enormous expanses of space.[33]

In Conclusion

As the Belgic Confession so clearly states in summarizing biblical truth, general revelation, the created world, allows us "to perceive clearly God's *invisible attributes, namely, his eternal power and divine nature*, as the apostle Paul says in Romans 1:20."[34] God is revealed in general revelation. When we speak of revelation from creation, then the Creator is the one who reveals himself in his greatness. His "fingerprints" are, so to speak, everywhere. Who else, for example, could have created the human brain with its incredibly complex neural networks with each of the 86 billion neurons being highly complicated information processing structures?[35] His power as revealed in storms, earthquakes, and other natural disasters is awesome (Judg 5:4 Ps 29; Nahum 1:4–5). He determines the pandemics (2 Chron 7:13). As we have seen, these are all events according to his command and will. We cannot order these events. Only God is sovereign.

There is a tragic irony in the fact that mainstream secular science studies God's handiwork in creation, but refuses to acknowledge the Creator. Working scientifically is for many by definition to ignore the One who has designed and made all things. However, the general revelation in the created world does reveal God and his greatness and to ignore him as a scientist is inexcusable and serious. "For the wrath of God is revealed from heaven against all ungodliness and unrighteousness of men, who by their unrighteousness suppress the truth. For what can be known about God is plain to them, because God has shown it to them. For his invisible

---

33 For more on the nature and limitations of science, see Van Dam, *In the Beginning*, 46–58.
34 Art. 2, *Book of Praise*, 499 (italics are original).
35 Cf. the report of A. Whitten, "How Computationally Complex is a Single Neuron?" mentioned in *Creation* 44, no. 1 (2022): 7.

attributes, namely, his eternal power and divine nature, have been clearly perceived, ever since the creation of the world, in the things that have been made. So they are without excuse" (Rom 1:18–20).

But God provides a way out for those who want to know him beyond what is revealed in creation. As the Belgic Confession states: God "makes himself more clearly and fully known to us by his holy and divine Word as far as is necessary for us in this life, to his glory and our salvation."[36] Scripture gives us all the information we need in order to know God as fully and clearly as is necessary. God's Word also gives us the necessary information to see the issues clearly with respect to what the Bible reveals as true and what limitations science has in affirming what is fact and not theory. Science does not give new divine revelation. We need to keep the distinctions clearly before us. The Psalmist said it well. "In your light, do we see light" (Ps 36:9).

---

36 Art. 2, *Book of Praise*, 499–500.

CHAPTER 8

A Lesson from Galileo's Trial

Some time ago someone wrote me expressing the hope that it would not take the church hundreds of years to catch up with science in the case of evolution as it did with Galileo with his view that the earth circled the sun. The name of Galileo is brought up more often when one argues that the church should accept evolutionary teachings on the origin of the human race and so avoid future embarrassment.

The background to mentioning Galileo is that in 1616, and again in 1633, the Roman Catholic Church condemned Galileo's view of an earth in motion. It was generally accepted that the earth had a fixed unmoving position and that the sun was the body which moved. However, eventually in 1992 the Roman Catholic Church acknowledged that Galileo had not been dealt with justly and restored his reputation.[1] So, the moral of this history is supposed to be that the church should not prevent science from doing its work. Rather, churches should take scientific findings seriously. Today that means that one ought to accept evolution because science has determined that this is how mankind was placed on earth.

But is this really the lesson of Galileo's trial? This famous dispute has spawned an unbelievable amount of scholarly literature and the topic still remains contentious. But what can Reformed believers learn from the events surrounding Galileo?

---

1 For some background on the 1992 papal action, see Michael Segre, "Light on the Galileo Case?" *Isis* 88 (1997): 484–504.

What Was the Issue?

The confrontation between Galileo (1564–1642), a scientist, and the Roman Catholic Church is often pictured as a conflict between inquisitive reason and the dogma of a narrow-minded church, or between current science and faith in an outdated book. It was, however, not quite that simple and there are good reasons to challenge this sort of understanding. As a Counter-Reformation Roman Catholic, Galileo probably took Scripture seriously and did not want to be seen as contradicting God's Word.[2] Furthermore, he was well regarded by the church and initially had the support of influential clergy for his scientific views. As a matter of fact, challenging the idea that the earth was at the center of the universe had already begun prior to Galileo's time.[3] What was it then that triggered this enormous conflict? A fact that needs to be highlighted is that the Roman Catholic Church did not begin the confrontation with Galileo. That was done by the academics at the universities. They did not want to hear of the latest discoveries. There was an academic inertia coupled with the fear that their edifice of astronomical learning, painstakingly put together over many years, might collapse.[4] The tension was further aggravated by Galileo's difficult character and his not being able to give sufficient proof for his ideas. Added to the mix were church politics and personal jealousies.

At the heart of the conflict was Galileo's challenge to the reigning Aristotelian worldview which had the earth at the center of the universe with the moon, sun, and planets revolving around it. He proposed and defended the notion, as Copernicus had done in 1543 in Latin,[5] that the sun and not the earth was at the universe's physical center. Galileo,

---

2   Richard J. Blackwell, *Galileo, Bellarmine, and the Bible* (Notre Dame, IN: University of Notre Dame Press, 1991), 81–82.
3   Arthur C. Custance, *Science and Faith*, Doorway Papers, vol. VIII (Grand Rapids, MI: Zondervan, 1978), 154; Arthur Koestler, *The Sleepwalkers: A History of Man's Changing Vision of the Universe* (New York, NY: Penguin, 1984), 362–63, 432–33.
4   Koestler, *The Sleepwalkers*, 433.
5   *De revolutionibus orbium celestium*, in an English edition as Nicolaus Copernicus, *On the Revolutions of the Heavenly Spheres*, trans. Charles Glenn Wallis, (Amherst, NY: Prometheus, 1995).

however, issued his challenge in the language of the people, Italian, and not in scholarly Latin, thereby setting his views before a very wide audience.[6] This angered the academics who wanted to maintain the Aristotelian cosmology. These people urged the ecclesiastical authorities to intervene. They did. Eventually, on March 5, 1616, the Congregation of the Index published a decree condemning Copernicanism without mentioning Galileo, apparently to allow Galileo's loyalty and obedience to the church to be tested. Pope Paul V had asked Cardinal Bellarmine to urge Galileo to drop his commitment to Copernicanism and to obey the church. He did not do so. Eventually, in 1633 Galileo was called to stand trial for disobedience and was found guilty.[7]

Rome took the challenge presented by Galileo's ideas very seriously. For centuries the Roman Catholic Church had embraced Aristotelianism in its dogma and it decided that it could not tolerate any questions or doubts about it. One needs to remember that at the time the authority of Rome was also under considerable pressure from the Reformation and any further perception of its authority being undermined was not to be tolerated. Scholars have suggested that at the center of the conflict was the fact that Galileo's views contradicted Scripture. In 1616, this was only partly true, but in 1633 there was little mention of the Bible. It was then a matter of Galileo not obeying the 1616 Decree. The underlying problem was that Galileo's views did not square with biblical interpretation as that was done according to Aristotelian principles. It is striking that the views of Galileo were officially censured and condemned in the first place on the basis of their being incompatible with Aristotelian philosophy and in the second place for contradicting Scripture. Galileo was opposing the reigning Aristotelian worldview as that was also articulated in biblical exegesis.[8]

---

6   *Dialogo sopra i due massimi sistemi del mondo* (1632), in an English edition as Galileo Galilei, *Dialogue Concerning the Two Chief World Systems—Ptolemaic & Copernican*, 2nd ed., trans. Stillman Drake, foreword by Albert Einstein (Berkeley, CA: University of California Press, 1967).
7   Blackwell, *Galileo, Bellarmine, and the Bible*, 59–82, 112–34; John C. Lennox, *God's Undertaker: Has Science Buried God?* (Oxford, UK: Lion, 2009), 24–26.
8   Blackwell, *Galileo, Bellarmine, and the Bible*, 120, 130–31; also see John Hedley Brooke, *Science and Religion: Some Historical Perspectives, Cambridge History of Science* (Cambridge, UK: Cambridge University Press, 1991), 37–38, 101–2.

So the trial of Galileo was at bottom a clash between an Aristotelian worldview that was not Christian but championed by the scientific establishment as well as by the Roman Catholic Church, and a scientist who on the basis of his observations and experiments proposed a different view of reality.[9] Galileo was convinced that his ideas could be interpreted as being in harmony with Scripture.[10] The church, however, disagreed and tried to retain the geocentric Aristotelian worldview by all the means at its disposal, including banning books it considered dangerous and prosecuting "heretical" teachers. It was a conflict between worldviews and not a struggle between science and the biblical faith.[11]

The Situation Today

In one way the situation today is very similar to that of Galileo's time. The reigning scientific paradigm today is the theory of evolution. Mainstream evolutionary science today is just as intolerant as Aristotelian science was in Galileo's day. It uses every means at its disposal, especially public education on all levels as well as mainstream media, to maintain its hegemony. Those who think differently and want to break out of the evolutionist model of science find themselves under attack, marginalized, and generally not taken seriously by evolutionists. It does not matter

---

9 The opposition to Galileo "had its roots in the hostility of the Aristotelians, and in a sense it was more for contradicting Aristotle than for contradicting the Bible that he was persecuted." R. J. P. Acworth, "Galileo," in *The Encyclopedia of Christianity*, eds. Edwin H. Palmer, Gary C. Cohen, and Philip E. Hughes (Marshallton, DE: National Foundation for Christian Education, 1964–72), 4:295.

10 We cannot enter here into a discussion of the different and sometimes contradictory aspects of how Galileo understood Scripture. For Galileo's views, see Maurice A. Finocchiaro, "The Biblical Argument Against Copernicism and the Limitation of Biblical Authority," in *Nature and Scripture in the Abrahamic Religions: Up to 1700*, vol. 37.2, ed. Jitse M. van der Meer and Scott Mandelbrote, Brill's Series in Church History 36 (Leiden, NL: Brill, 2008), 640–49; Charles E. Hummel, *The Galileo Connection: Resolving Conflicts Between Science and the Bible* (Downers Grove, IL: InterVarsity Press, 1986), 104–8; R. Hooykaas, *Religion and the Rise of Modern Science* (Grand Rapids, MI: Eerdmans, 1972), 124–26.

11 Reformed theology recognizes that Copernicanism or a geocentric cosmology is not against Scripture. See, e.g., Bavinck, *Reformed Dogmatics*, 2:484; Joel Beeke and Paul M. Smalley, *Reformed Systematic Theology* (Wheaton, IL: Crossway, 2019), 1:226; cf. John Byl, *God and the Cosmos: A Christian View of Time, Space, and the Universe* (Edinburgh, UK: Banner of Truth, 2001), 27–35.

whether one is a Christian who accepts the plain sense of Genesis 1 and 2 or an agnostic holder to Intelligent Design (ID); they get the same basic cold shoulder from the scientific establishment. Scholars who oppose the majority view are not given the same intellectual freedom that their mainstream colleagues enjoy. Too much is at stake for those who have invested heavily in the current evolutionist scientific paradigm. Their worldview is at stake and so they are hostile to all who oppose the evolutionist framework that has been so carefully built up over the years.[12]

In another way, for Christians who reject the theory of evolution, the situation today is quite different from Galileo's time. Whereas the Roman Catholic Church in the days of Galileo supported the mainstream scientists and tried very hard to impose the reigning Aristotelian scientific paradigm on those who thought differently, today it is the mainstream scientists who are at the forefront of trying to impose their evolutionary worldview on conservative Christians, and through them on their churches. As Arthur Custance noted, modern evolutionary authorities "are behaving more like the church [of Galileo's time] than the church ever did! The new Faith [evolutionary philosophy] has its cardinals and its archbishops and its colleges; its creeds and its encyclicals; and its prerogative of 'appointment' and its powers to silence opponents." Better-known publishers are discouraged to publish books critical of the evolutionary faith in an attempt to suppress all criticism.[13] Like those opposed to Galileo, mainstream scientists today have little tolerance or patience with those who disagree with their entrenched position.

Any who challenge the current scientific status quo, whether one is a creationist scientist or a promoter of Intelligent Design, is essentially condemned or shamed for being behind the times and for not acknowledging the so-called indisputable findings supporting evolutionary theory. Biologos, an influential Christian organization composed of scientists and biblical scholars, even makes it its mission to attempt in all sorts of ways to convince conservative Christians to embrace the evolution narrative of

---

12 See, e.g., a list of examples in "Discrimination against Creation Scienists (and ID Advocates)" at https://creation.com/discrimination-against-creation-scientists. The lack of fairness has led creationist scientists to set up their own scientific journals. Andrew S. Kulikovsky, "Creationism, Science and Peer Review," *Journal of Creation* 22 (2008): 44–49.
13 Custance, *Science and Faith*, 159–60.

earth's beginnings.[14] This insistence on maintaining the reigning scientific paradigm is just as reactionary as was the desire to retain the Aristotelian paradigm in Galileo's day. Mainstream scientists and organizations like Biologos should be encouraging scientists to think outside the current evolutionist box with its many problems and assist those who, like creationist scientists, try to do science in keeping with biblical truth and principles.[15]

In any case, to sum up this section, it is obvious that to say that the Galileo event of the seventeenth century teaches us today that the church should let science do its work is far off the mark. It was not the church in the first place but establishment science that was upset with Galileo's work and tried to suppress it. Today, it is not the church that is holding up scientific research, it is once again the scientific establishment.

The Question of Proof

An ongoing challenge for Galileo was to prove to his detractors that earth was actually moving around the sun. Prior to the condemnation of Copernicanism, he tried very hard to come up with such proof. According to the Aristotelian model of scholarship, science had to be completely sure about a matter for it to be counted as a scientific fact. In other words, proof meant absolute proof with no uncertainty. An attractive theory that seemed to meet the required criteria was not good enough (unlike evolutionary theory which is often in practice treated as factual).[16] Due to the nature of the case, an *absolute* proof for the position that either the sun or the earth is the fixed center of our universe is impossible. One

---

14 "Biologos invites the church and the world to see the harmony between science and biblical faith as we present an evolutionary understanding of God's creation." https://biologos.org/about-us/what-we-believe.
15 Critical problems for the theory of evolution are highlighted in resources such as: Douglas Axe, *Undeniable: How Biology Confirms Our Intuition That Life is Designed* (San Francisco, CA: HarperOne, 2016); J. P. Moreland, et al., *Theistic Evolution: A Scientific, Philosophical, and Theological Critique*, foreword by Steve Fuller (Wheaton, IL: Crossway, 2017); ed. Norman C. Nevin, *Should Christians Embrace Evolution? Biblical and Scientific Responses* (Nottingham, UK: Inter-Varsity Press, 2009).
16 Blackwell, *Galileo, Bellarmine, and the Bible*, 80–81, 107, 125.

would have to stand outside the universe on an absolutely fixed point of reference to observe whether the one or the other is a fact. On a scientific level the issue is ultimately rather inconsequential. For practical reasons, astronomers today also use the earth as their center of reference.[17]

Today, the dominant scientific paradigm is evolution. It too cannot be established as being true. The theory of evolution purports to deal with origins and how the present world came to be. But when it comes to trying to prove evolution, science really is in an area outside its competence. Science can speculate but it can never prove anything with regards to origins. More modesty as to what is certain would be appropriate. It is therefore a sad day when Christians are seeking to impose an evolutionist paradigm of origins on the opening chapters of Genesis. Speculative human ideas are forced on the clear authoritative Word of God to try to make it say what today's scientific paradigm wants to hear. This is not how to interpret Scripture. Let us rather celebrate the fact that God has told us how the heavens and the earth were created and encourage scientists to work on that basis. It is an incredible gift of God that he has told us in his Word what science can never reveal.

In Conclusion

One cannot appeal to the Galileo trial in order to urge the church to be more accepting of science. To the contrary, the trial showed how the church abused its position by forcing Galileo to agree to the reigning scientific paradigm so that he was compelled to recant and disown his views. The Galileo trial highlights an ecclesiastical intolerance that sought to impose a worldview that had its roots in pagan thinking and as such had no biblical warrant. The trial provides no rationale for the church to cave in to the current evolutionary consensus and so be "up to date." The church at the time was "up to date" to its shame by embracing the reigning Aristotelian scientific paradigm and interpreting God's Word through that lens.

---

17 For helpful observations on proof and geocentricity, see Byl, *God and the Cosmos*, 29–31, 180–81, 202–4.

The trial of Galileo does underline the need to work carefully with the Word of God so that scientific theories and worldviews foreign to Scripture are not imposed on it. That mistake is being repeated today, especially by those who interpret Scripture with an eye to making it compatible with the reigning evolutionistic paradigm. When the next revolution of scientific thinking occurs, their exegesis will have to be rewritten, just as the Aristotelian exegesis of the time subsequent to Galileo had to be redone. Any interpreter of Scripture is influenced by his own context and is as such a child of his times. But every precaution must be taken so that as much as possible the Word speaks for itself.

Given the nature of Scripture and its Author, we need to accept its plain and obvious meaning. We must also let the Word interpret itself. If the meaning of a text seems to be unclear, its meaning must be sought by comparing it with other biblical passages that deal with the same subject. Our understanding of the Bible must never be forced by the artificial constraints of an unproven scientific theory. God is an excellent communicator and he has clearly set forth how he created the world and sovereignly rules all creation. We must accept his Word in true faith.

CHAPTER 9

Faith and Reason

How do faith and reason relate to each other? The Lord our God has created us as rational beings who raise questions and want to think logically in all areas of life. At the same time we are to be as children, who accept on faith what he tells us in his Word. How do the two interact?

This is not a new issue. As a matter of fact it is one that has kept thinking Christians and scholars busy for hundreds of years. In the context of a single chapter, we will have to be very selective in addressing this issue. To set the stage, we will first look at a concrete historical example, namely, the situation in which Luther found himself as he struggled with this question. Using that as a springboard, we will move directly into our times and note the main answers that are being given today. After that we will try to set forth the position that seems to be most in accord with the Scriptures.

Luther's Ninety-Seven Theses

Luther is well known for his Ninety-Five Theses, those famous propositions against indulgences that were being marketed throughout Germany in his day. Tetzel, a prominent salesman, would assure buyers of an indulgence that "as soon as a coin in the coffer rings, a soul from purgatory springs."[1] In protest against this practice, Luther wrote his

---

1 Herman Selderhuis, *Martin Luther: A Spiritual Journey* (Wheaton, IL: Crossway, 2017), 96. The Ninety-Five Theses can be found in Luther, Martin, *Luther's Works*, ed. Jaroslav Pelikan, et al. (Saint Louis, MO: Concordia, 1955–2016), 31:17–33.

Ninety-Five Theses. Their publication on October 31, 1517, is widely considered the beginning of the Reformation. However, in the same year prior to composing these propositions, Luther also made available for public discussion his lesser-known Ninety-Seven Theses or Disputation against Scholastic Theology.[2]

These propositions were directed against scholasticism especially as seen in theology. The scholastic method was based on the application of techniques of logic. By reasoning and differentiating logically, one distinguished between different meanings of words and pronouncements and so answered questions and bridged apparent contradictions. In all of this, the philosophy of Aristotle (died 322 BC) was the highest authority. It should be noted that this scholastic method and the use of pagan philosophy meant that some of the presuppositions of Aristotle, such as the basic goodness of man, were imported into theology. Also, the dominant use of logic and pagan philosophy necessitated the presupposition that human reason is autonomous and can of its own accord come to knowledge and insight and does not need the illumination of the Holy Spirit. After all, how else could non-Christians have come to such wisdom and insight?[3] In discussing these issues later in correspondence with his former teacher, Jodocus Trutvetter, and his friend, George Spalatin, Luther pleaded for the eradicating of all reliance on reason and logic from the church, otherwise the reformation of the church would be impossible. After all, the human reason is an abyss of darkness and Christ is the true and only light.[4]

To appreciate Luther's vehemence against the use of logic in theology, one must realize the context from which he was speaking. He noted that already for 300 years the church had been subjected to the devastating

---

2   These theses can be found in Luther, *Luther's Works*, 31:9–16. According to Selderhuis, scholars now think there were ninety-nine theses. Selderhuis, *Martin Luther*, 91.
3   H.N. Hagoort, *Wijsheid van het vlees: over 97 onbekende stellingen van Maarten Luther* (Gouda, NL: Reformatorisch Instituut voor Cultuurwetenschappen, 1992), 12.
4   These sentiments were expressed in his letter (May 9, 1518) to Jodocus Trutvetter, Martin Luther, *D. Martin Luthers Werke: Kritische Gesamtausgabe: Briefwechsel*, ed. Ulrich Köpf (Weimar, DE: Hermann Böhlau Nachfolger, 1930), 1:170 (also see Luther, *Luther's Works*, 48:36–38) and in letters to George Spalatin, dated February 22 and May 18, 1518, Luther, *Luther's Works*, 48:57–59, 62; Hagoort, *Wijsheid van het vlees*, 18–19.

influence of scholasticism.[5] What was Luther referring to? He was referring to the Latin translations of the writings of the great Arabic Islamic scholar Averroes (died 1198) who had a tremendous influence in Christian Europe. Averroes believed that all truth was logical (i.e. as found in Aristotle), although he went beyond Aristotle in his use of logic. He even went as far as saying that no absolute truth could be found in any sort of revelation which for him was the Quran and for Christians, who adopted his philosophy, it was the Bible.[6]

At the same time, Averroes believed that the use of logic would lead to a harmony between religious faith and philosophical reason. The title of his most influential book is thus *The Agreement of Religion and Philosophy*. It is significant that in it he distinguished between the common people and the scholars or philosophers. The common people are more endowed with imagination than reason and they are addressed accordingly by the Quran. They believe because their feelings are stirred by the image of the truth that the Quran presents. These people are not touched by rational arguments for they cannot understand them. It is here where religion has its place. "Religion and Revelation are nothing but philosophical truth made acceptable to men whose imagination is stronger than their reason."[7] These common people can only believe. A second class of people needs to be assured that their believing what the Quran says is not against reason or verified scientific knowledge. Theology will assure them of that. It is easy to find reasons in favor of what we already believe.[8] A third group, the highest in the view of Averroes, are the philosophers and scholars. They will only accept what is consistently logical and reasonable. They can often go beyond the literal text of the Quran to the real truth by the use of logic. They should, however, not confront the simple people with this, but keep it to themselves. After all, the simple folk do not have the intellectual capacity for this and must do with the literal meaning of the

---

5   In his "Answer to the Dialog of Sylvester Prierias concerning the Power of the Pope" in Martin Luther, *D. Martin Luthers Werke: Kritische Gesamtsausgabe*, ed. Ulrich Köpf (Weimar, DE: Hermann Böhlau, 1883), 1:677; similarly in his "The Babylonian Captivity of the Church" in Luther, *Luther's Works,* 36:31.
6   Hagoort, *Wijsheid van het vlees*, 24–25; Etienne Gilson, *Reason and Revelation in the Middle Ages* (New York, NY: Scribner's, 1938), 39–40.
7   Gilson, *Reason and Revelation*, 43, also see 37–42; Hagoort, *Wijsheid van het vlees*, 24–25.
8   Gilson, *Reason and Revelation*, 43–46.

text. In this way, by each approaching the text in a manner suited for their temperament and by each minding their own business and not trying to tell others how to understand the text, everyone was to be happy and agreement was found between theology and philosophy.[9]

Needless to say, this approach when applied by Muslims or Christian disciples of Averroes did gross injustice to the Quranic or biblical text as it had been received and generally understood. For example, Scripture speaks of creation. According to Averroes, the simple Christian believer had to stick to that and believe it. The intellectual person, however, knew better. The thirteenth century rational believer knew that the world in reality originated through an eternal chain of causation and thus was not created. Since the simple believers could not grasp this understanding, they had to stick with the literal text of Genesis and believe in God's work of creation. Thus the harmony that Averroes proposed between faith and reason was basically a degradation of revelation to second rate knowledge.[10]

Not surprisingly there was official opposition to the approach of Averroes in Christian Europe, for not only was the truth of creation undermined, but many other biblical verities as well, such as the resurrection of the dead. Anything that could not be established by logic was suspect. The Bishop of Paris, Etienne Tempier, pushed back against this philosophy. He gathered Averroist statements, organized them into propositions, and solemnly condemned them in 1277. Such condemned statements included: "nothing should be believed, save only that which either is self-evident, or can be deduced from self-evident propositions" (Prop. 37); "theology rests upon fables" (Prop. 152); "one knows nothing more for knowing theology" (Prop. 153); "there are no wisdoms in the world except that of the philosophers" (Prop. 154); and "Christian Revelation is an obstacle to learning" (Prop. 175). Even though these and similar sentiments were officially condemned, the attraction of using logic and reason alone was so enticing that Christian theology was deeply influenced by it from the 13th century on.[11]

---

9   Gilson, *Reason and Revelation*, 45–49; Hagoort, *Wijsheid van het vlees*, 25.
10 Hagoort, *Wijsheid van het vlees*, 25–26.
11 Gilson, *Reason and Revelation*, 64–66; Hagoort, *Wijsheid van het vlees*, 27–31.

Thomas Aquinas (1224-1274) tried to counter the thinking of Averroes with the use of logic and not by turning to God's revelation. "We have written to destroy the error mentioned, using the arguments and teachings of the philosophers themselves, not the documents of faith."[12] But this approach was of no avail. Aquinas had sought a solution by making a separation between the things of God and the things of nature. However, truth is one; but the method of Aquinas assumed two kinds of truth. As Etienne Gilson has helpfully analyzed the thinking of Aquinas:

> To have faith is to assent to something because it is revealed by God. And now, what is it to have science? It is to assent to something which we perceive as true in the natural light of reason. ... I know by reason that something is true because *I see* that it is true; but I believe that something is true because *God has said it*. In these two cases the cause of my assent is specifically different, consequently science and faith should be held as two specifically different kinds of assent.
>
> If they are two distinct species of knowledge, we should never ask one of them to fulfill what is the proper function of the other.[13]

In this way Aquinas wanted to avoid all conflict. Revelation, which is accepted on faith because we cannot logically assent to it, is to be kept separate from scientific knowledge for which we do not need faith to assent to because we see that it is reasonable.[14]

The approach of Aquinas by which reality is split into two parts did not solve the issues raised by Averroes. Aquinas's efforts to oppose Averroes failed because he went into the confrontation accepting a basic presupposition of his opponent, namely, that there are two kinds of truth. As Gilson noted, the "Averroists were actually teaching a doctrine of two-fold truth; they were maintaining as simultaneously true two sets of contradictory propositions."[15]

---

12 Ralph M. McInerny, *Aquinas Against the Averroists: On There Being Only One Intellect* (West Lafayette, IN: Purdue University Press, 1993), 145 (= De unitate intellectus contra Averroistas", V.124).
13 Gilson, *Reason and Revelation*, 72–73.
14 Gilson, *Reason and Revelation*, 73–74.
15 Gilson, *Reason and Revelation*, 81.

The notion of a divided concept of truth is still with us today. Also in much current thinking, the truths of faith and religion are to be kept separate from scientifically verifiable truths. The net effect is that the assertions of faith and religion have nothing to do with what is considered to be the objective knowledge of science. In this way biblical truth has been marginalized and made irrelevant. To somehow make biblical truth relevant has for many meant trying to harmonize the clear statements of God's Word that contradict current scientific theory with human scientific insight. Often the net result is that the obvious teaching of Scripture is sacrificed for human wisdom and understanding as established by scientific methods. This approach has had a huge impact on how issues ranging from scientific ones like the origin of the earth to moral ones such as what constitutes marriage are viewed. The net result is that the wisdom of Scripture is jettisoned in favor of the current insights of the human scientific mind. Ultimately the concept of a divided truth means that very little of the Bible can be accepted or believed because what is true needs to be justified by natural reason and scientific findings as currently understood.[16]

As a result of the Averroist teaching of twofold truth and the inability of human reason alone to attain much biblical truth, there was a growing mistrust of philosophy during the Middle Ages. The list of truths revealed in the Bible that could be believed on the basis of rational proof shrunk to nothing. Philosophical reason cannot prove biblical truth. It needs to be believed, such as the immortality of the soul and the final judgment. So why should believers bother with philosophy that could not harmonize biblical revelation with itself? And so by the end of the fifteenth century, despair and reaction against scholasticism set in. Within this context, one gets a deeper appreciation why Luther hated scholasticism so fervently.[17]

For Luther, logic and rationality as derived from Aristotle was the source of all heresy. His Ninety-Seven Theses are to the point. Says Luther: "the

---

16 One can think, e.g., how the Genesis creation account is being understood through an evolutionist lens and how biblical sexual morals are reinterpreted to agree with current mainstream views which are supposedly based on science. See, e.g., Nancy Pearcey, *Total Truth: Liberating Christianity from Its Cultural Captivity*, Study Guide ed., foreword by Phillip E. Johnson (Wheaton, IL: Crossway, 2005), 20–24.
17 Gilson, *Reason and Revelation*, 81–94.

whole Aristotle is to theology as darkness is to light. This in opposition to scholastics."[18] Luther stressed that logical thinking is wisdom of the flesh and that if one studied Scripture depending only on reason then one would be following the wisdom of the flesh. The illumination of the Spirit is needed. As he wrote to George Spalatin: "there is no one who can teach the divine words except he who is their author, as he says, 'They shall all be taught by God.' [John 6:45] You must therefore completely despair of your own diligence and intelligence and rely solely on the infusion of the Spirit. Believe me, for I have had experience in this matter."[19] So passionate was Luther about the great danger of this use of reason in the church that in a sermon on Romans 12:3 he even called reason "the bride of the devil." Listen to parts of that sermon.

> So there must be preaching and everyone must also take care that his own reason may not lead him astray. ... The fanatics want to master both the Scriptures and faith by their own wisdom, and they perpetrate heresy. ... Usury, gluttony, adultery, manslaughter, murder, etc., these can be seen and the world understands that these are sins. But the devil's bride, reason, the lovely whore comes in and wants to be wise, and what she says, she thinks, is the Holy Spirit. Who can be of any help then? Neither jurist, physician, nor king, nor emperor; for she is the foremost whore the devil has. The other gross sins can be seen, but nobody can control reason. ... As a young man must resist lust and an old man avarice, so reason is by nature a harmful whore. But she shall not harm me, if only I resist her. ... Therefore, see to it that you hold reason in check and do not follow her beautiful cogitations. Throw dirt in her face and make her ugly. ... Trample reason and its wisdom underfoot and say, "you cursed whore, shut up! Are you trying to seduce me into committing fornication with the devil?" That's the way reason is purged and made free through the Word of the Son of God. ... This struggle will go on till the last day. This is what Paul wants; we are to quench not only the low desires but also

---

18 Luther, *Luther's Works*, 31:12 (thesis 50).
19 Luther, *Luther's Works*, 48:54; for more on the need of the Spirit, see A. Skevington Wood, *Luther's Principles of Biblical Interpretation* (London, UK: Tyndale Press, 1960), 13–17.

the high desires, reason and its high wisdom. When whoredom invades you, strike it dead, but do this far more when spiritual whoredom tempts you. ... Take heed to yourselves. Hereto you have heard the real, true Word, now beware of your own thoughts and your own wisdom. The devil will kindle the light of reason and rob you of your faith.[20]

Parts of this sermon can raise questions. Granted that too much reliance on reason is no good, but is there no place for one's use of rational gifts and intellect when reading and studying Scripture? What *are* the limits in the use of one's rational gifts? What is the relationship between faith and reason? How do we retain the use of logic and reason while insisting on the uniqueness of Scripture and the need for faith? In beginning to answer that question, it may be helpful to consider in very brief and simple terms three influential current streams of thought: fideism, the historical-critical approach, and evidentialism.

Three Approaches

Fideism

For our purposes, fideism can be understood as excluding the use of reason and relying on faith alone to seek truth. In this approach there is a deep-seated mistrust and disparagement of reason. Faith is a leap in the dark. "It is an act of trust in God which goes beyond the evidence, and in some cases goes against the evidence."[21] Alvin Plantinga noted that according to extreme fideism "reason and faith *conflict* or *clash* on matters of religious importance; and when they do, faith is to be

---

20 Luther, *Luther's Works*, 51:373–77. In a similar vein Calvin wrote: "The light of reason differs little from darkness" (in his commentary on Eph 4:17) and "Men ... choose to seek their safety in hell itself, rather than in heaven, whenever they follow their own reason" (in his commentary on Gen 19:19). These and other quotations of Calvin on reason can be found in J. Graham Miller, *Calvin's Wisdom: An Anthology Arranged Alphabetically by a Grateful Reader* (Carlisle, PA: The Banner of Truth Trust, 1992), 279–80.
21 P. Helm, "Faith and Reason," in *New Dictionary of Theology*, eds. Sinclair B. Ferguson, David F. Wright, and J.I. Packer (Downers Grove, IL: InterVarsity Press, 1988), 248.

preferred and reason suppressed."[22] This understanding is associated with existentialism. Religious truth is what matters for faith. It is existential and outside rational investigation. Consistent fideism, therefore, denigrates and denies the value of reason and scholarship and amounts to a kind of irrationalism.[23]

In contrast to this type of thinking, Cornelius Van Til argued that reason and logic have their place as we use our minds to bring order into our understanding of what God has revealed. "As God created us in accordance with his absolute rationality, so there must be a rational relationship from us to God. Christianity is in the last analysis, not an absolute irrationalism but an absolute 'rationalism.'"[24] This understanding of the important place of reason is a great encouragement for scholarly research, also theologically. Reason can be used in faith in seeking to broaden one's knowledge in understanding God and his revelation.

Not surprisingly, therefore, J. Gresham Machen wrote vigorously against anti-intellectualism in his classic work, *What is Faith?* Machen made the point that faith involves a person as its object. You believe in the Father and the Son. But, "it is impossible to have faith in a person without having knowledge of the person; far from being contrasted with knowledge, faith is founded upon knowledge."[25] Machen then continued by showing that Scripture teaches that faith includes the assent to doctrine. The author of Hebrews said that "whoever would draw near to God must believe that he exists and that he rewards those who seek him" (Heb 11:6). It is impossible to have confidence or faith in God without also assenting to doctrine and the accepting of a proposition, in this case, "that he exists and that he rewards those who seek him." This is a telling blow against all anti-intellectual mysticism.[26] Faith includes knowledge. The Heidelberg Catechism correctly confesses that "true faith is a sure

---

22 Alvin Plantinga, "Reason and Belief in God," in *Faith and Rationality: Reason and Belief in God,* eds. Alvin Plantinga and Nicholas Wolterstorff (Notre Dame, IN: University of Notre Dame Press, 1983), 87.
23 Richard H. Popkins, "Fideism," in T*he Encyclopedia of Philosophy*, editor in chief Paul Edwards (New York, NY: Macmillan, 1967), 3:201.
24 Cornelius Van Til, *The Defense of the Faith*, 4th ed., ed. K. Scott Oliphint (Philadelphia, PA: P&R Publishing, 2008), 64.
25 J. Gresham Machen, *What is Faith?* (Grand Rapids, MI: Eerdmans, 1962), 46.
26 Machen, *What is Faith?* 47–50.

knowledge whereby I accept as true all that God has revealed to us in his Word" along with also being a "firm confidence."[27]

How does faith involve the intellect? Before answering this question, let us first consider a movement in which no room is left for faith at all. The example will be taken from Biblical studies, namely the historical-critical approach. This is the current mainstream way of interpreting Scripture. It is taught or presupposed in virtually every secular institution of higher learning that offers courses dealing with the Bible.

The Historical-Critical Approach

According to this approach, Scripture must be scrutinized with the use of logic and reason to determine whether its claims are really true. The historical-critical approach does not accept the claims of Scripture on the basis of its authority as the Word of God. For example, the historicity of what is related in the Bible cannot be accepted at face value. One first has to determine whether the available evidence supports the notion that the events it recounts actually occurred. There is no room for faith. The historical-critical method results in a reconstructed Bible according to the canons of modern wisdom and logic. Nothing can be accepted on the basis of divine authority. This approach has enormous consequences in undermining the authority of Scripture. For example, according to this type of reasoning even the existence of Jesus as pictured in the gospels is questioned by those consistently faithful to the presuppositions of the historical-critical method. Indeed, the infamous Jesus Seminar (1985–2006) consisted of a group of scholars who were determined to find out what is or is not historical about Jesus. The result of their findings was that they rejected as myth the virgin birth, the miracles, and the resurrection of the Lord Jesus.[28] It is obvious that with the historical-critical approach there is no room for infallible revelation or faith in a trustworthy Word

---

27 Heidelberg Catechism, Q. & A. 21, *Book of Praise*, 523.
28 The official website is Jesus Seminar Forum at https://virtualreligion.net/forum/publish.html. A useful overview is found in "Jesus Seminar" in Wikipedia: https://en.wikipedia.org/wiki/Jesus_Seminar. For critical response see, e.g., Craig Evans, *Fabricating Jesus: How Modern Scholars Distort the Gospels* (Downers Grove, IL: InterVarsity Press, 2008) and Michael J. Wilkins and James Porter Moreland, eds., *Jesus Under Fire: Modern Scholarship Reinvents the Historical Jesus* (Grand Rapids, MI: Zondervan, 1995).

of God. This way of using reason without any place for faith must clearly be rejected.[29]

How then is faith to be integrated? This question brings us to evidentialism.

Evidentialism

Within the context of this chapter, evidentialism can be understood as holding that a belief in God and his Word is justified only if there is sufficient evidence for that belief. To state it differently, according to evidentialism you should not believe anything that is not supported or supportable by sufficient evidence.[30] This approach is very popular among conservative Christians. For example, Werner Keller's book, *The Bible as History*, in print since 1956, has sold more than ten million copies and remains popular. The point of the book is that all kinds of discoveries confirm that the Bible is true after all. The implication is that you can believe what it says.[31] Josh McDowell, an influential apologist and popular speaker, has defended Scripture on campuses and throughout the world using the evidential method. His many books have had and continue to have an enormous impact. There is much of value in his writing and if used properly gives much helpful material.[32] But, the evidential starting point is wrong.

This approach gives a normative function to the intellect. According to this view, it is basically our intellect that vindicates Scripture and makes the Bible acceptable. It is reason that ultimately saves you and not the

---

[29] For more on this approach, as well as resources, see, e.g., Richard N. Soulen and R. Kendall Soulen, *Handbook of Biblical Criticism*, edition no. 3, rev. and expanded (Louisville, KY: Westminster John Knox, 2001), 78–80; for critique see, e.g., Gerhard Maier, *The End of the Historical-Critical Method*, trans. Edwin W. Leverenz and Rudolph F. Norden, reprint, 1977 (Eugene, OR: Wipf and Stock, 2001) and Eta Linnemann, *Historical Criticism of the Bible: Methodology or Ideology?* trans. Robert W. Yarbrough, reprint, 1990 (Grand Rapids, MI: Kregel, 2001).

[30] K. Scott Oliphint, *Covenantal Apologetics*, forward by William Edgar (Wheaton, IL: Crossway, 2013), 113.

[31] Werner Keller, *The Bible as History*, 2nd revised ed., trans. William Neil, rev. Joachim Rehork and B. H. Rasmussen (New York, NY: William Morrow, 2015).

[32] His research culminating in his *Evidence that Demands a Verdict* books has been influential for over 40 years. This material has been updated, revised, expanded and co-authored with his son and is now available as Josh McDowell and Sean McDowell, *Evidence That Demands a Verdict: Life-Changing Truth for a Skeptical World* (Nashville, TN: Thomas Nelson, 2017).

Holy Spirit working through the self-authenticating Word. In a sense, the salvation of unbelievers depends on how well one has managed to present the truth rationally to them so that they can accept it. But, such a rationale for evangelizing is not biblical. With the fall into sin the human mind is incapable of receiving the truth of God's Word. Unbelievers are "darkened in their understanding, alienated from the life of God because of the ignorance that is in them, due to their hardness of heart" (Eph 4:18). According to evidentialism, also the believer only really prospers in his faith if the Bible can be proven again and again with rational arguments that the Word is true and that the heresies of the day are false. While this approach is to be rejected, it is beneficial to note the presence of evidence that supports the biblical account.

Although we must always begin with accepting in faith the Scriptures as the Word of God, embracing the Word in faith does not mean that we cannot use our powers of reason and any available evidence to defend the Bible. Happily this is being done by very capable and gifted scholars who rise to the challenge of current skepticism.[33] But why, when so much incontrovertible evidence is set before doubters of the veracity of Scripture, do they not believe and accept the Word and what it clearly states? The point is that you cannot make someone believe Scripture by means of visible proofs and logical reasoning. To be sure, our faith can be defended by the use of reason. Faith seeks understanding. God's Word is not irrational. We have a "reasonable faith" to quote the well-known title of a book by dogmatician Herman Bavinck.[34] However, you cannot make someone a believer by rational arguments.

This inability of proofs of the Bible's trustworthiness to convert someone to a true faith reminds us of the parable of the rich man and Lazarus. When they died, Lazarus went to Abraham's bosom, but the rich man went to Hades where he was in torment. Wanting to spare his brothers

---

33 See, e.g., the evidence presented in: K. A. Kitchen, *On the Reliability of the Old Testament* (Grand Rapids, NY: Eerdmans, 2003) and Craig L. Blomberg, *The Historical Reliability of the New Testament: Countering the Challenges to Evangelical Christian Beliefs* (Nashville, TN: B&H Academic, 2016).

34 Herman Bavinck, Our Reasonable Faith, trans. Henry Zylstra (Grand Rapids, MI: Baker, 1977; 1st publ. 1956); reissued as Herman Bavinck, *The Wonderful Works of God: Instruction in the Christian Religion According to the Reformed Confession*, foreword Herman Bavinck, trans. Henry Zylstra, intro. R. Carlton Wynne (Glenside, PA: Westminster Seminary Press, 2019; 1st publ. 1956).

the same fate, the rich man asked father Abraham to send Lazarus to warn them. But "Abraham replied, 'They have Moses and the Prophets; let them listen to them.'" The rich man, however, answered: "No, father Abraham, but if someone from the dead goes to them, they will repent." Noteworthy is what Abraham then replied: "If they do not listen to Moses and the Prophets, they will not be convinced even if someone rises from the dead" (Luke 16:29–31 NIV84). Not even a miracle as proof will make someone take Scripture seriously. Faith in God's Word is what is needed in the first place.

Thus, while there are good elements in the evidential approach, such as making one aware of the available indicators that support the claims of Scripture, this approach as a way of validating the claims of Scripture must be rejected. It places reason and logic on a pedestal where they do not belong.

How then shall we approach this whole topic of the relationship of faith and reason? What is the biblical way? An answer to this question must be molded and shaped by the Word of God.

A Reformed Understanding: Van Til's Contribution

When attempting to solve a problem, you need a point of orientation. Without such an unmoving point of reference you can easily get lost and disorientated. In our problem of how to relate reason to faith and vice versa our point of reference and our beginning point must be God. After all he has made us and he has given to us our ability to reason. He is the Creator and we are his creatures.

The Starting Point

In the debate on the relationship of faith and reason, one of the main difficulties is that of epistemology, the nature and grounds of knowledge. How you can be sure of something and its factuality? It is the problem of what is true knowledge. The basic fact with which we must start all our reasoning and with which everyone must begin their thinking on this issue is the fact of God. He is; he exists, and everyone knows it. He does not have to be proven. He is there. Everyone is aware of it, also those who do not believe in God. We read in Paul's letter to the Romans:

> For the wrath of God is revealed from heaven against all ungodliness and unrighteousness of men, who by their unrighteousness suppress the truth. For what can be known about God is plain to them, because God has shown it to them. For his invisible attributes, namely, his eternal power and divine nature, have been clearly perceived, ever since the creation of the world, in the things that have been made. So they are without excuse. For although they knew God, they did not honor him as God or give thanks to him, but they became futile in their thinking, and their foolish hearts were darkened. Claiming to be wise, they became fools, and exchanged the glory of the immortal God for images resembling mortal man and birds and animals and creeping things." (Rom 1:18–23)

Cornelius Van Til rightly stressed that our basic presupposition, which we do not need to argue about with anyone, is the existence of God. His existence is the basis for all human activity, also human reason and logic. This fundamental fact does not need to be debated. It is known as true to all humanity, in spite of protestations to the contrary. Therefore, and this is a critical point, one does not argue and reason with all kinds of evidence *to* God (as if God and his Word are on trial before human reason), but one starts with God and explains all reality *from* him in the light of his revelation. Van Til can thus say that: "the Bible has much to say about the universe. But it is the business of science and philosophy to deal with this revelation. Indirectly even science and philosophy should be theological,"[35] that is, related to God.

"All disciplines must presuppose God" and so there can be no neutral investigation.[36] Indeed, Van Til correctly notes that without God we could not know anything. All creation and all facts and all rationality are

---

35 Van Til, *Systematic Theology*, 1.
36 Van Til, *Systematic Theology*, 3.

dependent on God.[37] That reality indicates that they are also dependent on God for their meaning and place. Indeed, the existence and meaning of every fact must in the last analysis be related to the self-conscious and eternally self-subsistent God of the Scriptures. He created and assigned each fact their place for his glory (cf. Rom 11:36; Rev 4:11). It is only because of God that there is coherence in facts and that theorizing is possible.[38] Thus, in our reasoning and investigations, we must realize that God comprehends fully. That is encouraging and "God's full comprehension gives validity to our partial comprehension."[39] We may not comprehend the atom. It is mysterious for us, but not for God.

Implications of this Starting Point

Starting with God and recognizing him as the basic presupposition for all our logic and reasoning has several implications. The first is that we do not try to prove God or his Word. In the twentieth century Van Til's presuppositional approach was not well received by the evangelical community and it still is not.[40] Why not? Because people were accustomed to arguing towards the existence of God and a trustworthy Bible. For example, they would say, God exists or the Bible is true because this or that is true. But such reasoning is starting at the wrong end. We need to begin from the presupposition of God's existence and the truthfulness of his Word.

In this connection it is helpful to listen to a 1977 *Christianity Today* interview by David Kucharsky with Van Til on this issue.

> Question: Dr. Van Til, how do you know that what you believe is true?
>
> Answer: I am sure of my faith because its source is the Bible, the revealed Word of God.

---

37 Van Til, *Systematic Theology*, 9–10.
38 Van Til, *Systematic Theology*, 22–23.
39 Van Til, *Systematic Theology*, 24.
40 This is also the case with R. C. Sproul who, although dedicating the following book to Van Til, remained critical of his apologetics: R. C. Sproul, John H. Gerstner, and Arthur Lindsley, *Classical Apologetics: A Rational Defense of the Christian Faith and a Critique of Presuppositional Apologetics* (Grand Rapids, MI: Zondervan, 1984). For a review and critique, see John M. Frame, *Apologetics: A Justification of Christian Belief*, ed. Joseph E. Torres (Phillipsburg, NJ: P&R Publishing, 2015), 219–38.

Q: But doesn't it then become necessary to establish that the Scriptures are true, and that they are as we know them indeed the Word of God?

A: The problem with that question is that it shifts the starting point. I concede that the truth of the Bible is a presupposition. My argument is simply that this presupposition is the only one from which a Christian can begin without surrendering the sovereignty of God.

Q: Are you saying that any kind of human test applied to God and his Word violates the concept of God?

A: That is my basic position.[41]

God and his existence do not depend on our logical adeptness; neither does the authority or trustworthiness of Scripture. The Scriptures are self-authenticating. As the Belgic Confession articulates this truth:

> We believe without any doubt all things contained in them [the Scriptures], not so much because the church receives and approves of them as such, but especially because the Holy Spirit witnesses in our hearts that they are from God and also because they contain the evidence of this in themselves; for even the blind are able to perceive that the things foretold in them are being fulfilled" (Art. 5).[42]

The point is clear. We do not need to prove God and his Word. The Spirit works the conviction in our hearts that the Scriptures are from God. Yet, the confession also speaks of evidence. This evidence needs to be understood as supporting and confirming the faith that God had already worked in our hearts. Not even the most dramatic evidence will work faith. As Christ said in his parable of the rich man and Lazarus: "If they

---

41 Cornelius Van Til, "At the Beginning, God: An Interview," *Christianity Today* 22, no. 6 (30 December 1977): 19; for an excellent introduction and overview of Van Til's thought, see Greg L. Bahnsen, Van Til's *Apologetic: Readings and Analysis* (Phillipsburg, NJ: P&R Publishing, 1998).

42 *Book of Praise*, 500; also see Cornelis Van Dam, "Why Do We Believe the Bible?" *Clarion* 54 (2005): 578–80.

do not listen to Moses and the Prophets, they will not be convinced even if someone rises from the dead" (Luke 16:31 NIV84).[43]

The second implication of starting with God and recognizing him as the basic presupposition for all our logic and reasoning is that we must be aware of our fallen state and depravity. According to our nature as conceived and born in sin, our minds and understanding have been darkened (cf. Eph 4:18). "The natural person does not accept the things of the Spirit of God." Why? Because "they are folly to him, and he is not able to understand them because they are spiritually discerned" (1 Cor 2:14). Now all this has a very important consequence; namely, that we cannot talk about reason in a neutral sort of way and ignore the difference between the reasoning of a Christian and a non-Christian. Van Til notes that we have to distinguish clearly and he describes three types of consciousness.[44]

The first is the Adamic consciousness or human reason as it existed before the fall into sin. This reason was derivative and its knowledge was true, but not exhaustive. This reason was not in enmity against God, but in covenant with him. Its function was to interpret God's revelation. Adam could name the animals according to their nature, that is, according to the place God had given them in his universe. Adam could converse truly about the meaning of the universe. He wanted to know the facts of creation to help him fulfill his task as a covenant-keeper.

The second is the sinful consciousness, that is, human reason as it became after the fall into sin. It is dead in trespasses and sins. The natural person wants to be as God, judging good and evil for himself and being his own standard and norm. He sets himself up as the ideal for a comprehensive knowledge of reality. Rejecting God and the fact that all reality finds its reason for existence in him, the non-regenerate person takes for granted that the meaning of the world and its parts is immanent in itself and that he is its ultimate interpreter. The natural person does not want to interpret God's thoughts after him according to his revelation.

---

[43] See also, e.g., P. Y. De Jong, *The Church's Witness to the World* (St. Catharines, ON: Paideia Press, 1980), 1:130–34.
[44] What follows is based on Van Til, *Systematic Theology*, 25–30.

At this point a question can be raised. Is it not so that the natural, unregenerate person with the use of his reason can nevertheless make much sense out of the world and has even made astounding discoveries? Indeed, this is the case. However, the following factors need to be kept in mind. The natural person is in absolute ethical antithesis to God. If he cannot know God truly, neither can he know his creation truly. All knowledge is interrelated. Thus, although he may know much about the atoms, or the flowers, or whatever, as long as he does not recognize the purposes of God in these phenomena, he cannot know these things in the right overall perspective. Do not all things hold together in Christ (Col 1:17)? Denying God means denying a vital part of the truth that needs to be taken into consideration in order to get a proper view of reality. At the same time one must acknowledge that humanity is nevertheless allowed to do much with the use of his reason, even though it is hostile to the Creator. Perhaps we can see in this reality something of the tremendous gift of being created as crown of creation. Even sin does not undo all the gifts which God has given humans in distinction from the animal world.[45]

Van Til once put the situation this way:

The ultimate source of truth in any field rests in him [Christ]. The world may discover much truth without owning Christ as Truth. Christ upholds even those who ignore, deny, and oppose him. A little child may slap his father in the face, but it can do so only because the father holds it on his knee. So modern science, modern philosophy, and modern theology may discover much truth. Nevertheless, if the universe were not created and redeemed by Christ no man could give himself an intelligible account of anything. It follows that in order to perform their task aright the scientist and the philosopher as well as the theologian need Christ.[46]

Then there is the third category, the regenerate consciousness, reason restored in the regenerate person. This restoration is God's work and it makes people realize again their true place in God's world. The regenerate

---

45 Also see Henry Stob, *Theological Reflections: Essays on Related Themes* (Grand Rapids, MI: Eerdmans, 1981), 21–22.
46 Cornelius Van Til, *The Case for Calvinism* (Philadelphia, PA: P&R Publishing, 1968), 147–48.

consciousness is restored in principle but not in fullness. There is a constant struggle against the old nature in every Christian (cf. Rom 7). "If we say we have no sin, we deceive ourselves, and the truth is not in us" (1 John 1:8).

In summary, the unregenerate person will interpret reality in such a way that his basic presuppositions of unbelief and open or latent hostility to God cannot but influence his work and conclusions. In God's goodness, this hostility often does not prevent certain conclusions to be drawn in science or mathematics or other fields that can serve humanity and through which Christians can give glory to God. On the other hand, those whom God has regenerated will seek to "take every thought captive to obey Christ" (2 Cor 10:5).

Faith and Reason

When we believe in the Lord, we surrender ourselves completely to him. Faith is not something that can be put into a separate compartment of life. It pervades everything, also our thinking and reasoning processes. As believers, God has redeemed us and renews us, also our brains and logical powers. For a Christian, faith and reason are never set over against each other. We do, of course, have to respect the limits of our reason. We are creatures only. God is the Creator. There can be times when we admit that we do not know the solution for a particular problem. Perhaps we will know later, perhaps not. Something may seem contradictory now or irrational, but we know that God is a God of order and in him is no confusion. So faith sets the tone for our rational work and our powers of logic and analysis.

When we work in faith, then we try to think God's thoughts after him, to use a phrase Van Til loved to say.[47] Then we begin to see things in a right

---

[47] In using concepts such as "thinking God's thoughts after him," Van Til was indebted to Bavinck. Bavinck, *Reformed Dogmatics*, 1:44, 588; Cornelius Van Til, *Christian Apologetics*, 2nd ed., ed. William Edgar (Phillipsburg, N.J.: P&R Publishing, 2003), 77, 131, 140; Laurence R. O'Donnell, "Neither 'Copernican' Nor 'Van Tilian': Re-Reading Cornelius Van Til's Reformed Apologetics in Light of Herman Bavinck's *Reformed Dogmatics*," *The Bavinck Review* 2 (2011): 86–91.

manner. An unregenerate scholar of the natural world may have enormous knowledge. But if anyone can put things within a correct perspective, it will be only a Christian scientist who can do that because of his faith presupposition. It must, however, be stressed that also the knowledge of a Christian will be far from complete. Christians can also draw incorrect conclusions in spite of their faith commitment. But, to the degree that the Lord works in our hearts and minds through the Scriptures, he will order the believer's intellect by the way of faith. Faith brings order to our intellect and logic. Our thinking must be molded by the Word.[48]

Christian students and scholars must heed the call not to be conformed to the thinking according to the sinful nature, but to be transformed by the renewal of the mind (Rom 12:2). The Lord makes such renewal possible by the work of his Spirit (Eph 3:16; 4:23). This necessitates that the Spirit has the opportunity to shape our minds and hearts so that we are equipped as much as possible to think God's thoughts after him. It is a beautiful challenge to be a Christian student or scholar, a child of God, privileged to explore his world, his handiwork, his creation in all its complexity and glory. He is Lord of all and he promises that his truth will be a light on the path of those who honor him (cf. Ps 119:105). So we need to live close to the Word, and be renewed in mind by the Spirit so that we may reason in faith and so that faith may set the tone and limits of the use of our reason. Faith seeks understanding.

---

48 K. Schilder, "'F.Q.I.'," in *Almanak van het corpus studiosorum in academia campensi "Fides Quaerit Intellectum"* (Kampen, NL: Zalsman, 1951), 77.

PART D

A CHALLENGE FOR TEACHERS AND GRADUATES

CHAPTER 10

The Nurturing Rains

It is spring time—a season of new life, new beginnings, new hope, and new perspectives. What a wonderful time to have a graduation![1] After all, a graduation is an occasion for celebrating new beginnings as you put closure on a particular phase of your education and look forward to teaching as a profession.

On this happy occasion I would like to take a moment to consider some aspects of the awesome privilege and responsibility you will have as Christian teachers. I would like to do this by reflecting on a passage found in the Song of Moses which he recited to Israel before their entry into the Promised Land. In this his final instruction, Moses uses a comparison that is very striking. Moses said:

> Let my teaching fall like rain
>   and my words descend like dew,
> like showers on new grass,
>   like abundant rain on tender plants. (Deut 32:2 NIV84)

This teaching that Moses was about to give is obviously very important, for he even addresses heaven and earth so that they can witness this instruction:

> Listen, O heavens, and I will speak;
>   Hear, O earth, the words of my mouth. (Deut 32:1 NIV84)

---

[1] This chapter is a revision of a speech delivered on the occasion of the graduation exercises of Covenant Canadian Reformed Teachers College on Friday, May 25, 2001 in the Ebenezer Canadian Reformed Church in Burlington, Ontario.

A CHALLENGE FOR TEACHERS AND GRADUATES

The Truth from God

Now why would Moses speak of teaching God's people in terms of his words falling like rain and dew? What is there about teaching both specifically and in a general, more generic sense, that makes that type of comparison and figure of speech so apt? What can teachers today learn from likening teaching to the falling of a gentle rain as they seek to do their profession in a God-fearing manner?

To answer these questions properly, we must first notice that what Moses is doing, and has been doing all his life, is not passing on his own private views about something. No, he is passing on the truth from God! That is central in teaching as Moses understood it. His teaching is not a matter of some private musings or preferences, but it is a matter of instructing the people entrusted to him in the deeds and ways of the Almighty. Put differently, Moses does his utmost to have Israel see the reality of life and their own lives from God's point of view. Moses with his instruction tries to lift Israel up out of their narrow-mindedness and their immediate self-interests and point them to the greatness of their God.

And so, the focus, also of this song, is on the LORD and his great deeds. In this case, his attention is directed to God's loving care for his people, as well as his righteousness and mercy. In stark contrast to all of this stands Israel's selfishness, sin, faithlessness, and ingratitude. The teaching of Moses can, therefore, be briefly characterized as God-centered and covenantal because it speaks of that special relationship between God and his people which the holy nation was privileged to experience.

Like Rain, Like Dew

Now, to return to our initial question, why is this God-centered, covenantal teaching compared to falling rain and descending dew, "like showers on new grass, like abundant rain on tender plants"? Why this particular use of images? The short answer is because such teaching as Moses gave as spokesman for God was to be a teaching that was nurturing and life-giving. It was to be a teaching that was stimulating and encouraging for life with God in covenantal awe and obedience.

As any gardener or farmer knows, not all rain is the same nor is it all of equal value and benefit. A fierce thunderstorm, for instance, can do more damage than good to one's garden because it flattens everything in sight, crushes the flowers and pounds the young vegetation into the soil. And because of the ferocity of the storm, most of the water does not really penetrate into the soil and to the roots where it is needed. Instead, the downpour runs off, often dragging the precious topsoil and the valuable nutrients with it.

But such a negative scenario is definitely not what is in view here. This God-centered, covenantal teaching is to descend like a very gentle rain for it is to come down like dew. It drops down ever so gently and lovingly without washing away any soil and without doing any damage. This teaching is able to penetrate to the roots and so nurture and give life! It is like a fertilizing rain, like life-giving dew. Nothing can come down as gently as dew. Dew can appear in enormous quantities and soak the grass, but all this water comes on the tender blades with extreme gentleness and without hurting anything.

Now it is this life-giving and nurturing quality that Moses wants his teaching to emulate! He has good reason for such an expectation because his teaching is God-centered and covenantal. Specifically this means that Moses does not just come with some sweet-sounding words to Israel and only tell them what they wish to hear. Oh, no. He comes with the truth as it needs to be told—the truth according to Scripture and according to God's revelation of himself. His teaching, therefore, includes some very harsh words to Israel because of their sin against God. Moses does not spare God's people. He does not give them a "make-you-feel-good" address. No, where necessary, he hits them hard so to speak. But, he does not wish to hurt them. He simply passes on the truth of God and his salvation. It is, therefore, a teaching that is full of covenantal love and nurture for those who hear. It is like a refreshing dew for them because it enables them to know where they are at. It is teaching that helps them to orientate to what is true and what is important in life.

In this context it is interesting to note that the word Moses uses here for "teaching" in the original language has the idea of something that is readily grasped and is therefore persuasive.[2] His teaching is accessible and relevant. It is something that engages his audience. They will understand and should therefore be persuaded.

This element of reaching the audience with his instruction so that it can be grasped by them is also enhanced by the manner in which Moses gives his instruction here. He gives it in the form of a song. It is designed to be sung! Singing is intensified speaking. What is sung more readily penetrates the heart and mind. In this particular case, Moses' instruction is a matter of life and death for it is in essence a covenantal warning that the wrath of God will come if Israel does not abandon its sins and obey and acknowledge the Lord as God alone.

Important Principles

Now I do not want to imply that a teacher today stands in the sandals of Moses. But the principles of teaching, as seen in the image of rain and dew used at the beginning of Deuteronomy 32 are of vital importance also for your teaching task today. By September, the Lord willing, you will be in front of the classroom with members of the covenant community in your charge. They may be eager young beavers in their first enthusiasm for going to school or they may be adolescents pushing the limits and testing the boundaries. They may be students at peace with themselves or in inner turmoil for whatever reason. What is the underlying principle that is to govern all your teaching? It is this. Make your teaching to be as nurturing springtime rain and may it be as gentle as the dew that comes down without harming the most tender and vulnerable plant in your care.

In whatever subject area that you may be teaching you must never forget that you have precious lives in your charge whose overriding need

---

2 Clines, *The Dictionary of Classical Hebrew*, 4:575; Jeffrey H. Tigay, *Deuteronomy: The Traditional Hebrew Text with the New JPS Translation*, The JPS Torah Commentary (Philadelphia, PA: Jewish Publication Society, 1996), 299.

is to grow in knowledge and understanding, in wisdom and perception. As you know, all that can only be achieved if your teaching is done in the fear of the LORD, for only there is true wisdom and understanding to be found (e.g. Prov 1:7). Like the teaching of Moses your teaching is to be God-centered, covenantal and relevant.

That is a tall order and sometimes it may seem that Reformed teaching is out of touch with reality. While the world around us is dominated by narcissistic, self-centered impulses, postmodernism, and evolutionism, you will be teaching biblical attitudes to life, truth, and God's work of creation and providence by the sure and steadfast norms of Scripture. You will make it clear that you are not passing on some private views, but seeking to come with the truth that is consistent with God and his revelation. While secular education consciously does away with God, you will deliberately include him in your whole manner of teaching.

We may praise God for this radically different approach. For by God's grace you may be, in a very special way, God's voice for those in your charge. You are their figure of authority and direction. You will help them to orientate to what is true, meaningful, and important in life. You are the ones who have been charged with showing God's greatness, norms, the beauty of his holiness, and the glories of his creation. You may do all this in its dazzling fullness. You can teach his love as shown in his law, his handiwork as seen in the wonders of mathematics and the intricacies of biology, and his providential guidance as seen throughout history. You may be instrumental in exposing to your students the self-centered narrow-mindedness of the secular, post-modern world view that seeks to invade their consciousness in so many different ways. By making all your teaching God-centered, your instruction will be nurturing and life-giving, and relevant to the issues of the day!

Like a Rock, Like an Eagle

Mindful of the God to whom you are ultimately responsible, you will be able to do this with boldness and directness—saying what needs to be said. After all, as Moses went on to articulate in his teaching, our God is a rock (Deut 32:4, 15, 18, 30–31). He is solid and reliable. He cannot and will not change in his faithfulness to his people or to creation as a whole. What is true in his Word today will be so tomorrow. What is a given in creation today, will also be true tomorrow. We can trust his Word and his works and as teachers whose instruction is God-centered you build on a sure foundation. Your educating will be true and relevant! It will grab the attention of your audience!

When your teaching is God-centered, it will also be full of compassion, realizing the need to give your instruction as gently as the dew comes on the tender shoots, keeping in mind how vulnerable, sensitive, and confused students can be at a particular point in their lives. But your teaching will also be uncompromising and encourage growth in Christian knowledge and conviction using the biblical truths that are being taught. God is like a rock and his Word can be trusted and believed.

Indeed, your teaching is to reflect God's truth and love and, as Moses reminds us in his song, our God is like an eagle. That has two ramifications for our topic. First, an eagle is a very patient provider, takes care of its young and guards them as its most precious possession, keeping them safe in the lofty nests (Deut 32:10). Similarly God faithfully takes care of his people and is jealous for their well-being, watching over them as the apple of his eye. But, in the second place, like the eagle God is also not overprotective and neither should we be. An eagle will at a certain point of time push the young out of the nest so they will learn to fly. Such a push to new uncharted challenges is full of tension and scary. Teaching can be like that. There can be a moment of truth. But if the eagle parent miscalculated and the little one has not enough strength in the wings to handle the challenge and falls and plummets downward out of control, then quicker than the falling bird, the parent swoops underneath and catches the little one on its wings and carries it back for strengthening and eventually another try at flying.

May your teaching so be stimulating, bold, and relevant. As appropriate, with respect to age and ability, may your instruction challenge them to think through issues and to work at thinking biblically. There will undoubtedly be difficult moments. Students may stumble and lose their way in assimilating assigned material properly. But they need to know in what context their learning and their lives are to be lived out in and the challenges they will meet. But if they are not ready to fly, as evidenced in failed tests and exams, then you as teacher can help them and work further with them. After all, your teaching is also to be compassionate, life-giving and patient, preferably in easy to remember formats. Then under God's blessing your teaching will be as invigorating as the falling rain and gentle as the dew and under God's blessing it will eventually penetrate the dullest and most stubborn and unwilling hearts.

May the life-giving waters of your instruction so soak and fertilize and stimulate life in covenant with God for those in your charge. May they grow under your nurture. Then the Lord our God himself will be praised and glorified. May you so experience the joy and wonder of teaching!

CHAPTER 11

Getting Dressed for the Job

Different occupations require different dress.[1] If you wish to become a member of a police force, you look forward to the day when you can put on your official uniform. Then you are a police officer! Likewise, if someone studies to be a pharmacist, you train to put on the white garment that is the trademark of that profession. If you want to train to become a landscaper, you yearn to get out of your school clothes and don the attire fitting for that work. Usually your training is not finished once you have completed high school. You go on to an apprenticeship or college or university to further qualify yourself so that eventually you can arrive at the day when you can get dressed for the work as one who has completed his training. One could say you go to school in order to be able one day to dress for the task at hand. And on a joyful occasion like this commencement we wish very much for all of you that you will reach the goal you have set for yourself so that you too can put on the clothes of your life work.

The Decision

While looking forward to your ongoing preparations for your future work, there is an important element of your training and your dressing up for the job that does often come to an end by the time you graduate

---

1 This chapter is a revision of a speech delivered at the Guido de Brès Christian High School Commencement held on October 11, 1991 in the Bethel Gospel Tabernacle in Hamilton, Ontario.

from high school. The vast majority of you have already either come to the point or will soon arrive at the moment that you decide who will be the real overriding boss in your life, whom you will be working for above all else. At this stage in life you have benefited from many years of Christian parental instruction, of listening to sermons, catechism classes, and now Christian high school. By now you should know whether you want to serve the Lord, our God, or the great adversary, Satan. Choosing for the Lord and his service is a conscious decision that needs to be made in the full awareness of its life-long consequences. It can never be regarded as an automatic thing or as a matter of course that you should publicly profess your faith and become a communicant member of the church at a more or less predetermined time because that is expected of you. There should be nothing automatic about reaching that stage in life. A conscious responsible decision needs to be made. You are deciding whom you will ultimately be working for the rest of your life! Who will be your principal boss and authority? Christ or the evil one? In answering that question you are deciding how you will get dressed, metaphorically speaking, for your life task as a Christian—the task that is more important than all other labors in which you will be engaged. The real issue is whether you will be wearing clothes or garments dictated by the Lord or by those offered by the great adversary.

Getting Dressed as a Christian

Your teachers at Guido de Brès High School have been part of that process of your coming to a decision on this vital matter which has enormous consequences. It concerns not only this life, but also the life hereafter. The Bible, therefore, also instructs us about getting dressed for our task as Christians so we are equipped for the office of believers to which God calls us. These passages are undoubtedly well-known to you. Think of the admonition of the apostle Paul to the Ephesians in which he instructs us to

> put on the full armor of God, so that when the evil day comes, you may be able to stand your ground, and after you have done

everything, to stand. Stand firm then, with the belt of truth buckled around your waist, with the breastplate of righteousness in place, and with your feet fitted with the readiness that comes from the gospel of peace. In addition to all this, take up the shield of faith, with which you can extinguish all the flaming arrows of the evil one. Take the helmet of salvation and the sword of the Spirit, which is the Word of God (Eph 6:13–17 NIV84).

What a stirring passage! Onward Christian soldiers in combat gear! That is to be your uniform as Christians! Then you are dressed for your calling as a child of God. As the apostle Paul put it elsewhere: "Let us cast off the works of darkness and put on the armor of light!" (Rom 13:12). Christians are not children of darkness, the night, but of the day. Therefore, "since we belong to the day, let us be sober, having put on the breastplate of faith and love, and for a helmet the hope of salvation" (1 Thess 5:8). You are to be dressed as a warrior, a soldier in the service of our king!

This, however, is not all. Getting dressed for the task in this way implies several things that need to be spelled out. God's Word says that we must undress with respect to the old nature and dress up in the new nature. Scripture commands us "to put off your old self, which belongs to your former manner of life and is corrupt through deceitful desires, and to be renewed in the spirit of your minds, and to put on the new self, created after the likeness of God in true righteousness and holiness" (Eph 4:22–24).

So, putting on the breastplate of faith and love and the whole armor of God is only possible if you dress up in the new self or nature. Yes, the Greek verb used here means "to put on clothes" or in this case "to clothe oneself."[2] This same verb is used in Paul's letter to the Colossians when he gives a similar exhortation (Col. 3:10). Getting dressed up for service to God entails nothing less than putting on a new heart and a mind of holiness.

But there is more than that in which we have to get dressed. If Scripture did not itself explicitly command this, one would be hesitant to say it.

---

2   The verb is *'enduō*; F. W. Danker, rev. and ed., *A Greek-English Lexicon of the New Testament and Other Early Christian Literature*, 3rd ed. (Chicago, IL: University of Chicago Press, 2000), 333.

God tells us in his Word that if we are to be dressed properly for service to him, then the command is: "put on the Lord Jesus Christ" (Rom 13:14). One can also translate, "clothe yourselves with the Lord Jesus Christ" (NIV84)! The same verb is used here as was used in the exhortation to put on the whole armor of God and the breastplate of righteousness (Eph. 6:11, 14). "Put on Christ! Clothe yourselves with Christ!" What an awesome demand. Only then are you and I properly dressed for our life task as Christians! Only in one other place is such graphic terminology used. In Galatians 3:27 Christians are characterized as those who "have put on Christ" or, as one can also translate, "have been clothed with Christ" (NIV84).

But, what does it mean to clothe yourselves with Christ, you may ask. Judging from the figurative usage of this verb elsewhere in the New Testament world, it means that you have such a close relationship with Christ that you are not only completely wrapped up in Christ, so to speak, but that you think like him and act like him. For being dressed in him means that you are in a sense no longer yourself, but appear to be the one with whom you are clothed. To put it differently, "Clothe yourselves with Christ" means that you so closely identify with Christ that you have Christ's eyes and see the world and your situation as Christ sees it; that you have Christ's mind so that you think through life's problems as Christ would think through them if he were in your shoes.

But how are you to achieve this situation so that you are clothed with Christ? Consider that it is a demand. "Clothe yourselves with the Lord Jesus Christ" God's Word says (Rom 13:14 NIV84). The only way is to renounce the world's standards, lifestyles, and goals and to seek your direction and meaning for life, yes, your everything, in Jesus Christ. All this is clear from the context of the command to put on the Lord Jesus Christ (Rom 13:14). The apostle, after encouraging his readers with the prospect of the great day of Jesus Christ, writes: "Let us cast off the works of darkness and put on the armor of light; let us walk properly as in the daytime, not in orgies and drunkenness, not in sexual immorality and sensuality, not in quarrelling and jealousy. But put on the Lord Jesus Christ, and make no provision for the flesh, to gratify its desires (Rom 13:12–14).

In order to clothe ourselves in Christ, we need a strong and close relationship with our Savior. Christ must be everything for us. He demands our all! All our heart, our love, our time, our priorities. Know the cost of being clothed as a Christian and taking the whole armor of God so that you can stand in the evil day. It means to become as nothing and that Christ becomes everything! If we fulfill our responsibility, for that is the context, and put on Christ, then he takes possession of us. It is remarkable that when the Holy Spirit would come upon his chosen servants in the Old Testament, this action has even been described as dressing himself with them and so using them as his agents. The verb "to be clothed or dressed" is used in such instances.[3] One can think, for example, of Gideon. When Israel was threatened by the Midianites and Amalekites, "the Spirit of the LORD clothed Gibeon" (Judg 6:34). That is literally what it says. The Spirit dressed Gideon with himself. The Spirit enveloped and took possession of him. In a similar fashion "the Spirit clothed" Amasai (1 Chron 12:18) and Zechariah (2 Chron. 24:20).

In the New Testament, before his ascension Christ commanded his disciples: "stay in the city [Jerusalem] until you are clothed with power from on high" (Luke 24:49). Here too, the vocabulary of clothing or dressing[4] is associated with the Holy Spirit since he is in view (cf. Acts 1:8). Although the Holy Spirit enables, we have our responsibility not to quench the Spirit (1 Thess 5:19) or to resist and grieve him (Eph 4:30). Indeed, God commands us to put on or be clothed with Christ. In this way Christ wants to fill us with his Spirit and so use us as his instruments in his service. It must come to the point that the apostle Paul expressed with these words: "It is no longer I who live, but Christ who lives in me. And the life I now live in the flesh I live by faith in the Son of God" (Gal 2:20).

You graduates have been richly blessed. You have been nurtured by parents who taught you the ways of the Lord from an early age, took you to church, and sent you to Christian elementary and secondary schools. You have gone through the system and in several respects you have been sheltered from the most direct attacks of the evil one on your identity.

---

3 The verb is *lābaš*; Clines, *The Dictionary of Classical Hebrew*, 4:516–17.
4 The term is again *'enduō*.

Home, church, and school have prepared you to go out and get work or further qualify yourself for your task in life. You are graduating today as those who have fulfilled all the requirements of a high school education. You are graduates! But is that all? No, you are *Christian* graduates. At the very core of your identity you should be a follower of Jesus Christ—a Christian. But as you go forth from here you will need to reassert your identity as a Christian over and over again. It is the most important part of who you are.

The Critical Question

Undoubtedly you are busy preparing yourself for getting dressed for the job you hope to have in the future. That is good. God wants you to use your talents wisely. But, how far are you with dressing up in Christ, putting him on, and being totally governed by his Word and Spirit? Are you busy with that vital part of preparing for life in fullness? Actually, to ask such a question only of graduates is not really fair. Let me rephrase the question. All of us have our task in life. We dress in the morning to go to work. The appropriate clothes lie ready to be put on. Do we also take the time, day after day, to be clothed with Christ and to let our identity and outlook be totally determined by him?

Graduates, and for that matter, all of us, if we do not realize that we are naked and defenceless in a world of sin without being clothed by Christ, we are lost! If there is not that urgency that we need to get dressed with Christ, there is actually little meaningful life perspective for us. For only if we have the mind of Christ can we understand what being a Christian is all about. "Your attitude must be the same as that of Christ Jesus" (Phil. 2:5 NIV84). Having some head knowledge of Scripture and being aware of some basic Reformed or Christian principles for life have only a limited value. We need the mind of Christ. We need to be clothed with Christ and his Spirit. There must be that close personal relationship with our Savior so that we truly hate the sin of this world as he did and does. We need to think and reason as Christ would expect of us so that we too yearn for the holiness of the Father in our lives and in this world; so that we too strive in everything to do the will of Father; so that we too love the brotherhood, as he showed by example and taught us to; so that we too reach out to share the gospel and what we have received by grace wherever the opportunity arises, as Christ would have us do. Yes, to be so clothed with Christ that we can say with the apostle, "it is no longer I who live, but Christ who lives in me" (Gal. 2:20)! Graduates, that's what it's all about!

Congratulations on reaching the end of your high school education. It is a noteworthy milestone. We rejoice with you. Study and work hard for the occupational uniform of your choice. But do not forget to dress for the most important task our heavenly Father has given us, namely, to be Christians, to share in Christ's anointing and work. Don't forget to be clothed with Christ. There is no better way to show your gratitude to your parents who have sacrificed much for you. And there's no better way to show your thankfulness to the teachers at Guido de Brès High School, and above all to the Lord our God who has embraced you in covenantal love and from whom we have received all this. Then there will also be great rejoicing in heaven!

APPENDICES

Appendix A:

Decisions of Dort Regarding Education

The decisions of the great Synod of Dort (1618–19) concerning the education of the children and youth as formulated in their seventeenth session on November 30, 1618 are in abridged form as follows.[1]

In order that the Christian youth from their earliest years may be diligently instructed in the principles of the true religion, and be filled with true godliness, three modes of catechizing should be employed. **1.** In the home by parents; **2.** in the schools by the schoolmasters; **3.** in the churches by ministers, elders, and readers, or those visiting the sick. And in order that these may diligently do the duties of their office, the Christian magistrates shall be requested to promote, by their authority, so sacred and necessary a work; and all who have the oversight of churches and schools shall be required to pay special attention to this matter.

1. The office of parents is to diligently instruct their children and their whole household in the principles of the Christian religion, in a manner adapted to their respective capacities; earnestly and carefully to admonish them to the cultivation of true piety; to engage their punctual attendance on family worship, and to take them with them to the hearing of the Word of God. They should require their children to give an account of the sermons they hear, especially those on the Catechism; assign

---

[1] This translation is a version (edited by myself) of the English abridgement found in Barnard, "Scheme of Christian Education," 77–78. The full original Dutch text is in *Acta Dordrecht 1618–19*, 41–43.

them some chapters of Scripture to read, and certain passages to commit to memory; and then impress and illustrate the truths contained in them in an easily comprehensible manner, adapted to the tenderness of youth. In this way they are to prepare them for being catechized in the schools, to encourage them, and to promote their edification.

Parents are to be exhorted to the faithful discharge of this duty by the public preaching of the Word; but especially at the ordinary period of family visitation, previous to the administration of the Lord's Supper; and also at other times by the minister, elders, and those visiting the sick. Parents who profess the Reformed religion and are negligent in this work shall be faithfully admonished by the ministers. If required, they shall be censured by the Consistory so that they may be brought to the discharge of their duty

2. Schools, in which the young shall be properly instructed in the principles of Christian doctrine, shall be instituted, not only in cities but also in towns and country places where up to this time none have existed. The Christian magistracy shall be requested to see to it that well-qualified persons may be employed with adequate remuneration so that they can devote themselves to this service; and especially that the children of the poor may be instructed without payment and not be excluded from the benefit of the schools. Only members of the Reformed Church shall be employed for this teaching office. They are to be adorned with testimonies of an upright faith and pious life, and be well versed in the truths of the Catechism. They are to sign a document, professing their belief in the Confession of Faith and the Heidelberg Catechism, and promising that they will accordingly give catechetical instruction to the youth in the principles of Christian truth.

The schoolmasters shall instruct their students according to their age and capacity at least two days a week. In recognition of the different ages of the children and youth, they are to use either an elementary small catechism or the more detailed Compendium or the full Heidelberg Catechism. The schoolmasters shall take care not only that the students commit these Catechisms to memory, but that they have a satisfactory understanding of the doctrines contained in them and that their teaching is instilled into their minds. To this end, they shall clearly explain to everyone, in a manner consistent with their capacity, the material that is taught and frequently inquire if they do indeed comprehend it. Every schoolmaster shall bring the pupils committed to their charge to the hearing of the preached Word, and particularly the preaching on the Catechism, and require from them an account of the same.

3. It shall be the duty of the ministers, with an elder, and if necessary, with a magistrate, to visit frequently all the schools, private as well as public, in order to become knowledgeable about the diligence of the schoolmasters and the improvement of the youth and in order to stimulate the teachers to earnest diligence, to encourage and counsel them in the manner of catechizing, addressing them, questioning them, and stimulating them to diligence and piety. If any of the schoolmasters should be found neglectful or obstinate, they shall be earnestly admonished by the ministers, and, if necessary by the consistory, with respect to their office. The ministers, in the discharge of their public duty in the church, shall preach on the Catechism. These sermons shall be comparatively short, and as accessible as practicably possible, for the comprehension of children as well as adults. The labors of those ministers shall be praiseworthy who diligently search out country places, and see that catechetical instruction be supplied and faithfully preserved. Experience teaches that the ordinary instruction of the church, catechetical and otherwise, is not sufficient for many, to instill that knowledge of the Christian religion which should be expected among the people of God. In practice, it is clear that the living voice has very great influence and is the best mode of catechizing when suitable questions and answers, adapted to the apprehension of each individual, are used to impress the principles of religion upon the heart.

It shall be the duty of a minister to go, with an elder, to all those capable of being instructed, and to gather them in their houses, the consistory room, or some other suitable place, and explain to them the articles of the Christian faith, and catechize them according to the circumstances of their different capacities, progress, and knowledge. They shall also review the public Catechism sermons so that all may come to a clear and concise knowledge of the Catechism. Those who desire to unite with the Church shall be more carefully and frequently instructed three or four weeks before the administration of the Lord's Supper so that they may be better qualified and more capable of giving an account of their faith.

The ministers shall be diligent and careful to invite for instruction those who give any hopeful evidence of serious concern for the salvation of their soul. These meetings shall commence with appropriate prayer and exhortation. If all this shall be done by the ministers with that cordiality, faithfulness, zeal, and discretion that can be expected of those who must give an account of the flock committed to their charge, it is not to be doubted that in a short time abundant fruit of their labors shall be found in the growth of religious knowledge and holiness of life to the glory of God and the prosperity of the church of Christ.

Appendix B:

A Christian School's Mandate

A mandate or mission statement can be very helpful for seeing in a concise format the justification that Reformed Christians have for establishing Christian schools. For that reason, the mandate of Guido de Brès Christian High School in Hamilton, Ontario, is here given in full.[1]

Purpose and Foundation

Members of the Canadian Reformed Churches have established Guido de Brès Christian High School so that the schooling provided will assist the parents in the fulfillment of the promises made at the baptism of the covenant children entrusted to their care. Reformed education aims to realize this assistance by equipping the students to employ their talents in the service of God and his kingdom. The following statements indicate how this most basic aim is to be achieved and thus constitute the basis of the instruction which Guido de Brès Christian High School seeks to provide:

- The entire curriculum will be taught in obedience to the Holy Scriptures, the infallible word of God as confessed in the Three Forms of Unity (the Belgic Confession, the Heidelberg Catechism, and the Canons of Dordt).

---

[1] It can also be found on their website: http://www.guidodebres.org/info/mandate.html; reproduced here with permission.

- Each subject in the curriculum will have as its point of departure the cultural mandate: the command to subdue the earth as clearly stated in the book of Genesis and elaborated upon in the entire Scriptures.

- All teaching will take into account that this cultural mandate is to be exercised in a world which is lost in the misery and guilt incurred by man's fall into sin but overcome by the work of our Lord and Savior Jesus Christ.

Specific Aims and Objectives

It is the special task of Guido de Brès Christian High School to provide a program of instruction appropriate to the secondary level of education, and, in so doing, to:

- Teach the students about all aspects of God's created order, that they may stand in awe of their Maker and praise Him;

- Remind the students that their calling in this world is to know God as their Creator, Redeemer, and Sanctifier and to honor and serve Him;

- Help the students grow into mature human beings, prepared to employ their talents in the service of God and for the benefit of their neighbors, in all areas of life;

- Assist the students in recognizing their value and privileges as God's covenant children, and remind them that they are enabled by grace to respond in obedience to the call to serve;

- Help the students develop a Christian mind, so that they may discern the power and corrupting influence of secular or seemingly Christian philosophies and, in submission to the Lordship of Christ, with due humility begin to think in a Reformed way about all aspects of life;

- Remind the student that, because of the redeeming work of Christ, this world has not been abandoned by God and that their work as His followers and co-workers is therefore of value for the coming restoration of God's Kingdom on this earth;

- Show the students that knowing and fearing God is essential to attaining true knowledge and wisdom, since teaching and learning are bound up with one's relationship to God;
- Challenge students to demonstrate, in daily talk and action, a Christian heart sincerely responding to the call to follow Christ.

Appendix C:

Original Publication Information

The contents of much of this book consist of previously published material that is here reprinted, usually in revised or updated form.

Chapters 1 and 2

Material from "Wisdom, Knowledge, and Teaching" in C. Van Dam, *Fathers and Mothers at Home and at School*, Reformed Guardian 8 (Kelmscott, AU: 2000), 11–25 and previously published in *CRTA Magazine* 15:2 (1985); "Educating our Children within the Communion of Saints – Whose Task is it?" in C. Van Dam, *Fathers and Mothers at Home and at School*, 29–34; "A School of Sons and Daughters" *Clarion* 24:9 (1975) 2–4.

Chapter 3

Although previously published material has been included, this is basically a new chapter.

Chapter 4

A combination of two articles: "What's the Sense of Living with Severe Disabilities?" *Clarion* 59:20 (2010) 502–504 and an abbreviation and revision of "The Privilege and Challenge of Educating the Lord's Special Children" *Clarion* 50:16–17 (2001) 384–385, 406–408 which was a presentation given in various churches in Southern Ontario during 2000-2001 on the invitation of the Board of the ASC Committee (ASC = Assistance to the Special Child). The ASC Committee is a committee of the League of Canadian Reformed School Societies and functions as a type of think-tank which also creates awareness for and functions in the interests of children with disabilities.

Chapter 5

This is new material but some is from "Of Speaking a New Language" *Clarion* 22:1 (1973) 3–4; "Singing a New Song" *Clarion* 22:6 (1973) 2–4; "Language and Corruption" *Clarion* 37:5 (1988) 100–101; "Language and Redemption" *Clarion* 37:6 (1988) 124–126 (these last two were reprinted in C. Van Dam, *Fathers and Mothers at Home and at School*, 75–88); "Watch Your Language!" *Clarion* 44:10 (1995) 226.

Chapter 6

A revision of "Education in the Word in an Age of the Picture" in C. Van Dam, *Fathers and Mothers at Home and at School*, 57–88, originally presented in varying forms at a conference of Canadian Reformed Teachers in Langley, B.C. on August 30, 1988, in Chatham, ON, on October 28, 1988, and published in *Bible and Instruction: Proceedings of the Bible History Conference, August 1996* (CARE: Hamilton, ON, 1997).

Chapter 7

A revision of "How Does God Reveal Himself in His Works and Word?" *Clarion* 41:8–10 (1992) 154–156, 179–181, 201–202; "The King has Come!" *Clarion* 35: Year End (1986) 508–510.

Chapter 8

A revision of "A Lesson from Galileo's Trial" *Clarion* 65:4 (Feb 26, 2016) 90–92.

Chapter 9

A revision and expansion of "Faith and Reason" in C. Van Dam, *Perspectives on Worship, Law and Faith: The Old Testament Speaks Today* (2000) 95–111 and first presented on March 4, 1994 for the Fellowship of Canadian Reformed Students at their winter retreat near Paris, ON; "Why do we Believe the Bible?" *Clarion* 54:24 (2005) 578–580.

Chapter 10

A revision of "The Nurturing Rains" *Clarion* 50:19 (2001) 456–457

Chapter 11

A revision of "Getting Dressed for the Job" *Clarion* 40:23 (1991) 498–499

Select List of Works Cited

Alexander, James W. *Thoughts on Family Worship*. Philadelphia, PA: Presbyterian Board of Publication, 1847.

Allberry, Sam. *What God Has to Say About Our Bodies: How the Gospel is Good News for Our Physical Selves*. Foreword by Paul David Tripp. Wheaton, IL: Crossway, 2021.

Anderson, Ryan T. *When Harry Became Sally: Responding to the Transgender Movement*. New York, NY: Encounter Books, 2018.

Axe, Douglas. *Undeniable: How Biology Confirms Our Intuition That Life is Designed*. San Francisco, CA: HarperOne, 2016.

Bahnsen, Greg L. *Van Til's Apologetic: Readings and Analysis*. Phillipsburg, NJ: P&R Publishing, 1998.

Barclay, William. *Educational Ideals in the Ancient World*. Grand Rapids, MI: Baker, 1959.

Barnard, Henry, ed. "Scheme of Christian Education, Adopted at the Synod of Dort, on 30th of November, 1618." *The American Journal of Education* 5 (1858): 77–78.

Bavinck, Herman. *The Christian Family*. Edited by Stephen J. Grabill. Translated by Nelson D. Kloosterman. Introduction by James Eglinton. 1912. Grand Rapids, MI: Christian's Library Press, 2012.

———. *Our Reasonable Faith*. Translated by Henry Zylstra. Grand Rapids, MI: Baker, 1977; 1st publ. 1956.

———. *Reformed Dogmatics*. 4 vols. Edited by John Bolt. Translated by John Vriend. Grand Rapids, MI: Baker Academic, 2003–8.

———. *The Wonderful Works of God: Instruction in the Christian Religion According to the Reformed Confession*. Foreword by Herman Bavinck. Translated by Henry Zylstra. Introduction by R. Carlton Wynne. Glenside, PA: Westminster Seminary Press, 2019; 1st publ. 1956.

Beeke, Joel R. *Family Worship*. Grand Rapids, MI: Reformation Heritage Books, 2009.

Beeke, Joel, and Paul M. Smalley. *Reformed Systematic Theology*. Wheaton, IL: Crossway, 2019.

Blackwell, Richard J. *Galileo, Bellarmine, and the Bible*. Notre Dame, IN: University of Notre Dame Press, 1991.

Blamires, Harry. *The Christian Mind*. London, UK: SPCK, 1966.

———. *The Post Christian Mind: Exposing Its Destructive Agenda*. Foreword by J. I. Packer. Ann Arbor, MI: Servant, 1999.

———. *Recovering the Christian Mind: Meeting the Challenge of Secularism*. Downers Grove, IL: InterVarsity Press, 1988.

Bloom, Allan. *The Closing of the American Mind: How Higher Education Has Failed Democracy and Impoverished the Souls of Today's Students*. New York, NY: Simon and Schuster, 1987.

Bouwman, Clarence. *Spiritual Order for the Church*. Winnipeg, MB: Premier, 2000.

Brooke, John Hedley. *Science and Religion: Some Historical Perspectives*. Cambridge History of Science. Cambridge, UK: Cambridge University Press, 1991.

Buckingham, Janet Epp. *Fighting Over God: A Legal and Political History of Religious Freedom in Canada*. Montreal, QC and Kingston, ON: McGill-Queen's University Press, 2014.

Byl, John. *God and the Cosmos: A Christian View of Time, Space, and the Universe*. Edinburgh, UK: Banner of Truth, 2001.

Byl, John, and Tom Goss. *How Should Christians Approach Origins?* Winnipeg, MB: Word Alive Press, 2015.

Calvin, John. *Institutes of the Christian Religion*. Edited by John T. McNeill. Translated by Ford Lewis Battles. Library of Christian Classics. Philadelphia, PA: Westminster, 1960.

Chadwick, Owen. *The Secularization of the European Mind in the Nineteenth Century*. Cambridge, UK: Cambridge University Press, 1975.

Chomsky, Noam. *Language and Mind*. 3rd ed. Cambridge, UK: Cambridge University Press, 2006.

Copernicus, Nicolaus. *On the Revolutions of the Heavenly Spheres*. Translated by Charles Glenn Wallis. Amherst, NY: Prometheus, 1995.

Custance, Arthur C. *Science and Faith*. Doorway Papers, vol. VIII. Grand Rapids, MI: Zondervan, 1978.

de Graaf, S. G. *Christ and the Nations*. Vol. 4 of *Promise and Deliverance*. Translated by H. Evan Runner and Elisabeth Wichers Runner. St. Catharines, ON: Paideia Press, 1981.

De Jong, Peter Y. "Calvin's Contribution to Christian Education." *Calvin Theological Journal* 2 (1967): 162–201.

———. *The Church's Witness to the World*. St. Catharines, ON: Paideia Press, 1980.

Dwyer, James G., and Shawn F. Peters. *Homeschooling: The History and Philosophy of a Controversial Practice*. The History and Philosophy of Education Series. Chicago and London, IL: University of Chicago Press, 2019.

Ellul, Jacques. *The Humiliation of the Word*. Translated from the French. Grand Rapids, MI: Eerdmans, 1985.

Fesko, J. V. *Christ and the Desert Tabernacle*. Darlington, UK: EP Books, 2012.

Frame, John M. *Apologetics: A Justification of Christian Belief*. Edited by Joseph E. Torres. Phillipsburg, NJ: P&R Publishing, 2015.

Galilei, Galileo. *Dialogue Concerning the Two Chief World Systems—Ptolemaic & Copernican*. 2nd ed. Translated by Stillman Drake, Foreword by Albert Einstein. Berkeley, CA: University of California Press, 1967.

Gilson, Etienne. *Reason and Revelation in the Middle Ages*. New York, NY: Scribner's, 1938.

Grudem, Wayne. *Christian Ethics: An Introduction to Biblical Moral Reasoning*. Wheaton, IL: Crossway, 2018.

Hooykaas, R. *Religion and the Rise of Modern Science*. Grand Rapids, MI: Eerdmans, 1972.

Hummel, Charles E. *The Galileo Connection: Resolving Conflicts Between Science and the Bible*. Downers Grove, IL: InterVarsity Press, 1986.

Johnson, Phillip E. *Darwin on Trial*. 20th anniversary ed. Introduction by Michael Behe. Downers Grove, IL: InterVarsity Press, 2010.

Keller, Werner. *The Bible as History*. 2nd revised ed. Translated by William Neil, revised by Joachim Rehork and B. H. Rasmussen. New York, NY: William Morrow, 2015.

Koestler, Arthur. *The Sleepwalkers: A History of Man's Changing Vision of the Universe*. New York, NY: Penguin, 1984.

Lennox, John C. *God's Undertaker: Has Science Buried God?* Oxford, UK: Lion, 2009.

Lois, Jennifer. *Home is Where the School is: The Logic of Homeschooling and the Emotional Labor of Mothering*. New York, NY: New York University Press, 2013.

Lowe, Jane, and Alan Thomas. *Educating Your Child at Home*. London, UK; New York, NY: Continuum, 2002.

Luther, Martin. *Luther's Works*. Edited by Jaroslav Pelikan, Oswalk Hilton, Helmut T. Lehmann, Christopher Boyd Brown, Benjamin T. G. Mayes, and James L. Langebartels. Saint Louis, MO: Concordia, 1955–2016.

Machen, J. Gresham. *What is Faith?* Grand Rapids, MI: Eerdmans, 1962.

McDowell, Josh, and Sean McDowell. *Evidence That Demands a Verdict: Life-Changing Truth for a Skeptical World*. Nashville, TN: Thomas Nelson, 2017.

McKee, Elsie Anne. *The Pastoral Ministry and Worship in Calvin's Geneva*. Travaux d'Humanisme et Renaissance. Geneva, CH: Librairie Droz, 2016.

McKim, Donald K. *Everyday Prayer with John Calvin*. Phillipsburg, NJ: P&R Publishing, 2019.

Meade, Starr. *Comforting Hearts, Teaching Minds: Family Devotions Based on the Heidelberg Catechism*. Phillipsburg, NJ: P&R Publishing, 2013.

———. *Training Hearts, Teaching Minds: Family Devotions Based on the Shorter Catechism*. Phillipsburg, NJ: P&R Publishing, 2000.

Medawar, Peter. *The Limits of Science*. Oxford, UK: Oxford University Press, 1987.

Meijer, W. *Christ in the Family*. Edited by Debbie Lodder and Teresa Metzlar. Translated by G. Ravensbergen, revised by J. Moesker. London, ON: ILPB, 1985.

The Mishnah. Translated and edited by Herbert Danby. Oxford, UK: Oxford University Press, 1933.

Moreland, J. P., Stephen C. Meyer, Christopher Shaw, Ann K. Gauger, and Wayne Grudem, editors. *Theistic Evolution: A Scientific, Philosophical, and Theological Critique*. Foreword by Steve Fuller. Wheaton, IL: Crossway, 2017.

Mountney, Ross. *Learning Without School: Home Education*. London, UK; Philadelphia, PA: Jessica Kingsley Publishers, 2009.

Nevin, Norman C., ed. *Should Christians Embrace Evolution? Biblical and Scientific Responses*. Nottingham, UK: InterVarsity Press, 2009.

Oliphint, K. Scott. *Covenantal Apologetics*. Forward William Edgar. Wheaton, IL: Crossway, 2013.

Pathak, Jay, and Dave Runyon. *The Art of Neighboring: Building Genuine Relationships Right Outside Your Door*. Grand Rapids, MI: Baker Books, 2012.

Pearcey, Nancy. *Love Thy Body*. Grand Rapids, MI: Baker Books, 2018.

———. *Total Truth: Liberating Christianity from Its Cultural Captivity*. Study Guide ed., Foreword by Phillip E. Johnson. Wheaton, IL: Crossway, 2005.

Phillips, J. B. *Your God is Too Small*. London, UK: Epworth, 1952.

Plantinga, Alvin. "Reason and Belief in God." *Faith and Rationality: Reason and Belief in God*. Edited by Alvin Plantinga and Nicholas Wolterstorff, 16–93. Notre Dame, IN: University of Notre Dame Press, 1983.

Rushdoony, Rousas J. *Intellectual Schizophrenia: Culture, Crisis and Education*. Preface by Edmund A. Opitz. Grand Rapids, MI: Baker Books, 1961.

Safrai, S. *The Jewish People in the First Century: Historical Geography, Political History, Social, Cultural and Religious Life and Institutions*. Edited by S. Safrai and M. Stern. Compendia Rerum Iudaicarum Ad Novum Testamentum. Assen, NL: Van Gorcum, 1976.

Schuringa, Henry David. "Hearing the Word in a Visual Age: A Practical Theological Consideration of Preaching Within the Contemporary Urge to Visualization." Ph.D. diss. Kampen, NL: Theologische Universiteit at Kampen, 1995.

Schürer, Emil. *The History of the Jewish People in the Age of Jesus Christ* (175 B.C. – A.D. 135). Vol. 2. Edited and revised by Geza Vermes, Fergus Millar, literary editor Pamela Vermes, organizing editor Matthew Black. Edinburgh, UK: T. & T. Clark, 1979.

Selderhuis, Herman. *Martin Luther: A Spiritual Journey*. Wheaton, IL: Crossway, 2017.

Sikkema, Keith. "Home Schooling in View of John Calvin: A Study in Education and Communion of Saints." Unpublished Master of Education thesis. St. Catharines, ON: Brock University, 2004.

Silva, Moisés. *God, Language and Scripture: Reading the Bible in the Light of General Linguistics*. Foundations of Contemporary Interpretation. Grand Rapids, MI: Zondervan, 1990.

Snapper, J. Marion. "Memorization in Church Education." *Calvin Theological Journal* 16 (1981): 38–55.

———. "The Dethronement of Memory in Church Education." *Calvin Theological Journal* 13 (1981): 38–57.

Snelling, Andrew A. *Earth's Catastrophic Past: Geology, Creation, and the Flood*. Green Forest, AR; Petersburg, KY: Master Books; Answers in Genesis, 2014.

Stob, Henry. *Theological Reflections: Essays on Related Themes*. Grand Rapids, MI: Eerdmans, 1981.

Struthers, William M. *Wired for Intimacy: How Pornography Hijacks the Male Brain*. Downers Grove, IL: InterVarsity Press, 2009.

Tripp, Tedd. *Shepherding a Child's Heart*. 2nd ed., revised and updated. Wapwallopen, PA: Shepherd Press, 2005.

Van Dam, Cornelis. *The Deacon: Biblical Foundations for Today's Ministry of Mercy*. Grand Rapids: MI: Reformation Heritage Books, 2016.

———. *In the Beginning: Listening to Genesis 1 and 2*. Grand Rapids, MI: Reformation Heritage Books, 2021.

Van Til, Cornelius. *The Case for Calvinism*. Philadelphia, PA: P&R Publishing, 1968.

———. *Christian Apologetics*. 2nd ed. Ed. William Edgar. Phillipsburg, NJ: P&R Publishing, 2003.

———. *The Defense of the Faith*. 4th ed. Ed. K. Scott Oliphint. Philadelphia, PA: P&R Publishing, 2008.

———. *An Introduction to Systematic Theology*. Phillipsburg, NJ: P&R Publishing, 1979.

Wallace, Ronald S. *Calvin's Doctrine of the Word and Sacrament*. Grand Rapids, MI: Eerdmans, 1957.

Weeks, Noel. *The Christian School: An Introduction*. Edinburgh, UK: The Banner of Truth Trust, 1988.

———. *The Sufficiency of Scripture*. Carlisle, PA: The Banner of Truth Trust, 1988.

Whitney, Donald S. *Family Worship*. Wheaton, IL: Crossway, 2016.

Wood, A. Skevington. *Luther's Principles of Biblical Interpretation*. London, UK: Tyndale Press, 1960.

Wynia, John, Stephen Chase, Arthur Kingma, Judy Kingma, John Scott, Valerie Slaa, Karen Vander Deen, James Vanoostveen, and Janita Willis. *Conceptual Framework for the Language Arts*. Hamilton, ON: League of the Canadian Reformed School Societies, Inc, 2019.

Scripture Index

GENESIS

1	104, 128, 173
1: 3, 14-18	152
1: 5	104
1: 6-8	156
1: 8, 10	104
1: 14	155, 156
1: 14-18	152
1: 26	104
1: 27	151
1: 27-30	153
1: 28	107, 164
1: 28-30	126
2	173
2: 17	126
2: 18	153
2: 19	104
3	152
3: 1	106
3: 2-3	106
3: 4-5	106
3: 9	126, 153
3: 9-12	106
3: 15	107, 126
4: 23-24	107
4: 26	107
6: 5	108
6: 11	108
7	152
8: 8-17	137
8: 22	158
9: 8-11	159
9: 12-17	110
11: 1-9	107, 152
17: 1-2	127
18: 1-2	127
18: 19	12
25: 27-28	69

EXODUS

1: 15-2: 4	69
3: 2-6	127
3: 7-10	153
4: 15-16	126
4: 22	126
5: 1	126
12: 26-27	28, 135
13: 8	135
13: 21-22	127, 134
14: 16-18	153
14: 19, 24	134
15	119

15: 1-21	153
16: 10	127
19: 18	134
20: 4-5	138
20: 13	109
20: 16	108
20: 19	128
24: 9-11	135
24: 12	127
28: 3	19
31: 3	19
31: 6	19
31: 18	127
32: 4, 5	139
32: 19	127
33: 11	135
33: 18	128
33: 19, 21-23	128
34: 6-7	128
34: 28	127
35: 26	19
35: 31	19
40: 35-38	134

LEVITICUS

10: 11	13
18: 22	51
19: 14	82
23: 33-43	28

NUMBERS

9: 15-23	134
12: 18	135
14: 14	134
22: 5	154
24: 17	154
24: 17-19	154
35: 1-8	13

DEUTERONOMY

5: 4	134
6: 4-9	31
6: 5-8	122
6: 6-9	12, 17, 25, 43, 130
6: 7-9	26, 71
6: 9	14
6: 20-25	131
16: 9-12	28
27: 2-8	14
29: 5	160
30: 14	141
31: 10-13	13
32	119, 202
32: 1	199
32: 2	199
32: 4	139
32: 4, 15, 18, 30-31	204
32: 10	204
33: 10	14
34: 10	135

JOSHUA

4: 1-10, 20-24	28
4: 6	136
4: 9	136
10	159
10: 12-14	152
18: 4, 8-9	14
21	13

JUDGES

5	119
5: 4	166
5: 20	159
6: 34	211
8: 14	14

1 SAMUEL

2: 27	126
3: 1	13
7: 10	159
10: 9-13	13
19: 20	13
24: 11	15

2 SAMUEL

8-16	159
20: 22	19

1 KINGS

2: 6	19
3: 5	127
3: 28	19
7: 14	19
11: 29-31	136
17: 1	159
20: 35	13

2 KINGS

2: 3, 5	15
2: 3, 5, 7, 15	13
2: 12	15
6: 1-2	13
6: 21	15
11: 1-2	69

1 CHRONICLES

12: 18	211
26: 29-32	14

2 CHRONICLES

7: 13	166
17: 7-9	13
24: 20	211

JOB

38: 8-11	156
38: 31-35	158, 161
38: 33	162

PSALMS

1	120
8: 1, 9	149
8: 2	81
17: 15	135
19	157
19: 1	128, 149, 155, 156
19: 1-6	155
19: 3	156
19: 4	157
19: 5-6	157
19: 7-11	21
19: 7-14	155
19: 14	115, 155
23: 4	78
29	166
33: 2	122
33: 3	79
32: 8	120
33: 6	128
33: 9	104
34: 9	16
34: 11	16, 120
34: 11-14	21
34: 18	76
36: 9	167
37: 31	27, 118, 141
40: 3	79, 123
42	78
44	75
51: 13	120
65: 5-10	158

Reference	Page
68: 35	89
77	75
77: 18-19	26
78	119
78: 1	120
78: 4	7, 25, 71, 120
78: 5	46
78: 5-7	12, 43
78: 5-8	25
86	75
86: 11	82
88	120
88: 1-2	75
88: 14, 18	75
90: 12	19
95: 1-3	77
96: 1	79
103	120
104-106	120
104: 4	158
104: 6-9	159
118: 15	78
119	120
119: 11	27, 118, 141, 142
119: 89, 91	158
119: 91	159
119: 105	162, 196
130	120
130: 1-2	77
139: 1-4	70
139: 13	91
139: 13-16	70
139: 23-24	119
146: 8	87
147: 1-3	77
147: 3	76
148: 5	104
148: 5, 6	158
148: 7-8	159
149: 1	122

PROVERBS

Reference	Page
1: 2	19
1: 2-3	21
1: 2-7	18, 19
1: 7	17, 19, 21, 22, 203
1: 8	12, 16, 46
2: 1	16
2: 1-7	21, 22
3: 1	16
3: 1, 11, 21	16
4: 1	16
4: 1-7	20
4: 23	143
4: 23-24	118
7: 6-21	29
7: 22	29
8: 22-23	22
8: 27	22
8: 29	158
8: 35	22
9: 10	19
9: 20	12
10: 11	122
13: 24	24
15: 4	122
15: 7	13
20: 27	81
22: 6	63
23: 13-14	24
23: 26	30, 118, 142
26: 14	29
31: 1	12

ECCLESIASTES
4: 12 43
12: 9-11 13

ISAIAH
1-39 136
8: 16 13
19: 18 116
20: 3-6 136
28: 9-13 14
30: 8 127
38: 8 152
40: 8 165
40: 18, 25, 28 140
52: 8 134
55: 10-11 128
55: 11 .... 74, 105, 144

JEREMIAH
1: 4 126
1: 9 126
5: 24 158
17: 9 116
23: 29 105
30: 2 127
31: 33 144
31: 35-36 158
32: 39 82
33: 2 126
33: 20 158
33: 25 158

EZEKIEL
1 135
18: 31 116
11: 19 .... 82, 116
24: 15-27 137

33: 30-33 13
36: 26-27 116

DANIEL
2: 44 154
2: 48 154
7: 13-14 154

HOSEA
1: 1 126
1: 2 136
2: 18 159

JOEL
1: 1 126

AMOS
5: 8 159

NAHUM
1: 4-5 166

HABAKKUK
2: 2 127

ZEPHANIAH
3: 9 117

MATTHEW
2: 2 154
2: 3 155
2: 6 155
2: 9 155
5: 5 69
5: 18, 26 127
6: 7 76
6: 14 75
7: 9-11 99

9: 1-8, 18-38	153		9: 3	90
11: 29	69		14: 9	33
12: 27	16		14: 24	127
12: 34	116, 117		15: 7	141
18: 3	92		17: 17	129
19: 12	152		17: 15-16	118
20: 30-34	87			
22: 30	40		**ACTS**	
22: 37	65		1: 8	211
24: 37-39	108		2: 4, 6	117
28: 19	65		2: 6-11	131
			8: 26-39	70
MARK			14: 17	149
5: 4	131		17: 26	107
7: 21-22	116		23: 6	16, 70
7: 32-35	87			
7: 34	131		**ROMANS**	
14: 36	131		1: 16	73
15: 34	131		1: 18-20	167
			1: 18-23	190
LUKE			1: 19-20	149
1: 46-55	120, 122		1: 19-21	81
2: 14	120		1: 20	128, 149, 166
5: 1	127		1: 21	150
5: 18-25	87		5: 12	151
14: 21	87		6: 5	65
16: 29-31	189		7	195
16: 31	129, 193		8: 20	151
24: 49	211		8: 28	65, 90, 99
			8: 29	33, 140
JOHN			10: 17	105, 128, 133
1: 1, 14	127		11: 36	191
1: 14	105		12: 2	82, 196
3: 16	105		12: 3	183
3: 34	127		13: 12	209
6: 45	183		13: 12-14	210
8: 44	122		13: 14	210
9: 2	90			

1 CORINTHIANS

1: 24 22
1: 30 .... 22, 33
2: 12-16 81
2: 14 .... 133, 193
2: 15 162
6: 9 151
10: 31 100
11: 1 140
12: 13 42
12: 25-26 88
13: 4-8 122
15: 33 45

2 CORINTHIANS

3: 3 144
5: 17 133
10: 1 69
10: 4-5 121
10: 5 .... 118, 195
12: 7-8 152
12: 9 90

GALATIANS

2: 20 .... 71, 211, 213
3: 27 210
5: 22-23 69
6: 1 152

EPHESIANS

2: 10 93
2: 23 82
3: 16 196
4: 1-3 58
4: 7 91
4: 12-13 40
4: 18 .... 188, 193
4: 22 65
4: 23 196
4: 22-24 .... 140, 209
4: 29 115
4: 30 211
5: 4 115
5: 18-19 79
6: 4 .... 46, 73
6: 11, 14 210
6: 13-17 209
6: 17 121

PHILIPPIANS

1: 21 71
2: 4 55
2: 5 212
3: 8, 9 121
3: 17 140
3: 20 85
4: 4 85
4: 5-7 85
4: 7 121
4: 8 82

COLOSSIANS

1: 16-17 105
1: 17 194
2: 3 22
3: 5 65
3: 9-10 .... 82, 140
3: 10 .... 33, 209
3: 16 .... 79, 120, 141

1 THESSALONIANS

5: 8 209
5: 19 211

2 THESSALONIANS

2: 11-12 143

2 TIMOTHY
3: 16	127, 163
3: 16-17	129, 161

HEBREWS
1: 3	105
2: 17-18	70
4: 12	128
4: 15	70
4: 16	75
11: 3	152, 165
11: 6	185
12: 11	24

JAMES
3: 6	106, 115
3: 8	106, 115
5: 17	159

1 PETER
2: 5	59
3: 15	140
4: 17	59

2 PETER
1: 13-15	127
1: 21	163
3: 1-2	127
3: 5-10	159
3: 13	156

1 JOHN
1: 8	195
2: 15	65
2: 15-17	91
2: 20	162
3: 2	135

REVELATION
1: 11	127
4: 11	152, 191
5: 9	79, 123
12: 9	106
14: 1-3	80
14: 3	79, 123
14: 13	127
21: 5	127
22: 4	135
22: 20	84

Author Index

Adair, A., 154
Alexander, J. W., 73, 77
Allberry, S., 152
Anderson, R., 152
Aquinas, 181
Aristotle, 178, 179
Averroes, 179, 180, 181
Axe, D., 174

Barclay, W., 17
Bavinck, H., 85, 163, 172, 188, 195
Beale, G. K., 79
Beeke, J. R., 73
Bellarmine, C., 171
Blackwell, R. J., 170, 171, 174
Blarmires, H., 27, 113, 114, 143
Biesterveld, P., 38
Block, D. I., 159
Blomberg, C. L., 188
Bloom, A., 108
Bos, F. L., 36
Bouwman, C., 57
Bradley, G. V., 68
Bryant, K., 151
Byl, J., 165, 172, 175

Calvin, J., 23, 36, 39, 40, 58, 59, 78, 81
Chomsky, N., 103
Copernicus, N., 170
Custance, A., 170, 173

Dean, J., 67
De Boer, D., 89
De Graaf, S. G., 117
De Jong, P. Y., 40, 193
DeYong, T. A., 87
Dwyer, J. G., 35, 45

Ehrenpreis, S., 36
Ellul, J., 125
Eusebius of Caesarea, 154
Exiguus, D., 112

Fesko, J. V., 135
Finocchiaro, M. A., 172
Foreman, M., 151
Frame, J. M., 44, 89

Galileo, 169-176
Gilson, E., 180, 181, 182
Gispen, W. H., 16, 26, 134
Goss, T., 165
Grudem, W., 45

Hagoort, H. N., 178, 180
Hansen, C., 114
Helm, P., 184
Hess, R., 136
Holwerda, B., 39

Isserlin, B. S. J., 14

Jalsevac, J., 109
Johnson, P. E., 150

Keller, W., 187
Kempling, Dr. C., 110
Kistemaker, S. J., 117
Kitchen, K. A., 188
Koestler, 170
Koptak, P. E., 16
Kramer, S. N., 16
Kucharsky, D., 191
Kuhn, M., 112

Lemaire, A., 14, 15
Lennox, J. C., 171
Linnemann, E., 187
Lois, J., 47
Lowe, J., 56
Luther, M., 177, 178, 179, 182, 183

Machem, J. G., 185
Maier, G., 187
MacDonald, P. S., 56
Meade, S., 143
Meijer, W., 85
McDowell, J., 187
McHugh, Dr. P., 67, 68
McKee, E. A., 40
McKim, D. K., 76

McInerny, R., 181
Medawar, P., 165
Medlin, R. G., 48
Millard, A. R., 14
Monsma, M., 42, 43
Moreland, J. P., 174
Morris, J. D., 160
Morton, A. W., 15
Mosshammer, A. A., 112
Mountney, R., 51

Nevin, N. C., 174

Oliphint, K. S., 187
Oppenheim, A. L., 154

Pathak, J., 93
Panos, J., 132
Pearcey, N. R., 67, 114, 182
Peters, S., 35, 45
Peterson, D. G., 117
Phillips, J. B., 139
Pingleton, J., 24
Plantinga, A., 184, 185
Pope Paul V, 171
Popkins, R. H., 185
Pouwelse, W., 89

Ridderbos, N. H., 157
Rigby, K., 115
Runyon, D., 93
Rushdoony, R. J., 32

Safrai, S., 15
Schaeffer-de Wal, E. W., 130, 133
Schilder, H. J., 24, 132
Schilder, K., 196

Schurer, E., 131
Schurringa, H. D., 138
Segre, M., 169
Selderhuis, H., 177, 178
Sikkema, K., 49, 51, 52, 56, 57
Sikkel, J. C., 105
Silva, M., 103, 105
Singer, P., 89
Snapper, M., 27, 142
Snelling, A. A., 160
Soulen, R. N., 187
Spalatin, G., 178, 183
Sproul, R. C., 191
Stob, H., 194
Struthers, W. M., 83
Sullins, P., 151
Sullivan, B., 150

Templer, Etienne (Bishop of Paris), 180
Tetzel, 177
Thomas, A., 56
Thornton, B., 111
Tripp, T., 143
Trutvletter, J., 178

Ummel, D., 89

Van Dellen, I., 42, 43
Vander Plaats, D., 93
Vander Weij, E., 97
Vandooderwaard, R., 47, 48
Van Maren, J., 89
Van Meter, Q., 67
Van Oene, W. W. J., 42
Van Plaatsm, D., 93
Van Til, C., 26, 29, 185,190-195
Vos, C., 74

Wallace, R. S., 134
Weeks, N., 161
Welch, G., 78
Whitney, D. S., 73
Whitten, A., 166
Woelderink, J. G., 42
Wolters, A., 147, 148
Woudstra, M. H., 159
Wright, N. T., 82, 83
Wynia, J., 115

Young, E. J., 13

Zucker, Dr. K., 68

www.ingramcontent.com/pod-product-compliance
Lightning Source LLC
Chambersburg PA
CBHW061745070526
44585CB00025B/2804